SIERRA SOUTH

100 Back-country trips in California's Sierra

by Thomas Winnett and Jason Winnett

Wilderness Press
BERKELEY

First printing May 1968
Second printing January 1969
Third printing March 1970
Fourth printing January 1971
Fifth printing June 1971
Sixth printing March 1973
Seventh printing April 1974
SECOND EDITION March 1975
Second printing July 1977
Third printing April 1978
THIRD EDITION May 1980

Photos by the authors except as noted
Front-cover photo by Thomas Winnett
Back-cover photo by Howard Weamer
Design by Thomas Winnett
Map by Jeff Schaffer

Library of Congress card number 79–57593
ISBN: 911824–97–9
Manufactured in the United States
Published by Wilderness Press
2440 Bancroft Way, Berkeley CA 94704

ACKNOWLEDGMENTS

In preparing this third edition, I had input from a number of Sierra lovers who checked out some places where I hadn't been for several years. I deeply appreciate the help of Alan Bradley, the late Jim Jenkins, Jeff Schaffer and Andy Selters. My son Jason brought me reports on trips in this book even before he became the co-author of the third-edition-in-preparation. Cecelia Hurwich has, over the 12 years of this book's life, been a continual source of encouragement and information. My wife Lu walked wilderness trails with me, reminding me to take more pictures and then cooking delicious dinners while I reviewed the results of the day's trail-scouting.

T.W.

Although I am considered a very active Sierra enthusiast, I could not have succeeded in gathering all the necessary information for my parts of this book without the help of many people. National Park rangers, especially those stationed in the backcountry, have always been very eager to assist, as have been many packers. Bill, Vicki, Frances and Nathan Hoover have been very instrumental in my Sierra activities; I've walked thousands of miles with them, and much of this book would not have been possible without them. My father, Thomas Winnett, helped me integrate college and authorship activities and was very tolerant of any conflicts between the two.

J.W.

Other books by Thomas Winnett

Sierra North

Backpacking Basics

The John Muir Trail

The Tahoe-Yosemite Trail

Tennis Is an Unnatural Act (with Marion Fay)

The Comstock Guide to California Backpacking

The Comstock Guide to Pacific Northwest Backpacking

Backpacking in the Wilderness Rockies

The Pacific Crest Trail, Vol. 1 (with others)

Blackcap Mountain (with Ed Roberts)

Tuolumne Meadows

Matterhorn Peak

Mono Craters

Mt. Whitney

Mt. Abbot

SIERRA SOUTH

1984 Supplement

p. 16, Mosquito Flat trailhead. There is a Forest Service kiosk a short way up the Rock Creek road where you can get campsite reservations and wilderness permits.

p. 16, Lake Sabrina and North Lake trailheads. There is a Forest Service kiosk partway to these trailheads where you can get campsite reservations and wilderness permits.

p. 78, Sawmill Creek Roadend. Change "Black Rock Spring Road" to "Sawmill Creek Road".

p. 78, Courtright Reservoir trailhead. Change last sentence to end ". . . parking area across the dam and around a bedrock ridge."

p. 79. Delete the Little Rancheria Trailhead. It has been moved and no longer provides the shortest access.

p. 108, Trip 37, and p. 110, Trip 38. Begin at the Crown Valley Trailhead and connect with the described trail near Three Springs.

p. 186, Lodgepole Campround trailhead. Change the first sentence to end ". . . southeast on 198 to Lodgepole Village; turn east and go to a parking area near the Lodgepole Nature Center."

p. 186, Symmes Creek trailhead. It should read: Go 4½ miles west from Independence on the Onion Valley Road, turn left on Foothill Road and go 1.3 miles to a fork. Take the right-hand fork and go past an old corral on the left, then immediately cross Symmes Creek. In ½ mile take the right fork, and take the right fork again at the next two forks. Then proceed ½ mile to the trailhead near Symmes Creek. Some of these forks may have small signs.

p. 186, Cottonwood Creek and Horseshoe Meadow trailheads. It is easier if longer to go to Lone Pine and then take the Whitney Portal Road 3 miles west to the Horseshoe Meadow Road. This latter road is being repaved and extended to within 200 yards of the wilderness, with new campgrounds and parking areas near its end. This new construction near the end will not be completed until 1986, but you should know that changes are coming.

Contents

Introduction

The backcountry traveler knows the exhilaration of the out-of-doors in a rich, personal way that is beyond the ken of the ordinary car camper. Far from the crowds that infest the roadside campgrounds, he comes to realize the value of solitude, and he learns the calmness of spirit that derives from a fundamental relationship with the mountains. He comes to know the simple satisfactions of deep breaths, hardened muscles and a sound sleep under brilliant stars. But, above all, in renewing his bond with the wilderness he rekindles that cherished spark of childlike innocence that is so easily extinguished by the pressures of city life. It is these pressures that account for the dramatic increase in the demand for wilderness experiences. The Sierra, offering some of the finest and most spectacular wilderness in the United States, has drawn more than its share of the demand, and its backcountry sees thousands of new faces each year.

Together with the companion volume *Sierra North,* this book is a discriminating effort to meet the demands of both the newcomer and the "old hand." Taking up where *Sierra North* left off, this book describes backcountry trails between Mono Creek and the southern end of Sequoia National Park. Here are trips ranging in length from overnighters to two-week expeditions; trips that will sate the appetite of the most avid angler, naturalist or camera bug.

These trips were chosen after considerable screening that entailed interviews with rangers, packers and mountaineers, and substantial research. Finally, they were all walked. The final selections were made on the basis of (1) scenic attraction, (2) wilderness character (remoteness, primitive condition), and (3) recreational potential (fishing, swimming, etc.). After walking the trip, the author decided how long it should take if done at a leisurely pace, how long at a moderate pace, and how long at a strenuous pace. In deciding, he considered not only distance but also elevation change, heat, exposure, terrain, availability of water, appropriate campsites and finally, his subjective feeling about the trip. For each trip, then, we suggest how many days you should take to do it at the pace ("Leisurely," "Moderate" or "Strenuous") you prefer. Some trips simply don't lend themselves to a leisurely pace—maybe not even a moderate pace. Such trips have a blank in the number-of-days spot for the corresponding pace at the beginning of the trip. Some are not strenuous unless you do the whole thing in one day. Such trips have the word "Day" after "Strenuous."

The last decision about pace was the decision of which pace to use in describing the trip, day by day. Since this book is written for the average backpacker, we chose to describe most trips on either a leisurely or moderate basis, depending on where the best overnight camping places were along the route. The exceptions were the trips that involve an initial climb of more than 3000 feet—as much as 6000 feet—to get from the east side over the Sierra crest or from Mineral King into the Kern River drainage. We deemed all such trips strenuous.

The author's subjective consideration also carries over to the evaluation of campsites. Campsites are labeled "poor," "fair," "good" or "excellent." The criteria for assigning these labels were amount of use, immediate surroundings, general scenery, presence of vandalization, availability of water, kind of ground cover and recreational potential—angling, side trips, swimming, etc.

Angling, for many, is a prime consideration when planning a trip. The recommendations in this book are the result of (1) research into the California Department of Fish and Game's fresh-water fish-stocking program, (2) study of DF&G sponsored surveys ("Anglers' Guides"), (3) on-the-trail sampling and feed evaluations and (4) interviews with commercial packers. Like the campsites, fishing was labeled "poor," "fair," "good" or "excellent." It should be noted that these labels refer to the quantity of fish in the stream or lake, not the fishes' inclination to take the hook. Experienced anglers know that the size of their catch relates not only to quantity, type and general size of the fishery, which are given, but also to water temperature, feed, angling skill, and that indefinable something known as "fisherman's luck." Generally speaking, the old "early and late" adage holds: fishing is better early and late in the day, and early and late in the season.

Deciding when in the year is the best time for a particular trip is a difficult task because of altitude and latitude variations. Low early-season temperatures and mountain shadows often keep some of the higher passes snowbound until well into August. Early snows have been known to whiten alpine country in late July and August. Some of the trips described here are low-country ones, designed specifically for the itchy hiker who, stiff from a winter's inactivity, is searching for a "warm-up" excursion. These trips are labeled "early season," a period that extends roughly from late May to early July. "Midseason" is here considered to be from early July to late August, and "late season" from then to early October.

Most of the trails described here are well maintained (the exceptions are noted), and are adequately signed. If the trail becomes indistinct, look for blazes (peeled bark at eye level on trees) or "ducks" (two or more rocks piled one atop the other). Two other significant trail conditions have also been described in the text: (1) degree of openness (type and degree of forest cover, if any, or else "meadow," "brush" or whatever); and (2) underfooting (talus, granite, pumice, sand, "duff"—deep humus ground cover of rotting vegetation—or other material).

Two other designations used in the descriptive text warrant definition. "Packer" campsite is used to indicate a semi-permanent camp (usually constructed by packers for the "comfort of their clients") characterized by a nailed-plank table, sawn stumps to sit on, and a large, "stand-up" rock fireplace. "Improved" campsite is a U.S. Forest Service designation for places where simple toilets have been installed.

The Care and Enjoyment of the Mountains

The mountains are in danger, particularly the High Sierra. About a million people camp in the Sierra wilderness each year. The vast majority of us care about the wilderness and try to protect it, but it is still threatened with destruction.

Litter is not the problem! Increasingly, wilderness campsites, even when free of litter, have that "beat out" look of over-crowded roadside campgrounds. The fragile high-country sod is being ground down under the pressure of too many feet. Lovely trees and snags are being stripped, scarred, and removed altogether for firewood. Dust, charcoal, blackened stones and dirty fireplaces are accumulating. These conditions are spreading rapidly, and in a few years *every* High Sierra lakeshore and streamside may be severely damaged.

The national park service and the forest service are faced with the necessity for reservation systems, designated campgrounds, restrictions on fire building, increased ranger patrols, and even rationing of wilderness recreation. Not only the terrain but the wilderness experience is being eroded. Soon conditions may be little different from those we wanted to leave behind at the roadend.

The solution to the problem depends on each of us. We must change our habits so as to have as little effect on the terrain as possible. We must try to leave no traces of our passing. This was the rule in the wilderness when Indians and trappers traveled through other people's territory. It is still a good rule today. It does take a little trouble. In an earlier day, that extra trouble was the price of saving one's scalp or load of beaver pelts. Today it is the price of saving the wilderness. A few basic principles of wilderness preservation—particularly aimed at High Sierra conditions but applicable elsewhere too—are offered below.

Learn to go light. This is largely a matter of acquiring wilderness skills, of learning to be at home in the wilderness rather than in an elaborate camp. The "free spirits" of the mountains are those experts who appear to go anywhere under any conditions with neither encumbrances nor effort but always with complete enjoyment. John Muir, traveling along the crest of the Sierra in the 1870's with little more than his overcoat and his pockets full of biscuits, was the archetype.

Modern lightweight equipment and food are a convenience and a joy. The ever-practical Muir would have taken them had they been available in his day. But a lot of the stuff that goes into the mountains is burdensome, harmful to the wilderness, or just plain annoying to other people seeking peace and solitude. Anything that is obtrusive or that can be used to modify the terrain should be left at the roadend: gigantic tents, gas lanterns, radios, saws, hatchets, firearms (except in the hunting season), etc.

Pick "hard" campsites, sandy places that can stand the use. The fragile sod of meadows, lakeshores and streamsides is rapidly disappearing from the High Sierra. It simply cannot take the wear and tear of campers. Its development depends on very special conditions. Once destroyed, it does not ordinarily grow back.

Be easy with the trees! In the timberline country, wood is being burned up faster than it is being produced. The big campfires of the past must give way to small fires or no fires at all. Wood is a precious resource; use it sparingly. Where it is scarce use a gas stove, not a saw or hatchet. Trees, both live and dead, are part of the scenery. They should never be *cut*. The exquisite golden trunks left standing after lightning strikes should be left completely alone. Sadly, in some popular areas they have already been destroyed for firewood, and you would never know they *were* there. We recommend that you carry a stove and fuel (preferably liquid), and always use it when you are above 10,000 feet or in a place where wood is scarce.

In established, regularly used campsites a single, small substantial fireplace should serve for both cooking and warming. If kept scrupulously clean it should last for many years. Unfortunately, fireplaces (and campsites) tend to become increasingly dirty and to multiply. There are now, by actual survey, a hundred times as many fireplaces as are needed in the High Sierra. The countless dirty fireplaces should be eradicated. Many campsites situated at the edge of water should be entirely restored to nature and not used again. It is a noble service to use and clean up established campsites where they are present, and to restore them to nature where called for.

Elsewhere build a small fireplace, if one is legal, and always eradicate it and restore your campsite to a natural condition before you leave. This is facilitated if you build with restoration in mind: two to four medium-sized stones along the sides of a shallow trench in a sandy place. When camp is broken the stones are returned to their places. The coals are thoroughly burned down and pulverized under a heavy foot until nothing is left but powder. The trench is filled with clean sand. *Fires should never be built against cliffs or large boulders.*

Protect the water from soap and other sources of pollution. Abundant pure water is one of the joys of the mountains. Imagine having to purify every cupful before you drank it.

Scatter organic garbage in dry, out-of-the-way places. It disappears most quickly when dry and exposed to air. Talus slopes and dry brush are the best hiding places. Garbage should never be burned in the fireplace. Orange peels are an exception: they seem to be destructible only in a hot fire.

Thoroughly cold and pulverized charcoal may be broadcast away from camp in a fireproof site. Charcoal is part of the natural scene.

Pack cans and foil back to the roadend. Smelly or oily cans and foil can be cleaned easily in a hot fire but please do remove them. The accumulation of garbage, cans, and charcoal around fireplaces is the main reason campsites are abandoned and new, redundant fireplaces and campsites are created.

Latrines should be located at least 50 yards from any camping area, stream, or dry stream course. Again, a little extra trouble will alleviate one of the most annoying wilderness problems. Please be willing to walk a little farther and cover up a little more carefully.

Mirror Lake before it was closed to camping

Maps and Profiles

Today's Sierra traveler is confronted by a bewildering array of maps, and it doesn't take much experience to learn that no single map fulfills all needs. There are base maps (U.S. Forest Service), shaded relief maps (National Park Service), artistically drawn representational maps (California Department of Fish and Game), aerial-photograph maps, geologic maps, three-dimensional relief maps, soil-vegetation maps, etc. Each map has different information to impart (some have more information than others), and the outdoorsman contemplating a back-country trip is wise to utilize several of these maps in his planning.

For trip-planning purposes, the reader will find a plan map in the back of this book. Trails and trailheads used in the following trip descriptions are indicated on this map in red, and all the access roads are delineated in brown.

The profile of each trip in this book gives a quick picture of the ups and downs. All profiles are drawn with the same *ratio* of horizontal miles to feet of elevation, in which the vertical scale is exaggerated by 25 times. Since carrying a pack up a hill gets to be very gruelling sometimes, this exaggeration is probably appropriate.

On the trail most backpackers prefer to use a topographic ("topo") map, because it affords a good deal of accurate information about conditions of terrain and forest cover. Topo maps come in a variety of sizes and scales, but the best, because it covers the whole Sierra in one useful scale, is the U.S. Geological Survey's 15' Topographic Quadrangle series. The 15' series scale is approximately 1" = 1 mile; the contour interval (elevation difference between contour lines) is 80 feet in the Sierra; and the area covered by each map is about 14 X 17 miles. They show most of the maintained trails (exceptions are noted in the text of this book), the elevations, the relief, the water-courses, the forest cover and the works of man. Learning to read these maps takes a little practice, but the savings in shoe leather and frayed tempers make it a worthy undertaking. For the convenience of the reader, the appropriate 15' topo maps for each trip are cited in the text. (Wilderness Press publishes a 15' map of one quadrangle in the southern Sierra: *Mineral King* and *Triple Divide Peak*. They are far more up to date and accurate than the Government map.

A useful second map series is the ½" = 1 mile series published by the U.S. Forest Service. Being base maps, they lack the contour lines, but they are revised with some frequency, and show newer roads and trails. They also include markings for water, man-made structures and some elevations.

Anglers planning a fishing trip may wish to acquire the "Anglers' Guides" published between 1956 and 1968 by the California Department of Fish and Game. These include both artistically drawn representational maps and descriptions of the fishing waters as they existed at the time. Of this series, five guides apply to the regions of the southern Sierra covered by this book ("Mono Creek," "Bear Creek," "French Canyon/Humphreys Basin," "Upper Bishop Creek" and "Mineral King").

HOW TO ACQUIRE YOUR MAPS

USFS base maps:

U.S. Forest Service,
630 Sansome St.,
San Francisco, CA 94111
An index map is free.
Additional maps are 50
cents each.

DF&G "Anglers' Guides":

DF&G, Resources Building,
1416 9th St.
Sacramento, CA 95814
A single copy of any one
guide is free.

USGS 15' "Topo" maps:

U.S. Geological Survey,
Box 25286, Federal Center,
Denver, CO 80225
$1.25 each
A state index map is free.

Topo maps plus free state index maps can be obtained *in person* Monday through Friday 8 a.m. to 4 p.m. from USGS offices located at:

7638 Federal Building
300 North Los Angeles Street
Los Angeles, CA

345 Middlefield Road
Menlo Park, CA

504 Custom House
555 Battery Street
San Francisco, CA

Wilderness Permits and Quotas

The wilderness traveler will need a permit from the Forest Service (for federally designated wilderness areas) or from the National Park Service (for national-park backcountry). You may obtain a permit at a Park Service or Forest Service ranger station or office by indicating where you are going and when you will be there. The Forest Service requires a permit for a day hike as well as for a backpacking trip. The two services will reciprocally honor each other's permits for trips that cross a boundary between the two types of wilderness. Forest Service permits are also available by mail, and reservations for permits for the Sequoia-Kings backcountry are available by mail from February 1 through August 31. If you don't know the address of the nearest Forest Service office or station to your destination, write the Regional Forester, 630 Sansome St., San Francisco, CA 94111. The address of Sequoia-Kings Canyon National Park is Three Rivers, CA 93271. The Forest Service has also set up "entrance stations" on two east-side access roads leading to High Sierra trailheads—on the roads to Bishop Creek and Rock Creek. Information and permits—if you make the quota—are available there.

Quotas have been established for high-use areas in the region covered by this book, including all of Sequoia-Kings Canyon National Park. For example, in 1976, 30 persons per day were allowed to go up the Bubbs Creek Trail from Cedar Grove, on a first-come, first-served basis. Those who didn't "make the cut" either had to wait until they could be one of the 30 or had to choose an alternative trip. Group size anywhere in the wilderness is limited to 25, and camping is not allowed within 100 feet of lakes and streams. There are some special regulations for particular places. For example, a person may camp only one night at each camping place on the John Muir Trail within Rae Lakes Basin. Some places are closed to wood fires, such as the Kearsarge Lakes, and some places are entirely closed to camping, such as Mirror Lake on the Mt. Whitney Trail and Bullfrog Lake, near the John Muir Trail south of Glen Pass. Copies of all these special regulations are available from the government agencies that issue Wilderness permits.

A Word About Bears

Since the first edition of this book, more and more people have taken up backpacking. One result has been more and more unnatural food for bears—the food brought in by backpackers. Since this food is attractive to bears, and all too often easily available, the animals have developed a habit of seeking it and eating it. They patrol popular campsites nightly. As the bears have become more knowledgeable and persistent, backpackers have escalated their food-protecting methods. From merely putting it in one's pack by one's bed at night, and chasing away any bear that came, backcountry travelers switched to hanging the food over a branch of a tree. But bears can climb trees, and they can gnaw or scratch through the nylon line that you tie around a tree trunk. When they sever the line, the food hanging from the other end of the line of course falls to the ground. This happens all too often in the High Sierra.

To avoid food loss due to line severance, you can learn the *counterbalance* method of "bearbagging." First, put all your food in a stuff sack or other bag. Then tie two pots or metal cups to the bag that will tinkle and alert you if a bear should disturb them. Then tie a small stone to the end of a 30-foot length of nylon line (1/8" or so in diameter) as a weight to hurl up and over a likely branch. The branch should be at least 16 feet up, and long enough that the line can rest securely at a point at least 6 feet from the tree trunk. When you have the line over the branch, tie a rock that weighs about the same as your bag of food to one end of the line. (Instead of a rock, you could tie a bag containing half the food, if you have two appropriate bags.) Now pull the rock up to the branch that the line passes over. Then tie your food bag to the other end of the line, as high as you can conveniently reach, and stuff any extra line into the mouth of the food bag. Now push up on the food bag with just enough force—you hope—that the system will come to rest with the rock and the bag equally high. If they aren't equally high, take a long enough stick, preferably forked, and push up the lower of the two until they are even. If a 6-foot person could reach them standing on tiptoes, they are too low. Try again. Next morning, push up either rock or bag until one descends enough that you can reach it.

Anti-bear cables have been installed between trees at some popular camping areas in Sequoia-Kings Canyon National Park. If there's one where you camp, use it, following the instructions provided by the Park Service.

REMEMBER: If a bear does get your food, he will then consider it his, and he will fight any attempts you make to retrieve it. Don't try! Remember also never to leave your food unprotected even for a short while during the daytime.

A Word About Theft

Stealing from and vandalizing cars are becoming all too common at popular trailheads. You can't ensure that your car and contents will be safe, but you can increase the odds. Make your car unattractive to thieves and vandals by disabling your engine (your mechanic can show you how), hiding everything you leave in the car, closing all windows and locking all doors and compartments. Get and use a locking gas-tank cap. If you have more than one car, use the most modest one for driving to the trailhead.

Onion Valley roadend

Mono Creek country

Mono Creek to Glacier Divide

Part of the 500,000-acre John Muir Wilderness, this region towers between Mono Creek and the northern boundary of Kings Canyon National Park. It is a roadless vastness of incredibly rugged alpine beauty, a wilderness that beckons to all who hear of it. Barren summits rise above a dense mat of green conifers, and the landscape is stippled with a thousand blue-green lakes bound by connecting silver ribbons of mountain streams. Encompassing a small area of roughly 500 square miles, this section nevertheless contains enough trails and cross-country routes to satisfy the most dedicated backcountry traveler for several summer seasons.

The profile of this region is classic. It boasts the typical short, steep eastern escarpment, and the typical long, gradual western slope. The west side is cut by the drainages of Mono, Bear and Piute creeks—all tributaries of the South Fork of the San Joaquin. And the east side is cleft by the precipitous, hurrying waters of Rock Creek, Pine Creek and the North Fork of Bishop Creek—all tributaries of the Owens River. These watersheds are separated by spectacular divides, which, together with the main Sierra crest—if one uses a little imagination—form an interesting plan view. Seen from the air, the main crest and the ancillary divide spurs of this section take on the aspect of a very large frog: the head centers on Mt. Mills; Mono Divide and the Mt. Morgan/Wheeler Ridge make the forelegs; and the Mt. Hooper/Mt. Senger complex and the Mt. Tom/Basin Mountain divide are the two lower limbs. Naturalists would hasten to render this absurd analogy more "authentic" by pointing out that the frog's back is covered with warts (17 summits exceeding 13,000'), and that this mountainous region should therefore be analogized to a toad. The reader is free to make his own Rorschach of the topography, but in any case it is vitally important—particularly in cross-country travel—for him to have a working map knowledge of the country and its terrain.

One soon learns, however, that his map knowledge never does justice to the country. This awareness comes with one's first glimpses of the majestic prominences and the awesome, blue-hazed canyons. With awareness comes wonderment—a pause to ponder the colossal forces required to move, pluck and sculpt the rock on such a scale. Clarence King, a member of the famous Brewer Survey party of 1864, was among the first white men to look at this part of the Sierra and record his thoughts: "I believe no one can study from an elevated lookout the length and depth of one of these great Sierra canyons without asking himself some profound geological questions." Indeed, how did it happen?

The answer has mostly to do with ice—vast rivers of ice that ground, scoured and scraped their juggernaut way across the landscape. Were there an eye to witness it, in this area alone the fields of ice would have been seen to extend over 1500 square miles. Today there are but vestiges to mark the icefields' extent, reminders that hang like gray ghosts on the shady north-east faces of the higher peaks. But today's visitor has only to look about him to understand the land-forming powers of the glaciers. Huge U-shaped troughs mark the courses of the main glaciers that carved the canyons of Mono, Bear and Piute creeks, and of the South Fork of the San Joaquin River. Shallow side valleys, usually suspended hundreds of feet above the floor of the main canyon, mark the flow of tributary glaciers, and they have acquired the deserved appellation "hanging valleys." Equally interesting to the traveler is the inevitable chain of lakes that step-ladder down from the upper, amphitheaterlike cirque of a hanging valley. Called "paternoster lakes," they string down the valley floor much like the heads of a rosary, and they are the joy of the lazy angler who likes to alternate between stream and lake fishing.

Other important, but less spectacular, glacial traces include glacial polish and glacial smoothing caused by the abrasive action of sand and silt locked into the bottom and sides of a glacier. In these scoured areas one often finds long gouges or scratches rent there by boulders caught in the flow of the ice river. When the ice melted, all this material in it was deposited in the form of moraines.

The landscape is still changing. Streams have cut through sediments left by glaciers. Avalanche chutes and frost nivations flute vertical peak facades, and accumulations of scree and talus slope away at their feet. Subtler forms of weathering continue to attack the talus, reducing that rock to granules which then provide a suitable habitat for hardy plants. One can observe this ecological progression while walking the trails around timberline.

The presence of an ample and healthy plant life is necessary to animals, and one is sure to see many animals in this region's heavily wooded drainages. Birds are particularly plentiful, and the lakes and streams abound with fish. Among the most commonly seen mammals are mule deer. Early-season hikers working their way up Bear Creek are almost sure to come upon a grazing doe, and, with some luck, perhaps a pair of brand-new, spotted-back fawns. It should be noted that any wild-animal observation requires "freezing"—not necessarily stealth, but quietness and immobility. There isn't a naturalist observer worth his salt who hasn't experienced the dilemma of a hovering mosquito and a "once in a triptime" wild-animal observation opportunity. In early and mid-season both does and bucks have reddish coats, which are replaced in the fall with longer, gray hair. Because the buck is much warier, a sighting of him is rarer. One will also make trailside, passing acquaintance with the numerous squirrels that populate the heavily wooded areas, especially the fir belt. Easily recognizable because of the dual stripes running down his coppery-red back is the tiny golden-mantled ground squirrel. He is, perhaps, the most familiar squirrel, and is found in both the lodgepole and subalpine belts. His less distinguished cousin, the California ground squirrel, will be seen near the trailheads—generally below 8000 feet—and the Belding ground squirrel, or "picketpin," is seen in most of the meadows of this section. Constant companions to the high-country hiker are the cony, a small, rabbitlike creature, and the beaverlike marmot. Found in talus and other rocky areas, these somnolent rodents pipe and chirp excitedly whenever approached.

Other, less common, but consequently more exciting, sightings that one may make are of the black bear, mountain coyote, porcupine, flying squirrel and mountain lion. The black bear, contrary to impressions one might well have gathered in heavily camped national-park areas, is not often observed in the backcountry. The notable exception to this rule occurs when one leaves food lying about untended. (See page 10 for how to deal with this problem.)

The mountain lion, coyote and flying squirrel are more often heard than seen, and the happy occasion of hearing one of these animals usually occurs while one is busy setting up camp, bedding down or cooking a daybreak breakfast. A coyote's "singing" is a familiar sound to anyone who has watched a western movie, but the habitual birdlike whistling of a mountain lion is usually unrecognized because it seems totally out of character. This cat rarely screams, but he does meow, spit and growl in unmistakable feline fashion. Hearing a flying squirrel, contradictory as it may seem, is a fairly common occurrence. It takes place at night (the squirrel is nocturnal), usually with a whhhist . . . splat sound that characterizes his "flight" from one tree to another.

The most commonly seen animal in this region is man. He is usually quite domesticated, and is exceedingly easy to approach. A query like "Where've you been?" usually brings a flood of friendly information and advice that will keep the querying hiker shifting under his pack for 15 minutes or more. In the perspective of geologic time, this animal has been on the scene but a moment, and his written history consumes only a fraction of a second. Despite his relative newness, his effect has been great, and the mark of his passage is on the land—temporarily.

In this section, man's trails, usually following those of other animals, are plentiful, clearly marked and well maintained. The trail following Mono Creek and crossing Mono Pass, and the one following the South Fork of the San Joaquin River and branching over Piute Pass are old trade routes of the Mono Indian tribes. Paralleling these ancient trails is the relatively newer Italy Pass trans-Sierra crossing, and bisecting all three of these routes is the renowned John Muir Trail, which traverses the west slopes in a north-south direction.

There are seven trailhead entry points to this country that are used for trips in this book.

Mosquito Flat (10,250'). Go 24 miles north from Bishop on U.S. 395 and then 11 miles on paved and dirt road to road's end in Mosquito Flat beside Rock Creek.

Pine Creek Roadend (7580'). Go 10 miles northwest from Bishop on U.S. 395 and then 10 miles on paved road to a parking area near a pack station.

Lake Sabrina (9130'). Go 16 miles southwest from Bishop on State Highway 168 to the backpackers' parking area below the lake, at the North Lake turnoff.

North Lake (9200'). Go 16 miles from Bishop on State Highway 168 almost to Lake Sabrina and turn right on a dirt road. After a few hundred feet turn right again and go 2 miles to a backpackers' parking area just west of North Lake. You must walk the last ½ mile to the trailhead beyond the campground.

Vermilion Campground (7650'). Go east from Clovis (near Fresno) 81 miles on State Highway 168 to the Florence Lake/Lake Edison junction, then 8 miles north on a mostly paved road to Vermilion Campground.

Bear Dam Junction (7010'). Go 2¼ miles north from the Forence Lake/Lake Edison junction described above, to where the jeep road to Bear Diversion Dam leaves the paved road.

Florence Lake (7350'). Go 6 miles east from the Florence Lake/Lake Edison junction described above.

Bear Dam Junction to Twin Falls   **1**

TRIP   From Bear Dam Junction to Twin Falls (round trip). Topo map *Mt. Abbot.* Best early or late season; 11 miles.

Grade	Trail/layover days	Total recommended days
Leisurely	2/0	2
Moderate	....	....
Strenuous	....	....

HILITES   Few creeks in the Sierra possess the simple, primitive appeal of Bear Creek. Never constant, it cascades, chutes and then tumbles down its rocky course, interrupted at graceful intervals by deep, slow-moving, sandy-bottomed pools. Fine brown- and golden-trout angling makes this trip a good fisherman's choice early or late season.

DESCRIPTION (Leisurely trip)

1st Hiking Day (**Bear Dam Junction** to **Twin Falls**, 5½ miles): Lichen-covered, glacially scoured granite surrounds the trailhead for this trip. The rock, fractured in many places not by nature but by man, is more precisely granodiorite, which is typically black-flecked because it contains the minerals biotite and hornblende. The first two miles (to the Bear Diversion Dam) follow an unmaintained Southern California Edison Co. jeep road. After the jeep road leaves the Mono Hot Springs/ Lake Thomas A. Edison road (7000') it swings first east and then south, undulating gently as it traverses the long granite field that marks the southeast end of Bear Ridge. Rounding Bear Ridge, the jeep road ascends gently, and then drops down to the Bear Diversion Dam spillway.

This particular stretch of road overlooks the gorge of the river to the south, and gives the traveler a fine opportunity to watch the abundant population of birds that frequent these broken slopes. Among the birds one is most likely to see are Steller jays, mountain chickadees, juncos, dusky and olive-sided flycatchers, cliff and barn swallows, red-tailed hawks, and a variety of sparrows. Where the jeep road starts to descend to the spillway, one can see southeast to Ward Mountain and Mt. Shinn, and east to Bear Dome and the barren glacial cirques above. This route also offers the traveler on foot or on horseback a chance to absorb the feeling of this glacially scoured country. It is a feeling of openness that is emphasized by the scattering of the forest cover. The mountain juniper and Jeffrey pine occur in moderate stands amid broad expanses of granite, where they have taken root in the granular sand swales that have accumulated as a result of mechanical weathering. In turn, the sprouting of roots from pine, willow, ceanothus and manzanita accelerates the continual process of granite breaking up.

Beyond the parking area above the reservoir is a sign marking the beginning of the trail up Bear Creek. After the trail leaves the roadend area, it doesn't take one long to realize he has left that feeling of openness behind. The canyon walls close in, and the forest cover becomes moderate to dense.

Should one desire to try the fair-to-good fishing along the stream (they come in sizes up to 15"), he will also more than likely encounter small stands of water-loving cottonwood and aspen en route, as well as some lodgepole, oak, and the first fir. Near the creek, wildflower fanciers will relish the luxuriant growth of penstemon, lupine, paintbrush, monkey flower, and cinquefoil.

Bear Creek, in the stretch immediately above the reservoir, is a rock-bottomed, briskly flowing stream with a surprising penchant for suddenly eddying out into broad, emerald-green pools. Fortunately, the trail is never far from the creek's banks, and one can make several worthwhile forays to the water's edge without too much loss of trail time. For 1½ miles above the reservoir, the trail ascends very gradually, and then as the canyon narrows it begins to ascend more steeply. The duff trail gives way to rocky underfooting, which prevails for the rest of the trip, and about ½ mile farther this route encounters the boundary of the John Muir Wilderness. At the boundary, one can catch his first V-notched glimpse of Recess Peak directly up-canyon. The trail drops down for a short distance and then begins a steady, rocky ascent. Several good campsites dot the nearby banks of Bear Creek, and the traveler can take his choice of any of these primitive sites. Though the emerald-green pools occur less often, they stand in dramatic contrast to the plunging white water.

In this country slight changes in altitude entail significant changes in the plant and animal life. For example, as the trail ascends steeply, fishermen find golden trout as well as brown in their catch, and exploring naturalists discover that the predominant forest cover is now Jeffrey pine and the shrubs are now mostly gooseberry and snow bush. Arrival at the packer site is presaged by several "corduroy" bridge crossings of marshy sections, and a stock-drift fence. At the improved packer campsite (8000') there is a fine, large pool offering good fishing for brown and golden trout (8"–15"). Campers in this canyon are frequently serenaded by coyotes who range Bear Ridge. Swimming in mid or late season is excellent.

2nd Hiking Day: Retrace your steps, 5½ miles.

Recess Peak over Lake Edison

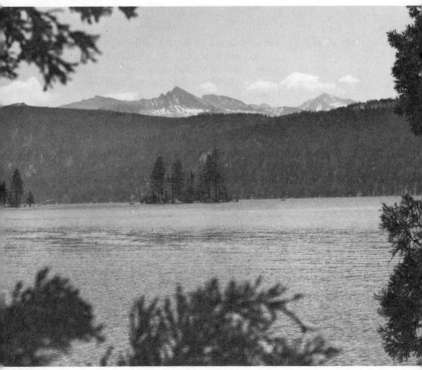

2 Bear Dam Junction to Upper Bear Creek

TRIP
From Bear Dam Junction to Upper Bear Creek (round trip). Topo map *Mt. Abbot.* Best mid or late season; 27 miles.

Grade	Trail/layover days	Total recommended days
Leisurely	4/1	5
Moderate	3/1	4
Strenuous	....	....

HILITES
This trip ascends Bear Creek beyond the densely forested flats at the site of Old Kip Camp. The angler seeking varied sport will find good fishing from the time he first sees Bear Creek at Bear Diversion Dam. Brown trout, a particular favorite of the serious fisherman, populate the lower waters of this trip, and justly famous golden trout inhabit the upper waters and nearby lakes.

DESCRIPTION (Leisurely trip)

1st Hiking Day: Follow trip 1 to **Twin Falls**, 5½ miles.

2nd Hiking Day (**Twin Falls** to **Upper Bear Creek**, 8 miles): An improved packer campsite marks the point where the trail veers north away from cascading Bear Creek. As you ascend steadily up the north wall of the canyon, you have good views of the jumbled cirque crest on the opposite side of the canyon to the southeast. Though rocky, this trail is well maintained as it rises above the floor of the valley. The moderate-to-dense forest cover of the creek bottom thins as the trail climbs to the slight granite-ribbed saddle that marks the start of the descent to a reunion with Bear Creek.

The floral display along this stretch of trail includes penstemon, larkspur, monkshood, lupine, goldenrod, paintbrush and western mountain aster. The descent reveals a marked change in the forest cover in that the predominant Jeffrey of the lower canyon has given way to lodgepole and juniper. Where the views during the ascent were of the down-canyon Bear Creek drainage, you now have views of the Mono Divide.

After descending from a low granite ridge, the trail meanders through dense forest cover and soon arrives at the flats of Old Kip Camp. The forest cover is now predominantly lodgepole, with some fir and aspen in the wetter areas and along the creek on the right. Now the trail begins climbing and soon we arrive at a junction with the John Muir Trail (9000′). Our route turns right onto this famous trail and ascends steadily along the east side of tumbling Bear Creek. Then we swing south through thinning forest on a moderate ascent that stays close to the stream, passing several campsites near the creek. About 2 miles beyond the Muir Trail junction our trail passes the Lake Italy Trail and soon fords the several branches of Hilgard Creek. About 1 mile beyond this creek are several good campsites far enough from Bear Creek to be legal stopping places.

3rd and 4th Hiking Days: Retrace your steps, 13½ miles.

Sign at Bear Dam Junction

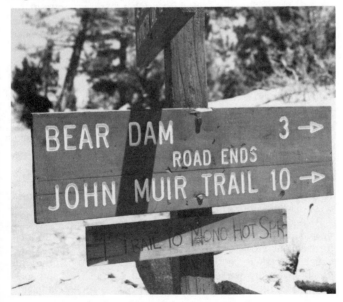

3

Bear Dam Junction
to Vermilion Campground

TRIP From Bear Dam Junction to Vermilion Campground via Quail Meadows (shuttle trip). Topo maps *Kaiser Peak, Mt. Abbot.* Best early or late season; 21 miles.

Grade	Trail/layover days	Total recom- mended days
Leisurely	4/1	5
Moderate	3/1	4
Strenuous	2/1	3

HILITES Varied scenery that ranges from the intimate confines of Bear Creek to the open expanses on Bear Ridge gives this long-weekend trip a universal appeal. The trek circumnavigates Bear Ridge, visiting the Bear and Mono Creek drainages, and the close proximity of the beginning and the end of this horseshoe-shaped route makes it a potential loop.

DESCRIPTION (Moderate trip)

1st Hiking Day: Follow trip 1 to **Twin Falls**, 5½ miles.

2nd Hiking Day (**Twin Falls** to **Quail Meadows**, 10 miles): Follow the 2nd hiking day, trip 2, to the John Muir Trail and turn left. Our route follows the Muir Trail as we traverse northward toward Bear Ridge. The trail soon makes a steady climb to top Bear Ridge. Views back into the Bear Creek drainage are excellent, including Recess Peak, Mt. Hilgard and Seven Gables. At the rocky summit of Bear Ridge, we pass a trail that goes west to Mono Hot Springs.

As the trail begins the steep series of 70 switchbacks that drop into the Mono Creek watershed, the traveler is treated to excellent views of the Silver Divide, the immediate Mono Creek watershed, and Lake Thomas A. Edison. When the trail finally levels off, we ford a tributary of Mono Creek and soon reach a bridge crossing of the creek. Several good campsites

line the north side of Mono Creek near Quail Meadows (7760´),
several hundred yards west. Additional campsites can be found
along the south side of the creek.

3rd Hiking Day (**Quail Meadows** to **Vermilion Campground**, 5½
miles): Our route leaves the John Muir Trail and proceeds
downstream toward Lake Thomas A. Edison. The first mile
of level going parallels the magnificent chutes and rapids that
precede Mono Creek's absorption by the Lake Edison reservoir.
These white waters are periodically interrupted by sandbottomed
granite potholes that offer excellent swimming to the mid or
late season traveler. One can easily imagine the members of
the famous Brewer Survey Party of 1864 stopping here for a
few moments of relaxation and refreshment. A few yards
beyond some potholes an indistinct path branches off to the left
and leads to the boat landing at the northeast tip of the lake.
Here a boat-taxi service operates during the summer months,
and one may obtain the ferry schedule by writing the Vermilion
Valley Resort/Lake Thomas A. Edison/Mono Hot Springs/CA
93642. The ferry service is based at the resort adjoining Vermilion Campground.

Those choosing to use the trail along the north side of Lake
Edison will find that the route undulates severely up and down
the north wall of Vermilion Valley. However, the worst of these
ascents and descents are over midway down the length of the
lake, and the point where our trail passes the Goodale Pass
Trail marks the beginning of relatively level going. Along these
more level stretches the forest cover of fir and pine becomes
somewhat denser. In one of the denser stands of lodgepole, a
few yards from the Goodale Pass Trail junction, our route meets
a second boat-landing trail. Continuing westward, our trail
crosses the Cold Creek bridge, passes the trail lateral to Devils
Bathtub, and winds down through a dense stand of Jeffrey pines
to meet the Forest Service access road that leads to Vermilion
Campground (7650').

4 Bear Dam Junction to Lake Italy

TRIP From Bear Dam Junction to Lake Italy (round trip). Topo map *Mt. Abbot.* Best mid or late season; 37 miles.

Grade	Trail/layover days	Total recommended days
Leisurely	6/1	7
Moderate	4/1	5
Strenuous	3/1	4

HILITES This trip is tailor-made for the traveler who wants to experience the high, alpine country of the mid Sierra without having to contemplate cross-country walking. Lake Italy, the aim of this trip, is a frequently used base camp for climbers, and a fine trip selection for the photographer.

DESCRIPTION (Leisurely trip)

1st Hiking Day: Follow trip 1 to **Twin Falls**, 5½ miles.

2nd Hiking Day (**Twin Falls** to **Hilgard Branch**, 7½ miles): Follow the 2nd hiking day, trip 2, to the Lake Italy Trail and turn left onto it to ascend steadily on rocky underfooting under moderate-to-dense lodgepole pines. In ½ mile the trail levels out and soon forest gives way to large expanses of meadow. Good campsites can be found at the lower end of this meadow.

3rd Hiking Day (**Hilgard Branch** to **Lake Italy**, 5½ miles): In the long meadow just beyond the campsites, one is apt to see much violet-colored Indian paintbrush. Then our route enters lodgepole forest and ascends moderately over rocky underfooting to the outlet of Hilgard Lake. Beyond, the trail swings southeast and traverses a long talus field where the traveler may see fat marmots sunning themselves atop large talus blocks. Beyond the talus, the trail crosses a very wet, meadowy area where seepage emanating from the base of Mt. Hilgard saturates the trail all season long, and it is very difficult to keep one's feet dry. The trail disappears in this area, but it is easily recovered once you reach drier ground.

Where the canyon turns east, the trail veers away from Hilgard Branch and begins a steep, rocky, switchbacking ascent. At the top of this climb the trail swings into a narrow canyon and follows the creek's course on a jumbled ascent high on the precipitous slope above crashing Hilgard Branch. The ascent becomes gentle and the trail enters meadowy sections with scattered clumps of whitebark pine. The stream flows relatively slowly here, but its velocity increases as the canyon floor steepens and the trail becomes fainter. You'll lose the trail here unless you follow a route very close to the one on the topo map. When the trail nears the creek one will see an enormous willow patch on its south side. There is a fairly clear line where the west side of the willow patch ends and sparsely forested slopes continue. Ford the creek at the edge of the patch and climb the south canyon wall. Our route crosses the top of the willowy area and ascends gently through meadow to a ford of the outlet from Teddy Bear and Brown Bear Lakes. The trail then passes clumps of whitebark pine, emerges above timberline, and stays closer to the creek as it crosses long granite ledges that alternate with grassy patches to the outlet of Lake Italy (11,150'). This large lake (124 acres) derives its name from its similarity to the European peninsula.

Rounding the curve of the lake just above the outlet, one can easily see the cirque basin where the feeder glacier had its beginnings. At the east end of the cirque, Bear Creek Spire marks the division between the western and eastern directional flows of the old glaciers. There are a number of fair exposed campsites along the turfy south shore of the lake near the outlet. However, the granitic scenery surrounding this large lake compensates for the lack of forest cover. To the west towers Mt. Hilgard; to the north, Mt. Gabb; and to the east are Bear Creek Spire and Mt. Julius Caesar. To the immediate north of Bear Creek Spire, filling the distant skyline, are Mts. Dade and Abbot. A mountaineer's heaven: every peak bordering on this lake towers well over 13,000 feet. The golden-trout fishery (8"–12") in Lake Italy is fair-to-good—a classification that applies to the surrounding Toe, Jumble, Brown Bear and Teddy Bear lakes as well.

4th, 5th and 6th Hiking Days: Retrace your steps, 18½ miles.

5   **Bear Dam Junction to Lake Italy**

TRIP   From Bear Dam Junction to Lake Italy via Hilgard
                  Branch, return via Vee Lake, East Fork Bear Creek
                  (semiloop trip). Topo map *Mt. Abbot.* Best mid or
                  late season; 41½ miles.

Grade	Trail/layover days	Total recommended days
Leisurely	7/2	9
Moderate	5/2	7
Strenuous	4/2	6

HILITES   For intermediate and experienced backpackers
                 only, this varied and exciting cross-country trip
                 seeks the kind of high country that is the exclusive
                 province of the knapsacker.

DESCRIPTION (Leisurely trip)

1st, 2nd and 3rd Hiking Days: Follow trip 4 to **Lake Italy,** 18½
miles.

4th Hiking Day (**Lake Italy** to **Vee Lake,** 5 miles, part cross country): Our route skirts the south side of Lake Italy, following
the ducked and sometimes faint Italy Pass Trail. As the trail
ascends on the west side of the outlet stream from Jumble Lake,
one has excellent views northeast along the Sierra Nevada crest.
The trail then fords the stream, and about ¼ mile above Jumble
Lake our route branches south away from the Italy Pass Trail
and, going cross-country, traverses the granite slope above
Jumble Lake. The route levels off before we reach the rocky
saddle that dents the ridge above White Bear Lake. At this
saddle, one can see the clear division that this ridge made between two small glaciers which once fed the main *mer de glace*
that flowed down Bear Creek canyon. White Bear Lake and

Black Bear Lake just to its east are the puddled remnants of the outermost extremities of the East Fork feeder glacier. By virtue of having come "through the back door," the hiker has the opportunity to trace the old glacier's path from its inception all the way to the main trunk. Anglers will probably want to try the fair-to-good golden-trout fishing at White Bear and Black Bear lakes before proceeding, but as a rule of thumb the fishing gets better as one descends into the East Fork drainage.

At the saddle a faint trail begins, and it continues to Big Bear Lake. The descent to White Bear Lake is not difficult if one doesn't stray too far west, where there are cliffs. Follow the west shore of White Bear Lake to its outlet, where the trail becomes more evident, and follow it down the intermittent stream to Big Bear Lake. At Big Bear Lake and Ursa Lake, just east of it, the angler will find the biggest fish of the trip— golden trout, rainbow trout and golden-rainbow hybrid (to 16").

To keep from getting lost, it is best to follow the rocky outlet stream from Big Bear Lake to Little Bear Lake. The route passes high above little Bear Lake on its south side, and then turns southwest over a low granite ridge and gently descends to the northwest shore of Vee Lake. A trail on this shore leads to the outlet, where a treeless but pleasant campsite is found. The views from here include Royce Peak and "Feather Peak" (Peak 13242) to the east, and Seven Gables to the west. Vee Lake makes an excellent base for exploring the upper part of the basin, and it also offers good fishing for golden trout (to 15").

5th Hiking Day (**Vee Lake** to **Upper Bear Creek,** 4½ miles): Keeping to the west side of the outlet stream, our route descends steeply to the Seven Gables Lakes basin. The intimate falls and chutes found along this outlet stream are a pleasant contrast to the brooding heights of Seven Gables peak to the west. At the confluence of the outlet creek and the Seven Gables branch of East Fork Bear Creek, our route turns downstream. However, anglers electing to first test the good fishing for golden trout at the largest of the Seven Gables Lakes will alter their route upstream—½ mile of gentle ascent. Those continuing downstream will find a faint trail on the east side, but travel here isn't much better than on the west side, and route-finding abilities may come in handy.

Descending steadily, the route continues northwest for a short quarter mile, then crosses by a shallow wade where the canyon narrows, and continues northwest to reach an obvious trail down the canyon which soon turns west. This steady descent encounters timberline just north of Seven Gables peak, and witnesses the typical hemlock-lodgepole-fir spectrum as it follows the length of a narrow canyon and emerges into the wide, more open expanses of Bear Creek canyon. Turning northward, the trail meets and turns right onto the John Muir Trail. Your descent becomes moderate to gentle as the trail winds through alternating meadows and lodgepole stands to the campsites on upper Bear Creek.

6th Hiking Day (**Upper Bear Creek** to **Twin Falls**, 8 miles): A mile of gentle descent leads to the fords of multibranched Hilgard Creek. A few yards beyond these fords the trail meets the Hilgard Branch Trail and then retraces most of the 2nd hiking day, trip 2.

7th Hiking Day: Retrace the steps of the 1st hiking day, 5½ miles.

Spotted sandpiper's nest with egg   *Jeff Schaffer*

Bear Dam Junction to Sandpiper Lake **6**

TRIP From Bear Dam Junction to Sandpiper Lake (round trip) Topo map *Mt. Abbot.* Best mid or late season; 33 miles.

Grade	Trail/layover days	Total recommended days
Leisurely	5/1	6
Moderate	4/1	5
Strenuous	3/1	4

HILITES This trip provides an unusual opportunity to trace a river's course from its inception. Much of this route follows the famous John Muir Trail, but most of our campsite recommendations avoid that trail's heavily used stopover places.

DESCRIPTION (Moderate trip)

1st Hiking Day: Follow trip 1 to **Twin Falls**, 5½ miles.

2nd Hiking Day (**Twin Falls** to **Sandpiper Lake**, 11 miles): Follow the 2nd hiking day, trip 2, to the campsites on upper Bear Creek. (This is a long uphill hiking day, and some people may want to stop somewhere on upper Bear Creek and continue on to Sandpiper Lake the next day.) The ascent is still gentle-to-moderate as it passes along open granite slab sections with meadowy breaks, and arrives at the trail junction where the Vee and Seven Gables Lakes Trail branches left (east). This junction is just a few yards short of a Bear Creek ford—a wade-across ford that is hazardous during high water. The trail then ascends steeply by switchbacks to the corduroy bridge crossing of West Fork Bear Creek at Rosemarie Meadow.

At an obvious junction, our route branches left, off the John Muir Trail, eastward over an easy ridge to Lou Beverly Lake. (This well-established trial is not shown on the topo map.) The moderate forest cover of lodgepole through which the trail winds shows the effects of the higher altitude. The two-needled trees take on a stunted appearance, and one begins to see clumps of red mountain heather. Lou Beverly Lake (10,050') is a tiny (5 acre), shallow, moderately forested lake with campsites at the southwest end. Fishing for golden (to 14") is good to excellent, which should be adequate reason for anglers to try their luck. For the camper who prefers a more protected and timbered lake, Lou Beverly is a fine alternative place to end this hiking day.

For the camper who prefers a high alpine feel to his campsite, the choice should be Sandpiper Lake. The trail to that lake crosses the marshy inlet of Lou Beverly Lake and ascends along the north and east side of the stream connecting the two lakes. This ascent, over rough, unmaintained trail, is steady until it reaches the abrupt granite face just below Sandpiper Lake, where the going becomes very steep. The waterfall outlet of Sandpiper Lake (10,450') makes a musical accompaniment to end the climb by, as one arrives at the good campsites near the outlet and along the west side of the lake. This fair-sized lake (about 25 acres) has a very sparse forest cover of stunted lodgepoles but the view of the surrounding granitic peaks is excellent —particularly from the granite shoulder just southwest of the lake. Despite fairly heavy fishing pressure, angling for golden (to 13") is often good, and this lake makes an excellent base camp for fishing and hiking excursions to the surrounding lakes on the headwaters of Bear Creek. The morning and evening sounds of Pacific tree frogs and Yosemite toads are welcome background music for the hustling cook at his chores.

3rd and 4th Hiking Days: Retrace your steps, 16½ miles.

Bear Dam Junction to Little Moccasin Lake   7

TRIP   From Bear Dam Junction to Little Moccasin Lake
via Sandpiper Lake, cross-country return via West
Pinnacles Creek drainage, Three Island Lake (semiloop trip). Topo map *Mt. Abbot*. Best mid or late
season; 47 miles.

Grade	Trail/layover days	Total recom-mended days
Leisurely	....	....
Moderate	6/2	8
Strenuous	5/2	7

HILITES   Loop trips that include the variety of country this
one does are rare. From the confines of Bear Creek,
this route climbs above timberline and circles two
rarely visited watersheds. The cross-country work
is often difficult, and this trip is recommended for
experienced hikers only.

DESCRIPTION (Moderate trip)

1st and 2nd Hiking Days: Follow trip 6 to **Sandpiper Lake**, 16½
miles.

3rd Hiking Day (**Sandpiper Lake** to **Little Moccasin Lake**, 6½ miles
cross country): Our rugged cross-country loop begins by rounding the west side of Sandpiper Lake (10,450') and fording the
inlet stream coming from Medley Lake. From here the route
ascends southeast by means of granite ledge systems. Following the south fork of the east inlet stream of Medley Lake, your
route ascends steeply over smoothed, barren granite slabs and
grassy pockets to a narrow, unnamed lake at the head of the
stream on the topo map. Views during the course of this climb
include Medley Lake, Mts. Senger and Hooper, and Seven

Gables. From the unnamed lake this route ascends up the drainage to the northeast to an obvious saddle. Just short of this
saddle, one has superlative views to the west, and these views
are matched to the east and north when the crest of the saddle
is reached, for from the saddle one can see Mts. Hilgard, Abbot,
Gabb, Dade, Bear Creek Spire, Julius Caesar, Royce, Humphreys
and Gemini.

Route-finding on these rugged talus slopes is difficult at best,
but the hiker will find the traverse around the steep north slope
of Gemini a moderate one that descends to a broad saddle and
down to the unnamed, scree-ridden lake just north of Aweetasal
Lake. This traverse offers excellent views down into the Seven
Gables Lakes cirque until it crosses a saddle. The rock cairn
at the saddle marks a point from which one can see the crest
as it dwindles away to the southernmost skyline, including
Glacier Divide, Emerald Peak, and Mts. McGee, Henry and
Goddard. Immediately on the right are the twin peaks of Gemini
and the spectacular jumbled crest of The Pinnacles. It is the
latter that dominate the views to the west for the remainder of
this hiking day's progress down the East Pinnacles Creek drainage. Descent into this drainage is first moderate (to the first
unnamed, talus-cluttered lake), and then steeper as one drops
down to shallow Aweetasal Lake.

Typical of most of the lakes on this drainage, Aweetasal has
poor fishing and virtually no timber, but tundralike grassy spots
between granite slabs. This rugged and somewhat sterile land
is the alpine Sierra at its best. Here, despite the harsh, exposed
environment, tough yet delicate grasses grow. Near the streams
one can rediscover the yellow columbine that is found only in
these rarified heights. There are, of course, the usual whorled
penstemon, paintbrush, yellow cinquefoil and shooting star, but
all are dwarfed, clinging close to the turf, as though they were
foreign to this clime. Here the margin for life is slim, and the
hardiest backpacker finds himself imitating the plant life. When
he rests or seeks sleep in the comfort of his bedroll, he instinc-
tively curls up to conserve his precious body heat. This is
perenially ice-touched land, always cold, and yet a place where
one can get a severe sunburn.

Harsh and uninviting as the land seems, the hiker soon finds
a beauty to wonder at as he progresses down the drainage.
Only those who dare this harshness manage to view The Pinnacles from the east side, and that rugged, spiring rock mass
towers on the right as one scrambles down the alternately moderate and steep granite slabs between Aweetasal and Jawbone
lakes.

Following the outlet stream from Jawbone Lake, one arrives at shallow, grassy Council Lake. Here route-finding becomes simpler as the going levels off, and by a series of grassy benches one passes Paoha and Negit Lakes, and, rounding a granite shoulder, comes to Big Moccasin Lake. Stunted and solitary whitebark pines dot the rock fringes of this shallow lake. From Big Moccasin Lake it is an easy descent to Little Moccasin Lake, where one has fine views of the Piute Creek drainage. Above its U-shaped valley one can see Pilot Knob and the complex of avalanche chutes on the north face of Mt. Henry to the south. Majestic Mt. Humphreys dominates the Sierra crest, and the adjacent subrange is crowned by Emerald Peak. From this viewpoint, our route veers due west, descending a grassy chute to the campsites along the outlet streams from the upper lakes. These campsites (10,800') are good, with excellent views.

4th Hiking Day (**Little Moccasin Lake** to **Sandpiper Lake**, 7½ miles cross country): From the west fork of East Pinnacles Creek this cross-country route swings around the south end of The Pinnacles on a long talus-and-boulder traverse to a point just north of Pemmican Lake. This scrambling traverse offers the views described in the 3rd hiking day until the drainage of West Pinnacles Creek is reached. A slight descent past several tarns unmarked on the topo map leads to Spearpoint Lake, which, unlike the lakes of the East Pinnacles Creek drainage, is deep, and populated by a few small golden trout (6–8"). The rugged terrain around the edges of Spearpoint Lake determines the best feasible route to be over the easy granite ridge separating Spearpoint and Pendant lakes, and thence north across the marshy section separating Pendant and Big Chief lakes. After skirting the east side of shallow Big Chief Lake, this route ascends on a moderate grade from the meadowed north end of the lake to Old Squaw Lake. This lake is barren of trout, but it offers some of the best views of The Pinnacles to be obtained on this trip. Glacially smoothed granite slabs line the lake's edge on all sides, and progress is fairly easy along the east shore. Following the inlet stream, the route ascends steadily to Wampum Lake, where anglers may try their luck for the fair fishing (golden 6–8").

At Wampum Lake the twin peaks of Gemini once more come into view, and one has reached the cirque-basined headwaters of West Pinnacles Creek. This bowl-like cirque presents route-picking problems, and some care should be exercised in crossing the sometimes steep west wall, which divides the West

Pinnacles Creek drainage from the South Fork Bear Creek drainage. At the top of this wall one has a panoramic vista of Seven Gables, Gemini, The Pinnacles, Emerald Peak, Mt. Henry, Mt. Senger, Mt. Hooper and the Bear Creek drainage.

Descent from this ridge presents no problems to the accomplished rock-climber, but the easiest route is to pick one's way westward around the head of the Three Island Lake cirque to the saddle just east of Sharp Note Lake, and then traverse down the steep slopes on the west side of Three Island Lake. Anglers will find fair-to-good golden-trout fishing in this large (80-acre) lake. These rockbound, deep waters provide a classic glacial setting for high-country enthusiasts, and they are a favorite of camera-carrying visitors. Following the outlet stream at the north end of Three Island Lake past Medley Lake, an easy descent along a ledge system of granite leads to the inlet of Sandpiper Lake, the beginning for this cross-country loop.

5th and 6th Hiking Days: Retrace the steps of the 2nd and 1st hiking days, 16½ miles.

Marie Lake from Selden Pass   *U.S. Forest Service*

Bear Dam Junction to Florence Lake

8

TRIP From Bear Dam Junction to Florence Lake via Sandpiper Lake, Selden Pass, Blaney Meadow (shuttle trip). Topo maps *Mt. Abbot, Blackcap Mountain.* Best mid or late season; 34 miles.

Grade	Trail/layover days	Total recommended days
Leisurely	5/1	6
Moderate	4/1	5
Strenuous	3/1	4

HILITES This popular shuttle trip circles the Mt. Hooper complex and visits some of the best creek and lake fishing in the Sierra. Part of this trip's popularity stems from the near proximity of the trailhead to the conclusion of the trip—making the shuttle fairly simple.

DESCRIPTION (Moderate trip)

1st and 2nd Hiking Days: Follow trip 6 to **Sandpiper Lake,** 16½ miles.

3rd Hiking Day (**Sandpiper Lake** to **Lower Blaney Meadows,** 10 miles —2 miles cross country): The first 2 miles of this hiking day are cross country. Starting from the campsites along the west side of Sandpiper Lake, this route ascends the easy, tarn-dotted swale at the southwest end of the lake and leads around the granite-slabbed nose of the ridge descending north from Mt. Senger. From this nose, one has excellent views down the Bear Creek drainage to Bear Ridge, and beyond to the barren tops of the Silver Divide. Immediately below is Lou Beverly Lake, and in its mirrorlike green surface one sees the reflection of Recess Peak. Looking north, views from left to right include Mt. Hooper, the Bear Creek drainage, and Lou Beverly Lake; and beyond, Graveyard Peak, Mt. Izaak Walton and Red and

White Mountain. Given a clear atmosphere, one can see all the way north to the Minarets and the Mammoth Crest. To the immediate right is the bouldery crest of Mt. Hilgard, and to the right of that towers multipeaked Seven Gables, with Mt. Gabb peeking over its left shoulder. Turning toward the south, one looks into the immense cirque basin capped by Mt. Senger.

From the top of this ridge, it is a moderate descent west to large, granite-lined Marie Lake, where our route skirts the meadowy northern edge. Walking the turfy fringes of the lake, one will find elephant heads and western mountain aster mixed among the heather. This lake is at timberline, and as our route turns south on the west side of Marie Lake, the mixed sparse forest is left behind. At the outlet of Marie Lake our route rejoins the John Muir Trail as it winds along the west banks of the lake. From the south end of the lake, the trail ascends on a gentle-to-moderate grade to Selden Pass (10,873'). Breather stops on this climb offer fine views back to Mt. Hilgard and the granitic Marie Lake cirque.

From Selden Pass the trail descends over short, steep switchbacks to Heart Lake. This rockbound, heart-shaped lake has a meadow-turfed fringe delicately colored with heather, primrose and yellow columbine. Continuing the moderate descent from Heart Lake along its outlet stream, the trail arrives at Sally Keyes Lakes. This short walk is lined with a great abundance of wildflowers including corn lily, Indian paintbrush, Douglas phlox, shooting star, yellow cinquefoil, yarrow milfoil, penstemon, lupine, red heather, wallflower, nude buckwheat and western mountain aster.

The trail crosses the short stream joining the two Sally Keyes Lakes and then descends on duff and sand through a thickening forest cover of lodgepole. There are several good, though heavily used, campsites at the outlet and along the west shore of the lower of the two lakes. In 1979 the main trail was rerouted around the large meadow that lies ¼ mile south of the lower lake, so you will have to find the old main trail southbound or go to this meadow via cross country to reach the start of the shortcut trail down to the South Fork San Joaquin River. Although this unmaintained trail is dusty and steep, one can enjoy an unusual cross section of Sierra flora in the course of a 3000-foot descent. At first, altitude-loving whitebark pines are mixed with the dense forest cover of lodgepole pines, but within a few miles the whitebarks disappear and fir makes a brief appearance, only to be replaced by Jeffrey pine at lower altitudes. Juniper is found in both the high and low altitudes; quaking aspen is not seen until the trail nears Senger Creek, near the foot of a descent. The dry canyon walls are generally brush-covered, with heavy manzanita around the middle of the descent, but with some surprise the trail traveler will also find many wildflowers along these same stretches. In the drier regions are Douglas phlox, streptanthus and Mariposa lily; in the wetter sections are shooting star, red columbine, corn lily, cinquefoil and penstemon; almost everywhere are lupine, white Mariposa, Bigelow sneezeweed, golden brodiaea and groundsel.

The switchbacking descent ends above Blaney Meadows (visible from the trail) and then this route turns right onto the Florence Lake Trail. From this junction the duff trail descends through a moderately dense mixed forest cover of lodgepole, juniper, Jeffrey and quaking aspen, and arrives at Lower Blaney Meadows and the public campground (7650'). Several fair campsites, including two improved packer sites, are available. Fishing in South Fork San Joaquin River for brook and some rainbow (to 12") is fair to good—mostly downstream.

4th Hiking Day (**Lower Blaney Meadows** to **Florence Lake**, 7½ miles): Following the well-used route west from Lower Blaney Meadows the trail ascends steadily over sand and rock to the footlog ford of the unnamed creek just east of Double Meadow. Here, the trail has been rerouted around the fringes of the grassland. Damage to fragile meadows like these, particularly during the wet early-summer months, has made a sufficient impression on the Forest Service and the National Park Service that they are now deemed worthy of appropriate conservation measures to guarantee their survival. As the trail rounds the north side of the meadow, it affords excellent views of Ward Mountain and high, pointed Mt. Shinn, and then it makes a moderate descent through a forest cover of Jeffrey, juniper and white fir to an improved campground above the head of Florence Lake. From here a bridge leads over South Fork San Joaquin River, just above the southeast end of Florence Lake. Crossing the smooth granite west of the bridge, this trail passes a short lateral branching right to the edge of Florence Lake, and a heavily used campground. At Boulder Creek the trail crosses by means of a footlog. The ford is dangerous during heavy runoff.

This route then passes the Thomson Lake/Hot Springs Pass Trail and commences a series of moderate-to-steep ups and downs through a mixed forest cover of Jeffrey and juniper, with occasional aspen, white fir and lodgepole. We skirt the west side of Florence Lake, sometimes ascending to granite ledges 150 feet above the lake's surface. Views to the southeast always include Mt. Shinn and Ward Mountain and glimpses up the South Fork San Joaquin River drainage. To the north is the Silver Divide, foregrounded by the blue waters of Florence Lake. Just before this route meets the Southern California Edison Dam Road (no public auto travel) the trail has climbed high on the ridge; it then descends steeply to the roadend. (A boat-taxi shuttles from the head of Florence Lake to the roadend in summertime, quitting around 7 p.m. each night. Write Muir Trail Ranch, Box 176, Lakeshore, CA 93634 for details.)

Florence Lake

Bear Dam Junction to Vee Lake

9

TRIP

From Bear Dam Junction to Vee Lake via Sandpiper Lake, cross country to Vee Lake, return via cross-country route to Lake Italy, Hilgard Branch (semiloop trip). Topo map *Mt. Abbot.* Best mid or late season; 45 miles.

Grade	Trail/layover days	Total recommended days
Leisurely	....	....
Moderate	7/2	9
Strenuous	5/2	7

HILITES

A fine fishing trip combined with a short, rugged cross-country segment, this route should appeal to the intermediate backpacker as well as the veteran.

DESCRIPTION (Moderate trip)

1st and 2nd Hiking Days: Follow trip 6 to **Sandpiper Lake,** 16½ miles.

3rd Hiking Day (**Sandpiper Lake** to **Vee Lake,** 5 miles cross country): This route circles the east side of Sandpiper Lake, goes up beside the eastern inlet stream to the elbow of this stream, and fords it. Shortly beyond, our route meets and follows the south fork of the east inlet stream of Medley Lake. This cross-country route crosses steep, glacially smoothed granite that is interspersed with grassy, wildflower-colored pockets, and arrives at the narrow, barren, unnamed lake that lies at the head of this stream fork. Along with the rarified air of the climb (crossing the 12,000' level) the route brings fine views of Mts. Senger, Hooper and Seven Gables. A rest break is probably in order before beginning the final flower-lined ascent to the obvious saddle on the northeast horizon. The climb begins easily, soon becomes steep, and concludes with a scramble to the crest.

At this saddle, one has unmatched views to the north and east. Besides the immediate summits of Seven Gables and the twin spires of Gemini, one can see Mts. Hilgard, Abbot, Gabb, Dade, Julius Caesar, Royce and Humphreys and Bear Creek Spire. Every one of these peaks towers over 13,000 feet. Also from this saddle, one can spy out the natural route to the southernmost of the Seven Gables Lakes. Though steep, this descent is made mostly over glacially smoothed rock. Route-picking, however, is sometimes made difficult by interruptions of talus and scree slides.

The upper lakes of the Seven Gables chain are talus-bound, shallow bodies of water having no fish, but anglers will want to try the good fishing on the lower lakes (golden trout to 12") before making the final ascent to Vee Lake. These lower lakes and the intersecting stream are a fly fisherman's paradise. The ascent to Vee Lake is made over granite and talus along the outlet stream from that lake. The ascent terminates at the turfy east end (11,120'), where there are fair campsites. (Hikers who do not care for the high, alpine kind of camping should plan on ending their day at the lowest of the Seven Gables Lakes, where there are several good campsites.) Fishing on large Vee Lake (50 acres) is good to excellent for golden (to 15"). Views from the campsites on the east and north sides of the lake are excellent of the striking, white-granite faces of Royce and Merriam peaks.

4th Hiking Day (**Vee Lake** to **Lake Italy**, 5 miles cross country): Beginning at the north side of the north arm of Vee Lake, this hiking day's route ascends a granite shoulder to the string of rockbound tarns just south of Little Bear Lake. This moderate ascent is accomplished over a granite ledge system broken by talus. Fishing on tiny Little Bear Lake for golden is fair to good, and this evaluation holds for Big Bear and White Bear lakes upstream. Following the inlet stream of Little Bear Lake, the route ascends to the outlet of Big Bear/Ursa/Bearpaw Lake basin, crosses the stream joining Big Bear and White Bear lakes, and ascends steeply along the east side of this stream. Above the abrupt northeast side of White Bear Lake, one can make out the obvious saddle that separates the drainage of East Fork Bear Creek from that of Hilgard Branch. Our route crosses this saddle, traverses the southeast end of the Jumble Lake cirque, and strikes the Italy Pass Trail, where it turns left.

The saddle and the traverse offer unusual end-on views of Mts. Julius Caesar, Dade, Abbot, and Mills and Bear Creek Spire. Descending the moderate-to-steep slopes above Jumble

Lake, one cannot help feeling awed by the forces that carved this basin. The smoothed rock is mute testimony to the grinding action of the glaciers that had their start here, and, as the trail continues to descend along the north shore of Jumble Lake, one pursues the course of the glacier as it forged its way into the much larger Lake Italy cirque. This descent fords the stream that joins Jumble Lake and Lake Italy and drops down to the shores of the latter about a mile above the outlet (11,150'). This very large lake (124 acres) is granite-enclosed, with narrow, meadowed fringes. Fair campsites that are quite exposed can be found along the south shore near the outlet, and there are superlative views of the surrounding peaks. Fishing for golden (8–12") is fair.

5th, 6th and 7th Hiking Days: Reverse the steps of trip 4, 18½ miles.

Douglas phlox

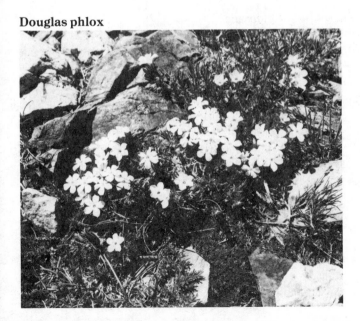

10   **Bear Dam Junction to Second Recess**

TRIP
From Bear Dam Junction to Second Recess via Hilgard Branch, Lake Italy, cross-country route to Lower Mills Creek Lake, Second Recess, return via Fish Camp, Quail Meadows (semiloop trip). Topo map *Mt. Abbot.* Best late season; 48½ miles.

Grade	Trail/layover days	Total recommended days
Leisurely	......	......
Moderate	7/2	9
Strenuous	5/2	7

HILITES
Another fine partly cross-country route, this trip is frequently used by climbers making ascents of the cluster of peaks that line the route. Anglers, photographers, naturalists and garden-variety trailpounders will all find something to excite them en route. Because of the cross country, this route is recommended for experienced backpackers only.

DESCRIPTION (Moderate trip)

1st, 2nd and 3rd Hiking Days: Follow trip 4 to **Lake Italy,** 18½ miles.

4th Hiking Day (**Lake Italy** to **Lower Mills Creek Lake,** 5 miles cross country): This scenic cross-country route rounds the granite-bound north side of Lake Italy to Toe Lake, and then ascends the increasingly steep north cirque wall to 12,250-foot Gabbot Pass (the saddle between Mt. Gabb and Mt. Abbot). The ascent involves a strenuous workout, but does not require rock-climbing skills. As a reward, the hiker acquires some of the finest views obtainable in this part of the Sierra. This route is generally considered a climber's access route for ascents of Mts. Gabb and Abbot, and is seldom used by casual hikers. Parts of it are slippery in early summer. Peaks in line of sight during the ascent and at the pass include, to the west, Mts. Hilgard and Gabb; to the south, Mt. Julius Caesar, Royce Peak and "Feather Peak"; to the east, Mts. Dade, Abbot and Mills, and Bear Creek Spire; and to the north, the crest of the Silver Divide.

From the pass, this ducked route descends just east of the Mt. Gabb glacier to the steep headwall of the Upper Mills Creek Lake cirque. Traversing the east side of this cirque, the route becomes a trail as it continues down the east side of the cascading creek between the lakes to the good campsites at the timberlined outlet of Lower Mills Creek Lake (10,840'), an outstandingly pretty lake. Both Upper and Lower Mills Creek lakes are meadow-fringed, though mostly rockbound, and offer good-to-excellent golden-trout fishing (to 13"). Views from the campsites are excellent of the Mono and Silver divides.

5th Hiking Day (**Lower Mills Creek Lake** to **Quail Meadows**, 9½ miles): Staying on the east side of Mills Creek, a faint fisherman's trail descends the sparsely timbered slopes below Lower Mills Creek Lake past two small lakelets (good fishing for golden to 10"). At the final drop into Second Recess Creek canyon, this faint, often washed-out trail switchbacks down steeply to the confluence of the two creeks. The forest cover alters during the course of this descent from stunted lodgepole and some whitebark to flat-needled fir, lodgepole pine, and occasional quaking aspen and Jeffrey pine.

Our route, now following a distinct trail, descends on a moderate slope along the east side of Second Recess Creek. As one nears the brink of Mono Creek canyon, one gets a clear picture of the glacial story that left these spectacular landforms. It is evident that the valley of the Second Recess was a secondary (or feeder) arm of the greater ice mass that once filled deeper Mono Creek canyon. After accomplishing the moderate-to-steep descent to the log crossing of Mono Creek, the traveler can look back whence he came and fully understand the nature of the geologic term "hanging valley." The greater ice mass of the main trunk ground deeper, leaving these valleys literally hanging.

At Fish Camp this route passes several improved packer campsites and turns left (west) onto the Mono Creek Trail. This creekside trail descends moderately, offering between-the-trees views into First Recess, and of the abrupt, dark, north face of Volcanic Knob. Frequent groves of quaking aspen line this route, and late season sees the banks of Mono Creek clad in golden hues. At the point where the canyon walls appear to be closing in, about 3 miles below Fish Camp, the trail veers away from the creek on a steep, switchbacking ascent that crosses the long-nosed ridge that separates the North Fork from the main canyon of Mono Creek. On the west side of this ridge, our route descends a short distance to the John Muir Trail junction, and turns left along the east side of North Fork Mono Creek. The trail then switchbacks down steeply to ford the North Fork a few yards above its confluence with the main stream. From this ford it is less than a mile of relatively level going through a dense lodgepole forest cover to the good campsites at Quail Meadows (7760').

6th and 7th Hiking Days: Reverse the 2nd and 1st hiking days, trip 3, 15½ miles.

Running Mono Creek below Quail Meadows   *Jeff Schaffer*

Mosquito Flat to Second Recess   **11**

TRIP   From Mosquito Flat (on Rock Creek) to Second
                Recess via Mono Pass (round trip). Topo maps *Mt.*
                Tom, Mt. Abbot. Best mid or late season; 32 miles.

| | Trail/layover | Total recom- |
Grade	days	mended days
Leisurely	6/2	8
Moderate	5/2	7
Strenuous	4/2	6

HILITES   The exciting eastern escarpment makes the first
                part of this trip a memorable experience. On this
                escarpment, the tral to Mono Pass offers sweeping
                vistas that vie for the traveler's consideration with
                the intimacy of the beautiful, cirque-bound lakes
                of Second Recess.

DESCRIPTION (Leisurely trip)

1st Hiking Day (**Mosquito Flat** to **Ruby Lake**, 2½ miles): The magnificent Sierra crest confronts the traveler at the very onset of
this trip. From the trailhead at Mosquito Flat (10,250´) the wide,
rocky-sandy trail starts southwest toward the imposing skyline
dominated by Mts. Mills, Abbot and Dade and Bear Creek
Spire. A short distance from the trailhead, our route tops a low
rocky ridge just west of Mack Lake. From this ridge one has
good views of the green-clad Little Lakes Valley, and one cannot help but feel a sense of satisfaction that this beautiful valley
enjoys protection as part of the John Muir Wilderness. Aside
from some early, abortive mining ventures, this region remains
relatively unspoiled.

The trail crosses the ridge and in a short distance comes to
a junction of the Little Lakes Valley Trail. Here our route
branches right (west) and ascends steeply on rocky switchbacks.
In the course of this switchbacking ascent, we see the moderate-
to-dense forest cover of whitebark and lodgepole diminish in

density as we near timberline. Views during the climb include
the glacier-fronted peaks named above, and, midway up the
ascent, imposing Mt. Morgan in the southeast. Immediately
below to the east, the deep blue of Heart and Box lakes and
some of the Hidden Lakes reflects the sky above, and the viewer
looking at the panorama of the valley can readily comprehend
the glacial history that left these "puddles" behind.

Near the meadowed edge of the outlet stream from Ruby
Lake is a junction, where we turn left. It becomes apparent
that a cirque basin is opening up, although one cannot see Ruby
Lake, which compeltely fills the cirque bottom, until one is
actually at water's edge (11,000'). This first breathtaking view
of the lake and its towering cirque walls makes the climb worth
the effort. Sheer granite composes the upper walls of the cirque,
and the crown is topped by a series of spectacular pinnacles,
particularly to the west. To the north, also on the crest, a notch
indicates Mono Pass, and close scrutiny will reveal the switchbacking trail that ascends the south ridge of Mt. Starr. The
lower walls of the cirque are mostly made up of talus and scree
that curve outward to the lake's edge, and it is over this jumbled
rock that ambitious anglers must scramble to sample the fair
fishing for brook, rainbow and brown (to 12"). Good campsites
can be found below the outlet of the lake.

2nd Hiking Day (**Ruby Lake** to **Fish Camp**, 9 miles): First retrace
your steps ¼ mile to the Mono Pass Trail. Following a general
east-to-west course, the trail climbs by long, steady switchbacks
up the north wall of the cirque, and after a long, steady traverse
veers northward by steeper switchbacks to the summit of Mono
Pass (12,000'). The best views from the pass area are obtained
by climbing the easy granite shoulder of Mt. Starr, to the east.
Views from this shoulder include Mts. Stanford, Huntington,
Crocker and Hopkins and Red and White Mountain to the
north; and Mts. Abbot, Dade, and Humphreys and Bear Creek
Spire to the south.

The trail continues north from the pass, descending steadily
over granite. It traverses the west side of rockbound Summit
Lake, and then descends more steeply to the slopes above Trail
Lakes. The westward descent around Trail Lakes turns northward, and the trail drops to a Golden Creek ford. Here this route
re-enters forest cover, and it continues to descend as it passes
the lateral to Pioneer Basin and the lateral to Fourth Recess
Lake. Serious anglers may wish to alter their hiking plan with a
rewarding excursion to the excellent brook (some rainbow and
golden) fishing obtainable at the lower Pioneer lakes. Fishing
at nearby Fourth Recess Lake is good for brook (to 14").

Beyond these laterals, the trail fords the outlet streams from Pioneer Basin.

Mono Rock towers on the left as our route passes the Third Recess Trail lateral, and, about a mile farther, the lateral to Hopkins Lakes and Hopkins Pass. Anglers who wish to sample the good fishing for brook, rainbow and occasional golden in Mono Creek will find many fine, deep holes along this stretch of trail. For the most part, Mono Creek rushes along briskly, but occasional potholes and level stretches in the stream bed contribute to the good spawning areas that any good Sierra trout stream requires. Anglers and hikers alike will appreciate the abundance of quaking aspens that line Mono Creek. For those with color film in their cameras, the best time to capture the aspen color is usually late September or early October. This route then passes the Grinnell Lakes lateral, and descends to the good improved campsites on both sides of a log spanning Mono Creek at Fish Camp (8550').

3rd Hiking Day (**Fish Camp** to **Lower Mills Creek Lake**, 4½ miles): Retrace the steps of part of the 5th hiking day, trip 10.

4th, 5th and 6th Hiking Days: Retrace your steps, 16 miles.

Bear Creek Spire

12 Pine Creek Roadend to Honeymoon Lake

TRIP

From Pine Creek Roadend to Honeymoon Lake (round trip). Topo map *Mt. Tom.* Best midseason; 11 miles.

Grade	Trail/layover days	Total recommended days
Leisurely	2/1	3
Moderate	2/0	2
Strenuous	day	....

HILITES

The steep, winding ascent to Honeymoon Lake offers breathtaking over-the-shoulder views of the Pine Creek watershed, and the Honeymoon Lake campsite views of the Sierra crest make this one of the best choices for a base camp location on the east side of the Sierra.

DESCRIPTION (Moderate trip)

1st Hiking Day (**Pine Creek Roadend** to **Honeymoon Lake**, 5½ miles): The trailhead (7400') is located at the pack station just south of Pine Creek. The dusty duff trail ascends steeply from the pack station through a dense, mixed forest cover of Jeffrey pine, juniper, red fir, quaking aspen and birch, and fords several branchlets of an unnamed creek that feeds Pine Creek. These fords are decorated by plentiful blossoms of wild rose, columbine, tiger lily and Queen Anne's lace. About ⅓ mile beyond these fords, the trail emerges from the forest cover, directly opposite the Union Carbide tungsten mill, and then merges with a recently rebuilt mining road for access to the Brownstone Mine, where new drilling was carried on in 1974. Although the slope into the Pine Creek canyon is steep, the road's grade is, for the most part, moderate, and this route segment is simply a matter of slog-and-pant. Three welcome streams break the monotony of the climb, and the view (despite the ugly roadcut that scars Morgan Creek) is spectacular. Through the Pine Creek valley that slopes away to the northeast, one can look across the Owens River drainage to the volcanic tableland and White Mountain (14,242') on the skyline. The road ends just above the scraps of metal marking the site of the Brownstone Mine.

There is one advantage to the presence of the mining activities in this canyon—and that is the dramatic contrast between industrial and recreational use of wilderness country. Coincident to this is the contrasting tempi of the lower and upper parts of the valley. One has only to watch the antlike scurrying of trucks and people across the way to fully appreciate the slow, peaceful pace of the wilderness traveler. From the mine, the trail ascends over talus and scree by short, steep switchbacks. Along this ascent one sees juniper, limber pine and lodgepole pine, and the juniper have left beautiful, weathered snags of a dramatic golden hue that are a constant delight to color photographers.

With the steepest part of the ascent behind, the trail fords another unnamed tributary, switchbacks past a sign at the boundary of the John Muir Wilderness, and veers north to join Pine Creek ⅓ mile below Pine Lake. Here, the creek alternates cascades, falls and chutes in a riot of white water. The trail fords the stream via logs and boulders, and amid a moderate forest cover of lodgepole pines arrives at the northeast end of Pine Lake. This medium-sized lake (16 acres) is a popular overnight camping place (campsites along the northeast shore), and fishermen may wish to tarry here to sample the fair fishing for brook (to 12''), but fishing is generally better at Upper Pine Lake.

Our trail skirts the rocky northwest side of Pine Lake and ascends through forest to the outlet stream from Birchim Lake, which we cross via logs. After climbing over a small ridge, the trail parallels the outlet stream from Upper Pine Lake and arrives at the north side of the lake (10,200'). Anglers will find that brook and rainbow (to 12'') frequent these waters, and angling is good. After skirting the meadowy areas at the north side of the lake, the trail crosses the multibranched inlet stream via boulders. Then, after a moderate ½-mile ascent, we arrive at the Pine Creek Pass/Italy Pass junction. Our route turns right, away from the Pine Creek Pass Trail and onto the Italy Pass Trail, and soon turns right again on the short lateral to the outlet of Honeymoon Lake (10,440'). This moderate-sized lake (10 acres) has good campsites near the outlet stream on the west side. Fishing for brook and rainbow (to 10'') is good. This lovely lake makes an excellent base camp for side excursions to 40 surrounding lakes in four drainages, or for climbing five nearby peaks that exceed 13,000' in elevation.

2nd Hiking Day: Retrace your steps, 5½ miles.

13   Pine Creek Roadend to Moon Lake

TRIP   From Pine Creek Roadend to Moon Lake via Pine Creek Pass (round trip). Topo map *Mt. Tom.* Best midseason; 20 miles.

Grade	Trail/layover days	Total recommended days
Leisurely	4/1	5
Moderate	3/1	4
Strenuous	2/1	3

HILITES   The snarling trucks that surround the trailhead belie the primitive country that lies beyond the first climb. Pine Creek, from its lower aspen-clad banks to its tundra-meadow birthplace, is a kind of stream that hiker, angler, photographer and naturalist can take a fancy to. At Moon Lake the visitor will experience memorable open, alpine surroundings at their finest.

DESCRIPTION (Leisurely trip)

1st Hiking Day (**Pine Creek Roadend** to **Upper Pine Lake**, 5 miles): Follow most of the 1st hiking day, trip 12.

2nd Hiking Day (**Upper Pine Lake** to **Moon Lake**, 5 miles): From the junction of the Italy Pass and Pine Creek Pass trails, our route bears left on a steady ascent toward Pine Creek Pass. Originally a Mono Indian trading route, this route and pass have been used by man for almost five hundred years. The moderate forest cover of lodgepole and then whitebark thins as the trail climbs. Tiny, emerald-green, subalpine meadows break the long granite slabs, and wildflower fanciers will find clumps of color that include wallflower, shooting star, penstemon, lupine, primrose and columbine. The trail comes to a small creek that is the headwaters of Pine Creek and ascends a long swale between two granite walls, before making the final steep, rocky climb to Pine Creek Pass (11,100') on the Sierra Crest. From the vicinity of the pass, one has excellent views to the north of Bear Creek Spire, to the northwest of Merriam and Royce peaks; to the south of Pilot Knob and Glacier Divide, and to the southeast of Mt. Humphreys. From the pass, the trail descends to a fairly level, rocky meadow, and then drops to French Canyon over lupine-dotted ledges. Soon our route meets the fisherman's trail branching left to Elba and Moon lakes.

Our route leaves the main trail, following this fisherman's trail as it ascends the fairly steep south wall of French Canyon. This 400-foot climb brings one to fair-sized Elba Lake (unnamed on the topo map). Typical of these high, montane lakes, Elba seems virtually devoid of vegetation and life. It is understandable that the first-time visitor to this country often refers to it as "moon country," but those who come to know and love the high country soon discover the beauty that hides close beneath the near-sterile veneer. Spots of green between the tumbled talus blocks indicate grassy tundra patches or clumps of willows, and occasionally the weatherered landscape is broken by a dwarfed lodgepole or whitebark pine. Steady, silent scrutiny will usually discover movement that indicates animal life. A bird is usually the first to be detected, and most likely it will be either a rosy finch or a hummingbird. Four-footed movement among the rocks is most likely a cony or a marmot, or it just might be a wolverine or a bush-tailed wood rat. Fishermen will soon find life in the lake, for Elba Lake has a good population of golden and golden hybrids (to 12").

Following the inlet stream, our route then ascends steadily to larger Moon Lake (10,998'). Fair campsites can be found along the southeast side of the lake. Fishing for golden (to 12″) is excellent, and, using Moon Lake as a base, anglers can explore eight more fishing lakes sharing this same bench system.

3rd and 4th Hiking Days: Retrace your steps, 10 miles.

14 Pine Creek Roadend to Bear Dam Junction

TRIP

From Pine Creek Roadend to Bear Dam Junction via Honeymoon Lake, Italy Pass (shuttle trip). Topo maps *Mt. Tom, Mt. Abbot.* Best mid or late season; 30 miles.

Grade	Trail/layover days	Total recom- mended days
Leisurely	6/2	8
Moderate	5/1	6
Strenuous	3/1	4

HILITES

This is one of the best and shortest routes for an ambitious intermediate backpacker desiring to get the "feel" of a trans-Sierra crossing, for the route embraces the steep eastern escarpment; the barren, glaciated granite of the Sierra crest; and the long, densely wooded slopes of the west side.

DESCRIPTION (Moderate trip)

1 Hiking Day: Follow trip 12 to **Honeymoon Lake**, 5½ miles.

2nd Hiking Day (**Honeymoon Lake** to **Lake Italy**, 6 miles): The trail to Lake Italy may require some route-finding skills, for it is almost nonexistent in places. A faint trail rounds the south shore of Honeymoon Lake and crosses an inlet in a willow patch just above the lake, and another one a few dozen yards above the foot of a small meadow (excellent campsites). From here the trail winds up the jumbled valley, sometimes steeply, on the north side of the creek that drains Granite Park. The route passes many lovely little swales and crosses sparkling creeks four times as it ascends through thinning whitebark pines. If you lose the trail, look for it in places with soil, since it mostly avoids crossing bedrock or talus. Where it does cross these, look for ducks.

The trail arrives in Granite Park in a lovely meadow at timberline where the brook-trout-filled stream momentarily flows slowly. The trail fords the creek here and then doubles back to cross it again at the highest stand of whitebark pines. Then the route winds up the open, rocky expanses of upper Granite Park, where the ducked trail is very faint at times. Soon we come to the northeast shore of the highest lake, and the hiker can admire the views to the east before beginning the last, straightforward climb to Italy Pass (12,300'). Views from the north side of this saddle are excellent, including—clockwise from the east—Mt. Tom, Mt. Humphreys, the Palisades, Seven Gables, Mt. Hilgard, Mt. Gabb, and, nearby in the north, Mt. Julius Caesar.

From the pass, the faint, ducked trail descends around the north side of a cirque and, after following a creek here for a short distance, drops down to the slopes above the north shore of Jumble Lake. Crossing this talus-covered slope to the edge of the hanging valley above Lake Italy, the trail may become lost amid boulders, but it becomes better defined as it winds down to the south shore of Lake Italy (11,454'). This large lake (124 acres) lies in a majestic basin surrounded by four of the highest peaks in this part of the Sierra. It was named Lake Italy by the USGS in about 1907 because of its resemblance to that country in shape. After skirting the lake's south shore (difficult when snow lingers late), our route arrives at the fair campsites near the outlet. Although the population of golden trout is somewhat depleted, their size (sometimes up to 12") makes this a fair lake for angling.

3rd, 4th and 5th Hiking Days: Reverse the steps of trip 4, 18½ miles.

15   Pine Creek Roadend to Sandpiper Lake

TRIP From Pine Creek Roadend to Sandpiper Lake via Honeymoon Lake, Italy Pass, Selden Pass, Hutchinson Meadow, French Canyon, Pine Creek Pass (loop trip). Topo maps *Mt. Tom, Mt. Abbot, Blackcap Mountain.* Best mid or late season, 53½ miles.

Grade	Trail/layover days	Total recommended days
Leisurely	....	....
Moderate	7/2	9
Strenuous	5/2	7

HILITES The intermediate trail traveler will find this long trip a rewarding choice. After leaving beautiful Pine Creek, this trail route tours Granite Basin and Italy Pass, and then joins the John Muir Trail. Traveling south, this singular trail crosses Selden Pass and ascends the South Fork San Joaquin River watershed. Leaving the Muir Trail at Piute Creek, this route then loops back to rejoin the Pine Creek Trail via Pine Creek Pass.

DESCRIPTION (Moderate trip)

1st and 2nd Hiking Days: Follow trip 14 to **Lake Italy**, 11½ miles.

3rd Hiking Day (**Lake Italy** to **Sandpiper Lake**, 11½ miles): The trail descends along the east bank of Hilgard Branch past the low ridge behind which lie Teddy Bear and Brown Bear lakes and then switchbacks down steeply to a ford of the creek. Then the trail levels out as it winds through a sparse forest cover of lodgepole. About a mile farther, it descends steeply once more, via rocky switchbacks, and after losing 500 feet levels out. The

loss of altitude brings an increase in density of the forest cover
—mostly lodgepole—and the individual trees no longer appear
gnarled and stunted. The route then fords the outlet stream
draining Hilgard Lake, and presently we make a final switchbacking drop into the main canyon of Bear Creek. Here we turn
left on the Muir Trail and follow the second part of the 2nd
hiking day, trip 6.

4th Hiking Day (**Sandpiper Lake** to lower **Sally Keyes Lakes**, 5
miles): Follow the first part of the 3rd hiking day, trip 8.

5th Hiking Day (**Lower Sally Keyes Lake** to **Hutchinson Meadow**,
12½ miles): An early start for this hiking day is advisable in
order to complete the long, sometimes steep, always dusty
descent into the South Fork San Joaquin River drainage. From
Sally Keyes Lakes (10,200'), the duff trail descends through
heavy stands of lodgepole interspersed with tiny meadows.
Colorful wildflowers, often in patches, dot this stretch of trail:
Indian paintbrush, Douglas phlox, shooting star, yellow and
white cinquefoil, penstemon, lupine, red heather, western wallflower, buckwheat, and western mountain aster. This route
swings eastward, and crosses two terminal moraine ridges.

The sometimes rocky trail then descends to ford Senger
Creek in a lovely forested flat, where it leave the heavy concentrations of lodgepole behind. Alternately steep and moderate descents characterize the southeastward course of the trail,
and the traveler soon finds that he is entering a drier area of
manzanita and fractured granite. Views are excellent to the
south and west of the resistant granite slopes of Mt. Shinn and
Ward Mountain. To the southeast, the skylined peaks of the
LeConte Divide and Emerald Peak dominate the view until the
trail passes the lateral to Blaney Meadows, and then makes
the final descent to a junction with the main Florence Lake
Trail. A prelunch swim in the nice holes on the South Fork
San Joaquin River to the west of the junction is in order, and
fishermen will find fair fishing for brook in the same vicinity.
Several fair-to-good primitive campsites and one packer camp-
site are near the junction.

From this junction, our route continues east on a duff-and-
granite-sand trail through a mixed forest cover of Jeffrey pine
and juniper interspersed with occasional red and white fir. The
trail crosses an easy series of ridges and descends past several
good campsites to the Piute Canyon Trail junction, where our
route branches left, away from the John Muir Trail. Sporadic
appearances of quaking aspen (in the wetter spots) line our
rocky ascent up Piute canyon. The trail keeps to the west side

of briskly flowing Piute Creek, and fords multibranched Turret
Creek. This climbing, rocky trail affords excellent views of
highly fractured Pavilion Dome and the surrounding, unnamed
domes composing the west end of Glacier Divide. The trail then
swings east through a narrowing canyon, fords tiny West Pinnacles Creek, and pursues a rocky course until it enters a moderate lodgepole forest cover before reaching the East Pinnacles Creek ford. Views of the cascading tributary streams
are frequent along this trail section. From the ford, the trail
ascends gently to beautiful Hutchinson Meadow (9439'), where
travelers will find excellent campsites near the Pine Creek Pass
Trail junction. Fishing for golden and brook is good-to-excellent (to 9"). The lovely meadow setting provides excellent
campsite views of several granite peaks (Pilot Knob and Peak
12,432') to the east and west.

6th Hiking Day (**Hutchinson Meadow** to **Upper Pine Lake**, 8 miles):
This hiking day's route leaves the Piute Pass Trail and ascends
moderately up French Canyon. Rocky stretches alternate with
the soft underfooting of grassy sections. Fishing along these
upper reaches of French Canyon Creek is good to excellent,
despite the diminishing size of the stream. The trail crosses
several unnamed tributaries draining the east and west slopes
of Royce and Merriam peaks, and soon climbs above timberline. The character of the canyon walls reflects the increase in
altitude. Barren granite, mostly white and heavily fractured,
scoops away to the east, making a broad-headed, typical cirque
basin. The footing becomes very rocky as the trail passes the
faint fisherman's trail to Moon Lake, and then veers north,
climbs steeply, and crosses a long granite bench. From the
bench, it is but a short, easy climb to the summit of Pine Creek
Pass, where there are excellent views of Bear Creek Spire,
Royce and Merriam peaks, Pilot Knob, the Glacier Divide and
Mt. Humphreys.

Directly ahead, the trail descends a long, talus-ridden swale.
This descent soon enters a sparse forest cover of lodgepole,
winding between large slabs of granite. Tiny subalpine meadows fill the gaps in the rock, and the traveler is sure to encounter western wallflower, shooting star, penstemon, lupine,
primrose and columbine. The trail veers away from the trickling
Pine Creek headwaters, crosses a slight rise, and then drops to
the hard-to-see junction with the Italy Pass Trail. Our route
keeps to the right, fords North Fork Pine Creek just above the
cascading inlet to Upper Pine Lake, and arrives at the excellent
campsites along the west side of the lake and below the outlet

(10,200'). Good fishing for brook, rainbow, and some golden (to 12") can be had on Upper Pine Lake.

7th Hiking Day: (**Upper Pine Lake** to **Pine Creek Roadend**, 5 miles): Retrace most of the steps of the 1st hiking day, trip 12.

Mt. Tom, Humphreys Basin   *E.P. Pister*

16   North Lake to Piute Lake

10 ⌐
9 ⌐

TRIP   From North Lake to Piute Lake (round trip). Topo
               map *Mt. Goddard.* Best mid or late season; 7 miles.

Grade	Trail/layover days	Total recommended days
Leisurely	2/0	2
Moderate	....	....
Strenuous	day	....

HILITES   This trip offers an easy walk into the high country
               and a lake with large trout. It is an excellent choice
               for beginning backpackers who want to sample the
               high country with only a modest effort.

DESCRIPTION (Leisurely trip)

1st Hiking Day: (**North Lake** to **Piute Lake**, 3½ miles): Shortly after
leaving the trailhead (9360'), this route enters the John Muir
Wilderness and then ascends gently along slopes dotted with
meadowy patches, aspen groves and stands of lodgepole pine.
In season the traveler will find a wealth of wildflowers in these
little meadows and in the sandy patches among the granite
slabs, including paintbrush, columbine, tiger lily, spiraea and
penstemon. After the trial fords and quickly refords North Fork
Bishop Creek, the ascent becomes moderate. Aspen is left
behind, the lodgepole becomes sparse, and some limber pine
is seen. The glaciated canyon is flanked by slab-topped Peak
12707 on the south and 13,225-foot Mt. Emerson on the north.
The newcomer to the High Sierra will marvel at how the great
granite slabs maintain their precarious perches atop Peak
12707, seeming to be almost vertically above him. But they all
topple eventually, due to the action of frost wedging, and add
to the piles of talus at the foot of the peak.

Approaching Loch Leven Lake, the trail levels off, and the
angler may wish to try the lake waters for brook, rainbow and
brown trout (to 10''). The trail then ascends moderately again,
through a cover of sparse lodgepole and whitebark, winds
among large, rounded boulders, and skirts a small lake before
arriving at the next bench up the canyon, which contains this
day's destination, Piute Lake (10,950'). The traveler may wish

to consider the wind in selecting a campsite, as it often blows stiffly in this Piute Pass country. There are overused campsites on the north side close to the trail. Fishing for brook and rainbow is fair (to 18"). Those who would go out of their way to find seclusion may elect to scramble southeast up a fairly steep slope to granite-bound Emerson Lake.

2nd Hiking Day: Retrace your steps, 3½ miles.

Mt. Humphreys   *E.P. Pister*

17   North Lake to Hutchinson Meadow

TRIP   From North Lake to Hutchinson Meadow via Piute Lake, Piute Pass (round trip). Topo maps *Mt. Goddard, Mt. Tom, Mt. Abbot.* Best mid or late season; 22 miles.

Grade	Trail/layover days	Total recom-mended days
Leisurely	4/1	5
Moderate	3/1	4
Strenuous	2/0	2

HILITES   Hutchinson Meadow is one of the finest meadows in the High Sierra, and the trail to it beside Piute Creek takes the traveler through several miles of wild mountain "lawns" and gardens, where Sierra wildflowers are at their best. Add the views of dominating Mt. Humphreys and the spectacular Glacier Divide, and this trip becomes one of the most scenic in all the Sierra. Yet Humphreys Basin is equally famous for its golden trout.

DESCRIPTION Moderate trip)

1st Hiking Day: Follow trip 16 to **Piute Lake**, 3½ miles.

2nd Hiking Day: (**Piute Lake** to **Hutchinson Meadow**, 7½ miles): From Piute Lake the trail ascends an open, rocky slope to timberline, and switchbacks up to the last traverse before Piute Pass (11,423'). Here the traveler in midsummer will probably pass through a "road cut" in a snowbank, created by packers using sand and shovels. At the pass there are grand views west to the canyon of South Fork San Joaquin River, south to Glacier Divide (the north boundary of Kings Canyon National Park) and north to Mt. Humphreys, highest peak this far north in the Sierra. (It if could acquire 14 feet from somewhere, Bishop residents would have their own 14,000-foot Sierra peak.) The rocky trail descends moderately to Summit Lake, and levels off as it fords a stream and enters the great, high lake bowl called Humphreys Basin, which contains 31 lakes that have golden trout.

In this basin the sandy trail contours through alpine grasses and then descends to ford the outlet stream of Big and Little Desolation lakes. There is good fishing in Big Desolation for golden to 20", reached by going 2 miles north on the trail that turns right from our route shortly after this ford. Or the angler may wish to sample the waters of Golden Trout Lake, just south of the trail, for the fair fishing for golden (to 10"). Several trails strike off toward Golden Trout Lake, and the main trail itself has several alternative branches in this area. Heading down-valley well above the creek will keep you on course. Entering timber, the route begins a moderate descent on a rocky trail through sparse lodgepole which soon becomes moderate. Breaks in the timber cover afford views of the residual glaciers that give the Glacier Divide its name.

About 4 miles from Piute Pass the display of flower-studded green "lawns" begins, and from here to Hutchinson Meadow the traveler is seldom out of sight of these subalpine gardens. The amateur botanist will discern paintbrush, shooting star, fleabane, swamp onion, red mountain heather, buttercup, cinquefoil, penstemon, buckwheat, yarrow milfoil, groundsel and Douglas phlox, along with Labrador tea, lemon willow and alpine willow. Rollicking Piute Creek is often close at hand, lending its music to complete this scene of mountain beauty.

Finally the trail levels out and fords the distributaries of French Canyon Creek, arriving at the good campsites at Hutchinson Meadow (9439'). Here beneath Pilot Knob and Peak 12432 the angler will find the riffles of Piute Creek good-to-excellent fishing for brook and some golden (to 9"), or he may cautiously approach the little pools on the distributaries of French Canyon Creek, which spread out through the east side of the meadow and offer equally good fishing.

3rd Hiking Day: Retrace your steps, 11 miles.

18   North Lake to Florence Lake

TRIP
From North Lake to Florence Lake via Piute Lake,
Piute Pass, Hutchinson Meadow, Lower Blaney
Meadows (shuttle trip). Topo maps *Mt. Abbot,
Blackcap Mountain, Mt. Tom, Mt. Goddard.* Best
mid or late season; 27½ miles.

Grade	Trail/layover days	Total recommended days
Leisurely	4/1	5
Moderate	3/1	4
Strenuous	3/0	3

HILITES
Following an old Indian trade route, this trip tours
nearly every life zone and type of forest belt found
in the Sierra. Well suited to foot or stock travel, the
trail crosses Piute Pass and descends the west
slopes via the San Joaquin drainage. Good angling
in the Humphreys Basin waters, fine views of the
Sierra crest and Glacier Divide, and well-maintained
trails make this a good, solid trip for the beginner
who has spent a few nights in the wilderness.

DESCRIPTION (Leisurely trip)

1st and 2nd Hiking Days: Follow trip 17 to **Hutchinson Meadow**, 11
miles.

3rd Hiking Day: (**Hutchinson Meadow** to **Lower Blaney Meadows**,
9 miles): Staying on the north side of Piute Creek, the alternately duff and rocky trail descends gently through a moderate
forest cover of lodgepole. After the easy ford of East Pinnacles
Creek, the timber thins, and the precipitous valley walls begin
to close in. There are excellent views of the cascading tributaries, and the green rock around Pavilion Dome in the southwest is but one of many beautiful parts of these canyon walls.

Meadowy patches of grass lace the rockier sections of trail, and it drops over a moderate slope to a tiny lakelet that interrupts the brisk, bouncing flow of Piute Creek. Although the fish are somewhat smaller than in the lakes passed on the 2nd hiking day, they are plentiful, and anglers may wish to sample some of these pan-sized golden.

Our route then swings west to ford West Pinnacles Creek, and south as it approaches the ford of multibranched Turret Creek. Crossing the easy granite nose protruding from the west wall of the canyon, the trail descends over steep and then moderate slopes to a junction with the John Muir Trail. Here our route turns right (west), and undulates via rocky trail down the South Fork San Joaquin River canyon. The mostly sparse forest cover has changed from a predominance of lodgepole to Jeffrey, juniper, some red and white fir, and the seepage-loving quaking aspen. The underfooting of this trail exhibits the effects of both chemical and physical weathering of the granite walls, with its deep pockets of heavy, coarse, quartz sand. Where this sand has mixed with alluvial deposits, trees and shrubs have taken root, and along these stretches the ground is frequently carpeted with a shallow layer of duff.

The trail junction where our Florence Lake route leaves the John Muir Trail, keeping to the left, makes an excellent lunch or swimming stop. In a forest cover that has become heavy, the trail from the junction continues by a series of moderate ups and downs to a junction with a trail climbing north, where signs indicate the Muir Trail is 1½ miles away, both to the east and to the north. In 200 yards you come to an unsigned trail on the left which leads south ¼ mile down to riverside campsites. From the campsites on the south side of the river a faint trail goes 150 yards southwest to a natural hot-spring pool. The fence right by this pool encloses the Muir Trail Ranch, and several of the outbuildings of this commerical establishment are in view as, back on the main trail, we skirt its boundary.

Soon we ford the noisy branchlets of Senger Creek and wind through the heavy forest cover surrounding Blaney Meadows. Then our trail continues around the fringes of the meadow to the fair campsites at Lower Blaney Meadows (7650'). Fishing for brook and some rainbow is fair to good (mostly downstream).

4th Hiking Day: (**Lower Blaney Meadows** to **Florence Lake**, 7½ miles): Follow the 4th hiking day, trip 8.

19

Lake Sabrina to Dingleberry Lake

TRIP		From Lake Sabrina to Dingleberry Lake (round trip). Topo map *Mt. Goddard.* Best mid or late season; 9 miles.

Grade	Trail/layover days	Total recom-mended days
Leisurely	2/0	2
Moderate	....	....
Strenuous	day	....

HILITES The sparkling blue lakes near the head of Middle Fork Bishop Creek, nestled close under 13,000-foot granite peaks, are among the most scenic on the Sierra Nevada's east slope. The favorite lake of all these, among many old Sierra trompers, is Dingleberry Lake.

DESCRIPTION (Leisurely trip)

1st Hiking Day (**Lake Sabrina** to **Dingleberry Lake**, 4½ miles): From the designated backpackers' parking area below Lake Sabrina, our route follows the Lake Sabrina road ½ mile to the trailhead, on the left about 100 yards below the Sabrina Dam. Soon the trail makes an easily missed left turn to the northeast, and then it rises above the blue expanses of Lake Sabrina. This dusty path undulates above the lake across talus slopes loaded with small aspen trees, which are evidence of a plentiful underground water supply on this sagebrush-dotted north-facing slope. From the trail we can see one of the finer panoramas in the Sierra: the shining waters of Lake Sabrina in the foreground, Middle Fork Bishop Creek cascading into the southwest end of the lake, and the jagged spires and ridges of the Sierra crest, often snow-streaked until late summer, as a backdrop.

A little more than a mile from the trailhead, not far beyond a pair of switchbacks, the trail enters a hillside area of low-growing aspen trees that look more like bushes. About 100 yards into this area you pass the George Lake Trail branching left, uphill. Not far beyond, you cross a major unnamed stream on logs where careful footing is required, and two switchbacks later the trail crosses another unnamed stream. Then the route enters a lodgepole forest and climbs steadily, emerging from the forest cover now and then for splendid views down over the Lake Sabrina basin. Presently the trail veers southeast into the canyon of Blue Lake's outlet stream, but stays high above this stream until we are almost at the lake. After threading an open area of jumbled boulders, we reach the north end of Blue Lake. This spot is a photographer's delight, with lodgepoles crowding the uneven shoreline and the rugged Thompson Ridge reflected in the clear waters of the lake.

The trail turns right and crosses the outlet creek via some well-placed logs, then veers left and traverses over and around a number of granite outcroppings and tarns just above the west shore of Blue Lake. About midway around the lake is an unmarked trail junction. The fork ahead goes to Baboon Lake, but we turn right and follow our trail over a low saddle, down across a rocky slope and back up granite ledges into a grassy valley spotted with lodgepoles. Just north of the northernmost of the Emerald Lakes, we cross their outlet below a beautiful pool and then climb a boulder-strewn ridge. Then the trail crosses the ridge and descends through broken terrain to the east shore of inviting Dingleberry Lake, where there are many good campsites near the stream above the lake (10,480').

2nd Hiking Day: Retrace your steps, 4½ miles.

Thompson Ridge over Blue Lake

20   Lake Sabrina to George Lake

TRIP   From Lake Sabrina to George Lake (round trip). Topo map *Mt. Goddard.* Best mid and late season; 6.4 miles.

Grade	Trail/layover days	Total recom- mended days
Leisurely	2/0	2
Moderate	day	....
Strenuous	day	....

HILITES   Few lakes reachable by trail and so close to a road offer as much solitude as George Lake. After the day-hiking fishermen leave, you may have the lake to yourself.

DESCRIPTION (Leisurely trip)

1st Hiking Day (**Lake Sabrina to George Lake**, 3.2 miles): Follow trip 19 to the George Lake Trail junction and turn left, uphill, onto that trail. This steep path switchbacks up an open, exposed hillside for more than ½ mile before it reaches the first clumps of welcome whitebark pines. When you come to the first stream, cross it and almost immediately recross it to continue on switchbacks up the steep hillside. As the forest cover grows thicker, the steep grade abates, becoming mild and then, very soon, level. On this level stretch you reach a flat meadow with George Lake's outlet stream meandering quietly through it, and in the clear waters you can see appealing brook trout slowly finning. At the head of this meadow, cross the stream to the right side and continue up the valley. Then the trail veers left to cross a sloping, willowed meadow, in the middle of which a guiding duck sits atop a house-size boulder. Beyond this meadow, the sandy trail rises steeply for about 100 vertical feet, and then sudenly you are at George Lake (10,700'). There are good campsites near the trail on the east side of the lake, and fishing is good for brook and rainbow (to 12'').

Lake Sabrina to Tyee Lakes   **21**

TRIP   From Lake Sabrina to South Lake Road via Tyee
                Lakes (shuttle trip). Topo map *Mt. Goddard*. Best
                mid or late season, 7.7 miles.

Grade	Trail/layover days	Total recom-mended days
Leisurely	2/0	2
Moderate	....	....
Strenuous	day	....

HILITES   The views from the plateau atop Table Mountain
                give one an ineffable feeling of grandeur that is not
                soon forgotten. Beyond and below, the numerous
                Tyee Lakes offer hundreds of bays and bowers to
                swim and picnic in.

DESCRIPTION (Leisurely trip)

1st Hiking Day (**Lake Sabrina** to **George Lake**, 3.2 miles): Follow
the 1st hiking day, trip 20.

2nd Hiking Day (**George Lake** to **South Lake Road**, 4½ miles): Before reaching the upper end of George Lake, the trail turns left
(northeast) up slopes of granite sand dotted with whitebark
pines. Although the tread is not always distinct on this slope,
the route is well-ducked. Switchbacking up the increasingly
steep trail, you have increasingly good views of George Lake
and the Sierra crest beyond. Near the summit is a small stream
that runs till midsummer, and one could camp beside it. The
trail becomes nearly level before reaching its high point, and
on this barren-seeming, rocky plateau grow many clumps of
white phlox and lavender whorled penstemon.

   Beyond the summit we head down the east side of a tributary
of Tyee Lakes creek and, following ducks, enter corn-lily country. The flowering plant that looks like a cornstalk grows pro-
fusely in dozens of soggy hillside gardens here. Where the little

valley narrows and steepens, a trail becomes obvious on the right side of the creek. Just before this creek drops into a gorge there is a beautiful lunch spot beside the stream with a commanding view of the fifth and largest Tyee Lake. Then the trail winds down to that lake, which has fair campsites on its north side under groves of whitebark pines. After we cross the outlet stream, the trail becomes more distinct, and it remains so to the end of this trip. We circle the fourth lake, keeping some distance from its shore until we near the outlet. Beside the outlet are some well-developed but otherwise good campsites near a very picturesque, rock-dotted pond.

Beyond these campsites the trail again crosses Tyee Lakes creek and then winds down-canyon far from the third lake, seen in the east, to the shores of small, partly reed-filled lake #2, whose campsites are poor. Lake #1 has practically no campsites, and we skirt its swampy west edge, then veer away from its outlet to begin a moderate descent through increasingly dense forest. In ½ mile the trail crosses Tyee Lakes creek, and then it switchbacks in a generally eastward direction, crossing another refreshing stream soon after. The descent continues on dusty switchbacks down an often steep hillside, finally ending at a sunken bridge across South Fork Bishop Creek just 0.1 mile downstream from a large turnout on the South Lake road where there is a large sign with words about the forest and, on top of it, a small sign saying *Tyee Trail*. This turnout is 4.4 miles up the South Lake road from the Lake Sabrina road.

A Tyee Lake

About 35 yards northeast of where the trail fords West Fork
Burnt Corral Creek for the second time, several very cold
springs provide a refreshing reason for the thirsty hiker to
pause before continuing down to the Long Meadow/Chamber-
lain's Camp junction. Taking the right fork at this junction, we
make a gentle-to-moderate ascent to serene Hobler Lake, where
good campsites can be found among the giant red firs and the
lodgepole pines. Ascending gently, the trail then leaves the
Muir Wilderness, crosses the outlet of a tiny lake to the west,
and meets the Courtright/Blackcap Basin Trail on a ridge above
Chamberlain's Camp. From here we retrace part of the 1st
hiking day, trip 25.

Middle Fork Bishop Creek above Dingleberry Lake

Glacier Divide to Bubbs Creek

This area is bounded by Glacier Divide on the north, Owens Valley on the east, Courtright and Wishon reservoirs on the west, and Bubbs Creek on the south, and it contains the greatest single block of unbroken wilderness in the southern Sierra. Still untainted by roads, the core of it enjoys the protection of National Park status, and the adjacent peripheral zones to the west, north and east are declared Wilderness Areas. Spread out over an area of roughly 1200 square miles, it boasts some of the most remote and scenic sections of the Sierra, and it is replete with scores of peaks that soar above 13,000 feet, hundreds of lakes and thousands of miles of sparkling streams. Were the hiker able to take every trip suggested in this section, he would have a solid sampling of four life zones ranging in altitude from 5000 feet to well over 12,000 feet. Further, he would have crossed ten major divides, visited three major watersheds, and enjoyed a wilderness experience perhaps unequaled anywhere in the world.

Topographically, the country divides neatly into three disparate types: the west slopes, Kings Canyon National Park, and the eastern escarpment. The Park, the heart of the high country, was established in 1940 when the Congress recognized the obvious need to protect this fragile wilderness from the increasing encroachment of stockmen and local, shortsighted business interests. Although the Park makes up the largest part of this section, the potential visitor should not ignore trips into the wilderness areas on the east and west sides of the Park.

The Park "heartland" is the rugged, comparatively barren, mostly alpine zone that lies between the Sierra crest and the LeConte/White Divide. Here are the headwaters of the South Fork of the San Joaquin and the Middle and South Forks of the Kings River. The latitudinal watershed divides, within the Park, are Goddard Divide (separating the South Fork of the San Joaquin Rover from the Middle Fork of the Kings River), and the Monarch/Cirque Crest divide (splitting the watersheds of the Middle Fork and the South Fork of the Kings River). Within the Park are several longitudinal divides that serrate the topography into a complex ridge-chasm conformation. Most outstanding among these secondary divides are White Divide, Ragged Spur, Black Divide and King Spur.

In contrast to the Park, the eastern escarpment enjoys a diverse and sometimes dense forest cover—a cover that diminishes toward the Sierra crest. All of the many eastside streams flow into the Owens River, and they are separated by towering spur ridges that protrude from the backbone of the crest. The escarpment is nowhere more severe and forbidding than the stretch from South Lake to Onion Valley—accounting in part for the absence of heavily used trailheads in this interval. Peculiar also to the east side is the lower juniper woodland belt replete with the scattered grasses, pinon pine, Utah juniper and brush plants associated with the Great Basin. Fortunately, for those who enjoy and would preserve the east escarpment's native primitive appeal, this region is protected by a long, narrow belt of Wilderness designation.

Similarly, the west slopes (west of the Park boundary) enjoy this immunity, but it is a sad political commentary that policy-makers and boundary-setters did not initially establish the Wilderness limit along the obvious demarcation indicated by the present roadends at Courtright and Wishon reservoirs. The terrain of these western slopes is remarkable for its absence of outstanding peaks. In general it is a gradual, steady ascent to the LeConte/White Divide and the timbered rise of Kettle Ridge. The pleasant, rolling landscape of Woodchuck Country and the several alpine basins nestled at the foot of the LeConte Divide make up the headwaters of North Fork Kings River, the sole drainage of this particular area.

Looking at topo maps of this section (Blackcap Mountain, Mt. Goddard) one can readily ascertain the comparative heavy forestation of the region west of the LeConte Divide. Travelers working their way up any one of the various dendritic tributaries of North Fork Kings River will discover for themselves the magnificent spectrum of Sierra flora that attends these westside entries to the high country. Beginning in the lower elevations around 6500 feet are the stately mixed conifers such as sugar pine, ponderosa pine and incense-cedar. Ponderosa pine, with its distinctive bark plates and its long needles, is frequently mistaken for its close cousin Jeffrey pine, which is usually of a higher elevation but sometimes found in the same locale. There are many distinguishing characteristics, but the surest is the difference in their cones. The naturalist's rule of thumb is, "If you can comfortably catch a tossed cone, it is a cone of Jeffrey pine." This differentiation arises from the fact that the prickle found on the end of each scale of the Jeffrey cone is turned inward, whereas the prickle on the ponderosa cone turns outward. But the most distinctive cone of all belongs to the sugar pine. Sometimes as long as a man's arm, it is an impressive fruit whether it be found on the ground or seen hanging in clusters at the ends of massive branches.

Climbing a little higher, one enters the fir belt. First comes the white fir, along with occasional groves of Jeffrey pine, and finally the noble stands of red fir. Being rather brittle, red firs are frequently associated with a heavily littered forest floor, but the atmosphere engendered by their open, parklike groves is entirely unique. Perhaps it is the soft, filtered green light that sifts through their dense, short-needled crowns, or it may be the gentle line of their graceful, down-sweeping branches. Whatever the reason, one feels a hush and a feeling of needing to tip-toe through these stands that one does not have in other kinds of forests. Standing in one of these cathedral-like groves, it is the easiest thing in the world to empathize with John Muir's bitterness when he wrote:

> Any fool can destroy trees. They cannot run away; and if they could, they would still be destroyed—chased and hunted down as long as fun or a dollar could be got out of their bark hides, branching horns, or magnificent bole backbones. Few that fell trees plant them; nor would planting avail much toward getting back anything like the noble primeval forests. During a man's life only saplings can be grown, in the place of the old trees—tens of centuries old—that have been destroyed. It took more than three thousand years to make some of the trees in these Western woods—trees that are still standing in perfect strength and beauty, waving and singing in the mighty forests of the Sierra. Through all the wonderful, eventful centuries since Christ's time—and long before that—God has cared for these trees, saved them from drought, disease, avalanches, and a thousand straining, leveling tempests and floods; but he cannot save them from fools—only Uncle Sam can do that.*

The "gentle country" of the trees continues as the trails wind upward through dense groves of the two-needled lodgepole pine. Near timberline, solitary gnarled sentinels in the form of Sierra junipers guard the ridges, and cling tenuously to rocky slopes. The slim lodgepole pine no longer appears in tall, dense stands—now its trunk is bent to the unchecked winds of alpine country. Occasional clumps of whitebark pine and mountain hemlock dot those spaces among the granite that are not already filled with the tender-yet-tough grasses of an alpine meadow.

This, then, is the land and the forests of the west slopes—an

*Our National Parks, by John Muir.

environment that has nurtured and awed man since his first acquaintance with it. It is an often-ignored fact that the first visitor to these slopes was the Indian, and there is adequate evidence to show that he was leaching his ground acorn meal at the sites of Simpson and Zumwalt meadows long before Europeans had settled the eastern shores of America. While Englishmen and Spaniards fought sea battles for supremacy of ocean trade routes, the Indians of the Mono and Monache groups were peacefully plying their primitive trade routes over Piute, Bishop and Kearsarge passes. Using laurel-wood bows and cane arrows that were dipped in a poison concoction of crushed, rattlesnake-venomed deer liver, Indian hunting parties ranged the upper watersheds of the Kings and San Joaquin rivers—this, while the white man was establishing the first Presidio-Mission complexes in Alta California. In Philadelphia, civilized men of 1776 used a bird feather and decomposed animal fat to paint their names on a piece of wood pulp—historians now refer to it as an historic document. At almost the same time, in Tehipite Valley, an unknown Indian artisan using a similar stain produced a series of amebalike figures—and today's archeologist-historian refers to them as primitive graffiti.

The first meetings of these original inhabitants and exploring white men had the seeds of disaster. Gabriel Moraga, among the first white men to penetrate this country, was called "the greatest pathfinder and Indian fighter of his day." Subsequent incursions by trappers, pioneer settlers and gold seekers brought the inevitable confrontation, and, to the white man's discredit, the inevitable eradication of the red man. Like the grizzly bear, he was judged a nuisance, and was considered "fair game." Today, both species are extinct in this region.

Early exploratory ventures from west to east into the heartland of this region were so arduous as to render their continuation impractical. This is quite understandable, as any examination of the topography will show. Numerous divides, nearly all exceeding 12,000 feet, cross-hatch the landscape, making passage even to this day lengthy and arduous. John C. Fremont, in December 1845, endeavoring to carry out a rendezvous with Theodore Talbot and Joseph Walker on the westside river they called "Lake Fork," led an unsuccessful sally into the reaches of North Fork Kings River. He was turned back by snow and "impossible" going. Jedediah Smith's party, in an earlier attempt during spring, had suffered the same travails, and the subsequent annals of the Brewer Survey parties of 1864 and 1870 tell a similar story.

The actual trail-blazers of currently used trails were, however, not the Spaniards or the trappers. The earliest trails were usually those of the sheepherders who grazed their flocks in the backcountry during the last half of the 19th century. Among the better known of these sheepherders were Bill Helm and Frank Dusy, whose early exploratory efforts on the west slopes culminated in the discovery of Tehipite Valley and in the building of the Tunemah Trail. W. Baird, operating in the same vicinity, established what is now known as the Hell-for-Sure Pass Trail, and although the 1864 Brewer Survey party was the first to visit the area, it is assumed that Portuguese sheepmen were the first to establish the current western access route to the Evolution region.

The locations of the trailheads for this part of *Sierra South* are given below.

South Lake (9760'). Go 12 miles southwest from Bishop on State Highway 168 to the South Lake turnoff, and then 7 miles to the South Lake parking area.

Taboose Creek Roadend (5460'). Turn west on a dirt road that leaves U.S. 395 12 miles south of Big Pine. Go right at a fork at 1.7 miles, pass through a gate at 2.4 miles, and continue to the roadend at 5.8 miles.

Sawmill Creek Roadend. (4600'). Turn west on a dirt road that leaves U.S. 395 18 miles south of Big Pine and go west on Black Rock Spring Road 1 mile to a junction. Turn north and follow Old U.S. 395 0.2 mile to an unmarked dirt road leading west. Pass through a gate and follow this poor road 2.3 miles to its end just north of Sawmill Creek.

Oak Creek roadend (6040'). Turn west from U.S. 395 2.3 miles north of Independence onto the paved Fish Hatchery Road and go 1.3 miles to a junction. Go right here, passing Oak Creek Campground, 5.8 miles to the roadend.

Onion Valley (9200'). Drive west from Independence 15 miles to the roadend parking lot.

Courtright Reservoir (8200'). Drive northeast 42 miles from Clovis (near Fresno) on State Highway 168 and in Shaver Lake turn right onto the Dinkey Creek Road, following it 28 miles to the Courtright/Wishon "Y," from where Courtright Reservoir is 7½ miles north, and there is a large parking area at the south end of the reservoir.

Wishon Reservoir (6720'). Follow the directions above to the Courtright/Wishon "Y" and from there drive east 2 miles to Wishon Dam and across the dam to the "Anderson" parking lot.

Crown Valley Trailhead (6750'). From Wishon Willage go 6 miles south on paved road almost to the roadend, to a large parking lot on the west side of the road.

Little Rancheria Trailhead (7600′). Use this trailhead for all eastbound hiking. However, the east end of the spur trail to this trailhead is hard to find, so trip 33 ends at the Crown Valley Trailhead. For the Little Rancheria Trailhead, go about 1 mile south from Wishon Corral and Wishon Work Camp. At the turnoff of the road to the Crown Valley Trailhead, take the left fork and drive 2 miles to its end.

Lewis Creek Trailhead (4580′). Go 77 miles east from Fresno on State Highway 180, to a parking area about ¼ mile east of the national park boundary.

Cedar Grove Roadend (5035′). Go 85 miles east from Fresno on State Highway 180 to the roadend.

John Muir Trail north of Rae Lakes

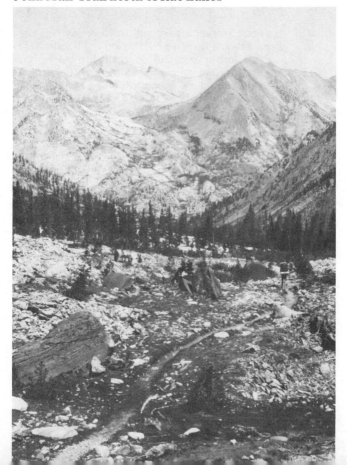

25 Courtright Reservoir to Post Corral Meadows

TRIP From Courtright Reservoir to Post Corral Meadows (round trip). Topo map *Blackcap Mountain*. Best early to mid season; 16 miles.

Grade	Trail/layover days	Total recom- mended days
Leisurely	2/0	2
Moderate	....	....
Strenuous	day	....

HILITES A fine weekend selection, this two-day trip visits enchanting Long and Post Corral Meadows. The dense forests of fir and lodgepole that line the route are a pleasant habitat for a variety of wildlife. This trip is an exellent selection for the beginning knapsacker.

DESCRIPTION Leisurely trip)

1st Hiking Day (**Courtright Reservoir** to **Post Corral Meadows**, 8 miles): From man-made Courtright Reservoir (8200') the route crosses the dam and, following a brief section of maintenance road, skirts the granite shoulder of the ridge that lines the east shore of Courtright Reservoir. Excellent views to the north of spectacular Maxson Dome greet the hiker crossing the dam, and the view down the Helms Creek gorge just below the spillway is a dizzying one. Beyond the dam, the rocky maintenance road descends for a few hundred feet and then turns left.

The road descends to the valley of East Fork Helms Creek and then ascends gently to a meadow where there's a sign saying that our route, which goes to the right, is closed to motor vehicles. Nevertheless, some jeeps go to Maxson Meadows on it. The trail now ascends moderately along the west side of East Fork Helms Creek under a dense lodgepole cover to the south end of Maxson Meadow, where we cross that fork. At the meadow's northeast end the trail passes a drift fence and the short lateral trail to Chamberlain's Camp before beginning a steep, switchbacking ascent up a dusty slope under a moderate canopy of fir and pine. At the top of this climb we pass the first of two trails to Burnt Corral Meadows, and then the trail fords an intermittent stream and descends gently to the head of beautiful Long Meadow. Aptly named, this grassland stretches away to the northeast for about a mile, and the route winds through the middle—seldom more than a few yards away from sluggishly flowing South Fork Post Corral Creek.

Midway through the meadow, our route passes a second Burnt Corral Meadow trail, fords South Fork Post Corral Creek, and then leaves the sandy-surfaced trail of the meadow behind as it swings east. Through the moderate-to-dense forest cover one can occasionally hear Post Corral Creek, and although it is out of sight, one can clearly hear the sound difference due to the increased volume of water resulting from the contribution of Burnt Corral Creek. Our route passes a faint trail branching left to a privately owned line cabin (Forest Service Multiple-Use land policy allows cattlemen to graze these lands), and then descends gently to the good campsites at the head of Post Corral Meadows (8201'). There are several primitive campgrounds at the head of the meadow, and one packer site. Other sites can be found at the foot of the meadow (ford Post Corral Creek) adjacent to the junction of the Hell-for-Sure Pass Trail. Fair-to-good fishing for pan-sized brook trout and some rainbow (to 7") can be had along Post Corral Creek.

2nd Hiking Day: Retrace your steps, 8 miles.

Woolly sunflowers

26 Courtright Reservoir to North Fork Kings

TRIP   From Courtright Reservoir to North Fork Kings
River via Post Corral Meadows (round trip). Topo
map *Blackcap Mountain.* Best early to mid season;
24 miles.

Grade	Trail/layover days	Total recom- mended days
Leisurely	4/1	5
Moderate	3/1	4
Strenuous	2/1	3

HILITES   The winding, horseshoe-shaped route-plan of this
trip tours magnificent backcountry meadows and
lush forests, and terminates alongside the racing,
pothole-dotted North Fork Kings River. Excellent
fishing and swimming on the river make this a good
trip selection for the beginner desiring maximum
wilderness exposure for a minimum of hiking days.

DESCRIPTION (Leisurely trip)

1st Hiking Day: Follow trip 25 to **Post Corral Meadows**, 8 miles.

2nd Hiking Day (**Post Corral Meadows** to **North Fork Kings River**,
4 miles): From the campsites at the lower end of Post Corral
Meadows (8201'), the trail passes the Hell-for-Sure Pass Trail
branching left and winds through a densely forested stretch of
mixed stands of red fir and lodgepole and silver pine. The duff-
and-sand trail surface makes for very pleasant walking, and the
relatively level going allows the trail traveler to keep a sharp
eye out for the commonly seen mule deer and the sometimes
seen black bear. Tiny meadowy sections interrupt the dense
forest sections, and the experienced silent hiker will pause at
the fringe of these fens to watch for betraying movement. The
general southward progress of the trail changes to an upward
slog eastward as the trail ascends a rocky, moderate slope, and
finally emerges on an open, manzanita-covered ridge above the
North Fork Kings River drainage. This open slope is a fine
point from which to view the unfractured granite river chasm
to the west and the dramatic **U**-shaped valley to the southeast.

From this point, it is interesting to speculate on the probable route followed by Captain John Fremont, the "Pathfinder." Historians are still speculating on this subject, but on one thing they do agree—Fremont's party got lost in the upper reaches of North Fork Kings River. They suffered terribly during an early winter storm, were forced to eat their saddle stock, and finally retreated. From this ridge, the trail descends on a traverse over infrequently jointed granite to the banks of the river (8029'). Excellent campsites can be found a short distance up or downstream, but one should remember that it is illegal to camp within 100 feet of the stream. Angling for brook, rainbow and some brown (to 12") is excellent. Swimming in some of the finest sand-bottomed potholes in the Sierra is available just downstream, and photographers seeking a worthy subject will find Sue Falls about ¼ mile downstream.

3rd and 4th Hiking Days: Retrace your steps, 12 miles.

Swimming in the Kings' North Fork

27   Courtright Reservoir to Rae Lake

TRIP   From Courtright Reservoir to Rae Lake via Post
            Corral Meadows (round trip). Topo map *Blackcap
            Mountain*. Best mid to late season; 26 miles.

Grade	Trail/Layover days	Total recom-mended days
Leisurely	4/2	6
Moderate	3/2	5
Strenuous	2/2	4

HILITES   Rae Lake, an alpine gem surrounded by meadows
               on two sides and tumbled granite slopes on the
               other two, has long been a favorite of anglers and
               other high-country visitors. Situated beneath Flem-
               ing Mountain, this lake's innate beauty and its prox-
               imity to 25 other lakes and the intervening streams
               make it a choice base camp for discovery explora-
               tions of Red Mountain Basin.

DESCRIPTION (Leisurely trip)

1st Hiking Day: Follow trip 25 to **Post Corral Meadows**, 8 miles.

2nd Hiking Day (**Post Corral Meadows** to **Rae Lake**, 5 miles): Our
route leaves the Blackcap Basin Trail at the campground at the
foot of Post Corral Meadows (8201') just beyond the crossing of
Post Corral Creek. Ascending the divide that separates the
Fleming Creek and Post Corral Creek drainages, we climb eastward, pass a Forest Service maintenance camp, and then cross
several unnecessarily dynamited sections of granite. To dynamite these granite slabs is a policy decision—an unfortunate
and unrepresentative policy that sees the Forest Service main-
taining backcountry trails for horses and pack animals when the
overwhelming use of the trails is by hikers on foot.

Beyond these blasted sections, the trail crosses the John Muir
Wilderness boundary, switchbacks over the crest of a divide,
and begins a long, steady, rocky ascent through a moderately
dense forest cover of lodgepole, incense-cedar and red fir. As
the trail nears Fleming Creek it climbs steeply, and there are

spots along this ascent from which the passerby has beautiful views of the long, silver chutes of West Fork Fleming Creek as it plunges over the glacially smoothed, unfractured granite of this upper basin. The lodgepoles begin to take on the stunted look characteristic of high country as the trail emerges at the subalpine meadows surrounding Fleming Lake. Itchy anglers may wish to sample the fair-to-good brook-trout fishing (to 10") at Fleming Lake, but fishing is generally better as one ascends the drainage.

The trail passes a packer campsite at the outlet of Fleming Lake and then crosses a lovely subalpine meadow to the Indian Lakes Trail junction. Here, our route branches left and ascends steeply to the spur trail to Rae Lake. This rocky, morainal trail brings us to the excellent campsites along the south and east sides of charming Rae Lake (9894'). Almost ringed by meadow, this lake exhibits a timbered east wall, a mostly meadowed south side, and precipitous rocky faces on the west and north sides. Originally named "Wolverine Lake," 13-acre Rae Lake makes a fine base camp for day-hiking excursions to Lower Indian Lake, Upper Indian Lake, and the lakes of Red Mountain Basin. Fishing for brook (to 12") is good.

3rd and 4th Hiking Days: Retrace your steps, 13 miles.

28   Courtright Reservoir to Devils Punchbowl

TRIP   From Courtright Reservoir to Devils Punchbowl;
return via Meadow Rock and North Fork Kings
River (semiloop). Topo map *Blackcap Mountain.*
Best mid to late season; 35 miles.

Grade	Trail/layover days	Total recommended days
Leisurely	6/2	8
Moderate	5/2	7
Strenuous	4/2	6

HILITES   Traveling what was originally known as the "Baird
Trail" (an old sheepherder's trail that remained for
years the primary access to the Evolution Valley
country), this route culminates at regal Devils
Punchbowl Lake. Here, excellent fishing and magnificent views greet the visitor, and a prolonged
stay—using the lake as a base camp—will compensate the hiker with excellent fishing and views at
the surrounding lakes.

DESCRIPTION Leisurely trip)

1st and 2nd Hiking Days: Follow trip 27 to **Rae Lake**, 13 miles.

3rd Hiking Day (**Rae Lake** to **Devils Punchbowl**, 4 miles): Descending from Rae Lake (9894'), our trail meets and joins the trail
from Lower Indian Lake, and a few hundred yards farther (in
the meadow) joins the Hell-for-Sure Pass Trail. Our route turns
left, fords West Fork Fleming Creek, and ascends the steep
moraine divide to the east. The forest cover diminishes as the
trail ascends, and through the thinning timber one has good
views of the northern reaches of the LeConte Divide and of
Fleming Mountain. Then the trail veers somewhat more southward, and rounds a granite-nosed ridge before ascending a
grassy swale to the Devils Punchbowl Trail junction. From this
junction, one can look up the benched drainage containing Hell-
for-Sure Lake to the notch that marks Hell-for-Sure Pass.

Our route turns right onto the Devils Punchbowl Trail, skirts
a ridge, and descends past several streamside campsites at the

headwaters of East Fork Fleming Creek. After climbing out of this drainage, the rocky trail reaches the good campsites at the north end of Devils Punchbowl Lake (10,110'). Timber cover on three sides of this charming, fairly large (33-acre) lake is moderate-to-sparse lodgepole mixed with willow in the wetter areas. Fishing for brook (to 13") is excellent. Anglers with extra layover days may wish to use this lake as a base camp for further angling adventures in Red Mountain Basin. Angling varies from excellent at Horseshoe and Hell-for-Sure lakes to fair at Blackrock Lake. Equally varied is the range of trout. At Blackrock Lake there is a fair population of rainbow, while Horseshoe has a mixed fishery of brook, rainbow and (says the DF&G) golden hybrids. Whether the reason for excursions into Red Mountain Basin be angling or just enjoying the rugged, alpine country, the basin merits investigation.

4th Hiking Day (**Devils Punchbowl** to **North Fork Kings River**, 6 miles): Walking around the west fringe of Devils Punchbowl, the hiker should take time out to step a few yards to the right of the trail for the breathtaking view west to the two tiny lakes ("Tall Jigger" and "Short Jigger") and the wooded upper drainage of East Fork Fleming Creek. The trail then crosses the rocky saddle at the southwest end of Devils Punchbowl, and descends the heavily timbered slopes to the rolling meadows of Meadow Brook. These meadows exhibit an unusual amount of seepage, and it is well that the winding, duff trail keeps to the lodgepole forest fringe on the west side. Along the trail and on the fringes of the stream, one will find a luxuriant growth of shooting star, swamp onion, and lupine.

There is a serene quality to a rolling alpine meadow that touches all who visit it, and the meadows that stepladder down with Meadow Brook are a particular delight. The brief 2 miles of trail that wind in and out of these grasslands are a rare pleasure. There is, however, a disturbing factor, which grates on the sensitivities of all experienced high-country travelers. That factor is the presence of privately owned cattle that summer-graze here. Because of heavy seepage, these grasslands are vulnerable, and they are undergoing irremediable harm. A close-up examination will reveal the torn turf and polluted waters caused by this stock. Further, the presence of these domestic bovines dramatically detracts from the meadow's magical wilderness quality.

The trail passes a second large meadow section, swings away from Meadow Brook, and makes a final, steep descent into the North Fork Kings River valley. Views during this descent include large segments of Woodchuck Country, Nichols

Canyon, and the **U**-shaped cross section of the North Fork Kings
River valley. As we approach the valley bottom, the trail becomes quite dusty, and the forest reflects the lower altitude,
with the reintroduction of golden, shaggy-barked incense-cedar
and vanilla-scented Jeffrey pine. Our route then meets and turns
right onto the North Fork Trail. A short distance downstream,
the trail crosses granite slabs, and then passes a snow-survey
cabin with a nearby waterfall and a fine, deep pool (good swimming). Immediately leaving the vicinity of the river, the trail
swings right, crosses a rocky granite ridge, and then descends
through a heavy stand of lodgepole, Jeffrey, and occasional red
fir and incense-cedar. This route fords Fleming Creek and
arrives at the excellent riverside campsites situated at the point
where the trail begins to climb out of the North Fork Kings
River watershed. Fishing for brook (to 12") is excellent, and
swimming in the nearby potholes (just downstream) is also excellent.

5th and 6th Hiking Days: Reverse the steps of trip 26, 12 miles.

Devils Punchbowl   *U.S. Forest Service*

Courtright Reservoir to Guest Lake   **29**

TRIP   From Courtright Reservoir to Guest Lake via Post
Corral Meadows, North Fork Kings River (round
trip). Topo map *Blackcap Mountain.* Best mid to late
season; 37 miles.

Grade	Trail/layover days	Total recom- mended days
Leisurely	6/3	9
Moderate	5/2	7
Strenuous	4/2	6

HILITES Of the three lake basins lying close under towering
LeConte Divide, Bench Valley is the least known
and least visited. This is surprising in view of the
excellent angling at McGuire Lakes and Guest
Lake. The other lakes of this basin are among the
most picturesque in the Sierra, and the angler with
an inclination to visit stirring subalpine scenery en
route should give this trip serious consideration.

DESCRIPTION (Leisurely trip)

1st and 2nd Hiking Days: (Follow trip 26 to **North Fork Kings River**,
12 miles.

3rd Hiking Day (**North Fork Kings River** to **Guest Lake**, 6½ miles):
From the river's edge the trail swings left through a dense stand
of lodgepole, Jeffrey, and occasional red fir and incense-cedar,
and fords Fleming Creek just above its confluence with North
Fork Kings River. In these shady timber stands, heavy coats
of green moss cover rock and tree alike; bright orange shelf
bracts flash like great eyes against the forest green; and sounds
seem muted on the carpet of pine needles. But the soft duff
trail is soon left behind as the route climbs above the river valley
over the granite nose of a ridge, and then descends to snow-
survey cabin nestled in granite slabs at river's edge. A nearby
waterfall on the river and the pool below make a nice spot for a
fast prelunch swim, and anglers will find good fishing for brook
trout (to 11'') immediately up- or downstream. The trail then

passes the Meadow Brook Trail branching left to Hell-for-Sure Pass before fording an unnamed tributary and then Meadow Brook. Ascending gently up-river, this trail route winds through moderate-to-dense stands of lodgepole and red fir.

After fording Fall Creek, the route leaves the Blackcap Basin Trail by branching left onto an unmaintained shortcut trail that ascends along the south side of Fall Creek. The route is gentle at first, and easy to follow, but this condition changes as soon as the area of the broad granite walls is reached. Now the route becomes quite steep and rocky, and the hiker keeps on course by staying within a few hundred yards of the creek on the south side. Where ledges interrupt the stream's flow, pockets of wild-flowers have taken root, and a well-deserved lunch break is in order here.

After gradually levelling off into dense lodgepole forest, the trail meets a trail ascending from North Fork Kings River above Big Maxson Meadow. Soon our route winds along the luxuri-antly foliaged banks of Fall Creek, where shooting stars, pen-stemon, larkspur, monkshood, monkey flower, columbine, wall-flower and paintbrush nearly fill the valley floor.

After traveling a short distance beside the creek, our trail climbs steeply for a short time and then moderately for a while, to reach the outlet from McGuire and Guest lakes. Here the trail begins a series of short switchbacks which soon become rocky and steep, but soon also we arrive at the outlet of meadow-fringed lower McGuire Lake. The lake's waters appear suddenly only a few feet from the precipitous drop-off, and from this point one can indeed ascertain the true meaning of the term "hanging valley." Our route passes several primitive and packer camp-sites as it rounds the north side of lower and upper McGuire Lakes. Both of these lakes afford excellent fishing for brook (to 15"). Through moderate-to-sparse timber, the trail crosses an easy ridge to the fisherman's lateral that turns off the main trail and leads to Guest Lake (10,160'). Good packer and primi-tive campsites with unobstructed views of Blackcap Mountain line the north shore of this lovely granite-lined lake, and it is a fine choice as a base camp for excursions to 20 nearby lakes in this basin. At Guest Lake fishing for brook trout (to 12") is good. Fishing in the lakes of the upper Bench Valley Basin varies from good to excellent, and offers the angling sportsman a creel of both brook and rainbow trout.

4th, 5th and 6th Hiking Days: Retrace your steps, 18½ miles.

Courtright Reservoir to Guest Lake **30**

TRIP   From Courtright Reservoir to Guest Lake via Post
Corral Meadows, North Fork Kings River; return
via cross country to Devils Punchbowl, then by trail
to North Fork Kings, Post Corral Meadows (semiloop trip). Topo map *Blackcap Mountain.* Best mid
or late season; 43 miles.

Grade	Trail/layover days	Total recom- mended days
Leisurely	7/2	9
Moderate	5/2	7
Strenuous	4/1	5

HILITES   This looping trip traverses two of the finest angling
basins on the west side of the Sierra. The rugged
cross-country route between the basins makes it a
choice limited to experienced hikers, and the grand
vistas encountered along this route more than compensate for the skill and energy required. The return leg of this trip through Meadow Brook valley
is an exposure to subalpine meadows that will kin-
dle an appreciation of and a dedication to preserving
beautiful grasslands like these.

DESCRIPTION (Leisurely trip)

1st 3 Hiking Days: Follow trip 29 to **Guest Lake**, 18½ miles.

4th Hiking Day (**Guest Lake** to **Devils Punchbowl** via cross country,
6½ miles): The trail from Guest Lake is a fisherman's trail that
joins the main Bench Valley Basin Trail ascending to Horsehead
Lake. This ascent winds north through a moderate cover of
whitebark pines and passes Colt Lake before it descends to the
southeast shore of Horsehead Lake, where there is an improved
packer campsite. After the trail arrives at the grassy fringes
above Horsehead Lake, the traveler has excellent views to the
east and northeast of the barren crest of LeConte Divide. From

this lake's open shores one can readily see that he has sur-
mounted a series of hanging valleys, and that this hanging-
valley chain continues in the tiny cirques carved out of the
granite divide to the east and northeast.

Beyond the marshy inlet to Horsehead Lake, this route rounds
the east side of the lake, fords the east inlet (from Filly Lake),
and parallels the north inlet stream as it ascends. Faint fisherman's routes crisscross this drainage, and the conflicting
ducks placed by misguided but well-meaning visitors should be
taken with a grain of salt. Anglers passing through this country
will be able to sample the brook and rainbow (to 10") at Horsehead Lake; brook (to 8") at Roman Four Lake; rainbow (to 11")
at West Twin Buck Lake (East Twin Buck Lake is barren); and
rainbow (to 7") at Schoolmarm Lake.

From the west side of Twin Buck Lakes we ascend northward to the outlet of Crabtree Lake. From the outlet our trail
climbs northeast and emerges above timberline in a high, rolling
valley. After crossing two small creeks, our route ascends
steeply to the saddle just north of Peak 11398. From this point
the route contours around to the notch just to the northwest
and makes a rather steep descent into the cirque just above
Devils Punchbowl. This descent should be undertaken only by
experienced hikers with rudimentary climbing skills. Our route
passes a small, golden-trout-filled lakelet and then makes another less steep descent down to the first of the two little lakes
above Devils Punchbowl, called Little Shot and Big Shot. After
descending past Big Shot Lake, our route arrives at the moderate-to-dense forest cover at the east side of Devils Punchbowl.
There are several good campsites here, and fishing for brook
(to 13") is good. This lake is a perennial choice among anglers
as a base camp for side trips into Red Mountain Basin.

5th Hiking Day (**Devils Punchbowl** to **North Fork Kings River**, 6
miles): Follow the 4th hiking day, trip 28.

6th and 7th Hiking Days: Retrace the steps of the 2nd and 1st
hiking days, 12 miles.

Courtright Reservoir to Portal Lake

31

TRIP From Courtright Reservoir to Portal Lake (Black-cap Basin) via Post Corral Meadows, North Fork Kings River (round trip). Topo map *Blackcap Mountain*. Best mid or late season; 45 miles.

Grade	Trail/layover days	Total recom-mended days
Leisurely	6/2	8
Moderately	5/2	7
Strenuous	4/1	5

HILITES Portal Lake lives up to its name. It is indeed the door to Blackcap Basin, a beautiful, austere, granite basin forming the headwaters of North Fork Kings River. This trip boasts an encompassing look at west-slope ecology over a 2500-foot elevation span.

DESCRIPTION (Leisurely trip)

1st Hiking Day: Follow trip 25 to **Post Corral Meadows,** 8 miles.

2nd Hiking Day (**Post Corral Meadows** to **Big Maxson Meadow,** 8 miles): Follow the 2nd hiking day, trip 26, to North Fork Kings River. Then proceed to the junction of the trail to Bench Valley as described in the 3rd hiking day, trip 29. From this junction, the Blackcap Basin Trail continues south along North Fork Kings River. Fishing along the river continues to be good for brook and rainbow (to 12"), and occasional pools, usually located at the foot of a chute or a fall, make for fine late-season swimming. The narrowing canyon walls open briefly as the trail reaches wide Big Maxson Meadow (8480'). Formerly a sheep-herders' camp, and more recently grazed by cattle, this meadow offers fair-to-good campsites at its northwest end. If used as a base-camp location, these meadow campsites are central for side trips to Halfmoon Lake and to the alpine lakes of upper Bench Valley. The trail to Halfmoon Lake, not shown on the topo map, leaves the meadow right across the river from the cabins.

3rd Hiking Day (**Big Maxson Meadow** to **Portal Lake**, 6½ miles): As the trail leaves the open flats of the meadow, the traveler has excellent views east-southeast to the glacially smoothed, narrowing walls of the canyon. Immediately beyond a drift fence at the southeast end of the meadows, you can turn right to reach a fair campsite. Bearing in the direction of these canyon narrows, our duff trail passes the main Bench Valley Trail. The louder river sounds on the right reflect the steepening slopes as our trail makes a steady climb. Half a mile from the last junction the trail returns to riverside near some fine campsites under lodgepole pines with views of beautiful pools in the North Fork. Very soon, the trail veers away from the stream again, then leads southeast for about ⅔ mile before once more approach-the river across some expansive granite slabs. Beyond these boulder-dotted slabs we traverse a bog for about 100 yards to a ford of the North Fork which is difficult in early season. Immediately beyond the ford is a junction with the Blackcap Basin Trail, coming over from Halfmoon Lake.

Beyond this junction the trail swings east, following the North Fork, and passes a campsite with a table and a label "Snow-slide Camp." This gentle-to-steady ascent through moderate-to-dense lodgepole forest traverses some areas that have been swept by avalanches and the lodgepoles replaced by willows. The North Fork on our left, sometimes near and sometimes far, sometimes meandering slowly through meadows and sometimes tumbling down large slabs, contains an adequate population of golden, brook and brown trout.

About 1½ miles beyond Snowslide Camp the trail steepens, veers south toward Portal Lake, and joins its outlet stream. The trail climbs to a meadowy area where there is an improved packer campsite on the right beside the junction with the Crown Basin Trail. Just beyond this campsite is the easy-to-miss rock ford (difficult in high water) of the outlet from Portal Lake. Beyond the ford, our trail climbs via short switchbacks to the poor-to-fair campsites on the north shore of jewellike Portal Lake. Other campsites may be found by following the trail a short ½ mile to the unnamed lake northeast of Portal Lake.

4th, 5th and 6th Hiking Days: Retrace your steps, 22½ miles.

Courtright Reservoir to Florence Lake   **32**

TRIP From Courtright Reservoir to Florence Lake via Post Corral Meadows, Hell-for-Sure Pass, John Muir Trail, Blaney Meadows (shuttle trip). Topo maps *Blackcap Mountain, Mt. Abbot.* Best mid or or late season; 39½ miles.

Grade	Trail/layover days	Total recom- mended days
Leisurely	6/2	8
Moderate	5/2	7
Strenuous	4/1	5

HILITES Crossing the LeConte Divide at Hell-for-Sure Pass, this fine shuttle trip tours the headwaters of two major Sierra drainages—North Fork Kings River and South Fork San Joaquin. Unparalleled scenery and excellent angling recommend this trek for hiker and angler.

DESCRIPTION (Moderate trip)

1st and 2nd Hiking Days: Follow trip 27 to **Rae Lake**, 13 miles.

3rd Hiking Day (**Rae Lake** to **Lower Goddard Canyon**, 11 miles): Proceed to the Devils Punchbowl Trail junction as described in the 3rd hiking day, trip 28. From this junction our trail ascends steadily above the meadowed basin to the barren granite bench north of Disappointment Lake. Far from being a disappointment, anglers will find the brook-trout fishing in this lake to be good to excellent (to 15″).

The trail then fords the outlet of Chagrin Lake (10,440') and ascends gently, then moderately, to the north end of barren Hell-for-Sure Lake. This large (58-acre) lake with its narrow northern meadow fringe is a long-time favorite of people using this three-quarters-of-a-century-old sheep trail. A fine fishing

spot for rainbow trout (to 10''), this lake takes up the largest
part of the upper cirque of Red Mountain Basin. Smoothed and
polished slab granite rises from the lake's waters, broken only
by an occasional glacial erratic or a small patch of green. Just
beyond the slab granite, the broken slopes of talus and scree
lead up to abrupt, metavolcanic-topped LeConte Divide. The
notch to the northeast of Hell-for-Sure Lake marks Hell-for-
Sure Pass (11,297'), and the climb to this saddle is a steep,
switchbacking, rocky slog. The climb is not as bad as the name
would suggest, and one soon arrives at the windswept saddle
of Hell-for-Sure Pass. From the pass, Hell-for-Sure Lake and
the bold north face of Peak 11998 make up most of the scenery
to the south, but one can see a good part of the way down the
Fleming Creek drainage. The most impressive view, however,
is that of Goddard Canyon, Emerald Peak, Peter Peak and Mt.
McGee to the east and northeast. Made of the dark gray volcanic rock characteristic of the Goddard area, the steep canyon
walls plunge uninterrupted nearly 2500 feet to the valley floor
below.

This breathtaking view lasts most of the switchbacking way
down to the ford of the first unnamed tributary feeding South
Fork San Joaquin River. From this ford (about halfway down
the vertical distance) the trail traverses the west canyon wall on
a long, rolling descent that crosses two more tributaries, and
then doubles back along the South Fork. The subsequent steady-
to-moderate descent stays on the west side of the river and
refords the tributaries cited above. The trail crosses over mostly
rock, some talus and scree, and occasional meadowy sections.
Willow clumps along the river always ensure the presence of
birdlife, and the passerby is likely to encounter Brewer black-
birds, hummingbirds, flycatchers, fox sparrows, Lincoln Sparrows, nuthatches, robins, and an occasional finch. This descent,
leveling near the confluence with Evolution Creek, re-enters
forest cover with the appearance of lodgepole and aspen. The
trail then passes a drift fence a short way upstream from the
John Muir Trail junction, and arrives at the fair-to-good campsites south of a bridge (8600'). Fishing for brook and some rainbow in the river remains fair-to-good despite heavy angling
pressure.

4th Hiking Day (**Lower Goddard Canyon** to **Lower Blaney Meadows**,
8 miles): Quickly stepping onto the John Muir Trail, we make a
gentle descent on dusty underfooting through stands of quaking
aspen, lodgepole and some juniper. Underfoot, gardens of wildflowers line the trail, including sneezeweed, penstemon, yellow
cinquefoil, pennyroyal, Mariposa lily and lupine. As the trail

approaches a bridge crossing of the South Fork San Joaquin River, the canyon walls narrow and rise **V**-shaped from the canyon floor. On the north wall one can make out the unmistakable striations carved there by ice-driven rocks in the last glacial stage. Our route passes several more campsites on the right, and then, just before we cross the bridge, a short spur trail leads west to some campsites on the south side of the river. Beyond the bridge, we descend a short, rocky stretch over morainal debris. This steady descent levels out through a densely forested flat ("Aspen Flat") that is made up of postglacial alluvial deposits. An occasional Jeffrey and juniper add variety to the forest cover as the route leaves the flat and descends steeply on a rocky, dusty trail. Looking back, one has a last look at Emerald Peak, **V**'d by the steep canyon walls. Our route passes a sign indicating one's exit from Kings Canyon National Park and then crosses Piute Creek on a wood and steel bridge and passes the Hutchinson Meadow Trail branching right. From this junction one has good views of the domes to the east, the most notable being Pavilion Dome. This route continues as described in the 3rd hiking day, trip 18.

5th Hiking Day (**Lower Blaney Meadows** to **Florence Lake**, 7½ miles): Follow the 4th hiking day, trip 8.

Under Piute Creek bridge on the John Muir Trail

33   Courtright to Crown Valley Trailhead

TRIP   From Courtright Reservoir to Crown Valley Trailhead via Post Corral Meadows, North Fork Kings
River, Blackcap Basin, cross country to Blue Canyon, then by trail to Cabin Creek (shuttle trip).
Topo maps *Blackcap Mountain, Mt. Goddard,
Marion Peak, Tehipite Dome*. Best mid or late season; 48 miles.

Grade	Trail/layover days	Total recom-mended days
Leisurely	....	....
Moderate	8/2	10
Strenuous	6/1	7

Hilites   Employing a challenging cross-country route (*for
experienced backpackers only*), this trip joins Blackcap
Basin with Blue Canyon. Where it crosses the Le-
Conte Divide, it offers breathtaking views to each
side. The trailed segments of this trip touch a full
range of flora and fauna representative of the exciting west slopes of the Sierra.

DESCRIPTION (Strenuous trip)

1st 3 Hiking Days: Follow trip 31 to **Portal Lake**, 22½ miles.

4th Hiking Day (**Portal Lake** to **Blue Canyon Cabinsite**, 7 miles cross
country): Staying on the north side of the outlet stream from
Midway Lake, our route ascends the steep, fractured granite
slope above Portal Lake. One can follow ducks and other signs
of use up the short headwall to arrive at Midway Lake. After
skirting the north shore of this lake, our route follows up its

inlet stream past several rocky tarns to medium-sized (32 acres) Cathedral Lake. Fair fishing for rainbow and some brook trout (to 10") is available here. This high, alpine lake is typical of the lakes of Blackcap Basin: situated in a granite pocket, ringed by cirque walls on three sides, characterized by deep, cold waters, and relieved only by an occasional clump of willow, heather or stunted lodgepole. Our route rounds the north side of the lake, then turns up southeast and climbs talus and steep granite slabs to a jagged notch, the top of a scree slope on the White Divide north of Finger Peak. From the notch views are excellent, especially to the east, with Goddard Creek's canyon, Ragged Spur, Wheel Mountain, Devils Crags and, on the Sierra crest far to the east, Split Mountain.

From the notch, walk right a few yards down a narrow ledge and descend into the talus-strewn cirque on the north side of Finger Peak. The traverse to Blue Canyon Pass requires little elevation loss but a large amount of boulder-hopping, which should be done with caution. After a good mile of rugged cross-country walking, we arrive at Blue Canyon Pass, the first saddle to the east of Finger Peak. Views from this saddle are superlative of the White Divide, Goddard Divide and Ragged Spur, and into southern Kings Canyon National Park. Thence our route descends by chutes to the northernmost, unnamed lakes of the Blue Canyon Creek drainage, and follows the southwest course of this drainage over slab granite that is broken by welcome grassy pockets. The route veers left and drops down to the west side of granite-bound Lake 10364. From the outlet of this lake, our route crosses the stream and descends into lodgepole forest at about the 10,000-foot level, and soon we pick up a trail on the south side of the creek. From the slopes on the left, the hiker is very apt to hear the piping of a marmot as he rounds the turn in the canyon that gives him a view of the lovely, open meadows below. This trail scrambles down to the head of these meadows, skirting the eastern fringe, and arrives at the log ford leading to the good campsites up and downstream from the landmark cabinsite (8430'). Fishing for brook (to 10") in Blue Canyon Creek is good.

5th and 6th Hiking Days: Reverse the steps of trip 39, 18½ miles.

34 Wishon Reservoir to Halfmoon Lake

TRIP   Wishon Reservoir to Halfmoon Lake (round trip).
                  Topo map *Blackcap Mountain*. Best early or mid
                  season; 22 miles.

Grade	Trail/layover days	Total recommended days
Leisurely	4/1	5
Moderate	3/0	3
Strenuous	2/0	2

HILITES   Halfmoon Lake, beside an unnamed trail, nestled in
                  a cirque below an unnamed peak, can serve as a
                  hideout for the city-dweller who—temporarily—has
                  had it. On the way to this fine lake, Mooreboys
                  Meadow offers a campsite where the flora and
                  fauna are plentiful and fascinating.

DESCRIPTION (Leisurely trip)

1st Hiking Day (**Wishon Reservoir** to **Mooreboys Meadow**, 5½ miles):
From the parking lot east of the dam, the trail angles northeast
up a ridge on steep, dusty switchbacks under a mixed forest
cover of pines, firs, cedars and occasional black oaks. In less
than ½ mile we cross a dirt road and look down on a parking
area that one can reach by continuing 1 mile south on the road
beyond the dam to the eastern loop of a long **s**-curve and then
turning left onto a dirt road, which ends at this parking area.
Now our trail passes into deep forest to make a short, strenuous
climb before bending north and leveling out to begin a long,
contouring traverse above Wishon Reservoir. Many tiny streamlets provide thirst-quenching relief on this moderately shaded
traverse, and a near-continuous band of wildflowers periodically
expands into a garden in an open spot, enhanced by many species of butterflies in an aerial array of blues, oranges and yellows.

Finally we round a ridge and descend quickly to Woodchuck Creek (fair campsites). Follow the *TRAIL* signs a short way downstream; don't cross immediately and take the trail, visible across the creek, which peters out a few hundred feet upstream. After boulder-hopping Woodchuck Creek, you travel northwest on a closed, sandy road to the foot of a steep slope. A number of well-graded switchbacks (not the straight-line trail of the topo map) lead up under merciful conifer shade to a lesser slope where your route veers east and continues to climb moderately, then gently, up a dusty, much rutted trail. Just beyond North Fork Woodchuck Creek, which may be dry by late August, you re-meet gurgling Woodchuck Creek beside a fair campsite.

Then the trail climbs steeply through a moderate forest cover understoried by copious greenery up to a junction with the Chuck Pass Trail. Climbing north from here, in ½ mile you reach beautiful Mooreboys Meadow (8780'), named for the people who built the collapsing cabins and the still-standing hewn table and benches here. This large meadow is filled with thousands of corn lilies and other flowers in season, and marmots live on the rocky slope to the east side of the meadow. The best campsites are at the meadow's north end. (There may be no water supply here in the late summer of a dry year.)

2nd Hiking Day (**Mooreboys Meadow** to **Halfmoon Lake**, 5½ miles): Just beyond the meadow, the trail passes a lateral leading left across the creek and up to Woodchuck Lake. Our trail bears right and ascends a taxing ridge to an overview of a fine meadow where mule deer often graze. Soon we pass a trail that goes north (left) past Chimney and Marsh lakes on its way to Woodchuck Lake. Our trail continues to climb, sometimes steeply, on alternating dusty ground and slab granite. As the forest turns from lodgepole to whitebark pine, we have more and more open views, and a feeling of spaciousness and expansiveness prevails. A mile from the last junction is yet a third lateral to Woodchuck Lake. From here we ascend east gently to moderately, and climb the southeast ridge of an unnamed granite dome, where views are great in all directions. Only a hiker totally dedicated to pushing on up the trail could pass up the exhilarating panorama from the top of this rock island: an east-west spectrum from the LeConte Divide and Kettle Ridge down to the forested sloped west of Wishon Reservoir, and a north-south range from the Minarets near Mammoth to the high peaks of the Great Western Divide and the Kings-Kern Divide. Seen through a notch in the latter divide, Mt. Whitney doesn't seem to be the highest thing in California, but it is.

From this granite ridge the trail drops steeply to the saddle of Crown Pass (Point 10188) and a junction with a steep trail down to Crown Lake. In a moment we pass an unmaintained, rough trail leading left down Nichols Canyon. Past these junctions, we follow the ridge north to a beautiful overlook of Half-moon Lake before descending steeply down a lodgepole-forested slope to the north end of the dramatic lake (9422'). Good campsites are on the north side and the east bay of this striking lake.

3rd and 4th Hiking Days: Retrace your steps, 11 miles.

Chimney Lake

Wishon Reservoir to Portal Lake   **35**

TRIP   From Wishon Reservoir to Portal Lake via Halfmoon Lake (round trip). Topo map *Blackcap Mountain.* Best mid season; 35 miles.

Grade	Trail/layover days	Total recommended days
Leisurely	6/1	7
Moderate	4/1	5
Strenuous	3/0	3

HILITES   Blackcap Basin is a worthy goal of any vacation trip,
but this long route to it offers additional attractions
along the way, from the serene forests of Woodchuck country to the dramatic cliffs surrounding
Halfmoon Lake.

DESCRIPTION (Leisurely trip)

1st and 2nd Hiking Days: Follow trip 34 to **Halfmoon Lake**, 11
miles.

3rd Hiking Day (**Halfmoon Lake** to **Portal Lake**, 6½ miles): From
the muddy junction north of Halfmoon Lake, our trail leads
north down the valley of the lake's outlet. As the trail steepens,
the forest cover thickens, and we begin to lose the good views
of the LeConte Divide and Bench Valley that have enhanced
the walking to this point. After a wading ford ½ mile below
Halfmoon Lake, our trail plunges via many switchbacks down
to North Fork Kings River at Big Maxson Meadow. The sound
of the river heralds our approach to a ford (difficult in early
season) which takes us across to a junction with the Courtright/
Blackcap Basin Trail near some cabins at the northwest end of
the meadow. From here we follow the 3rd hiking day, trip 31,
to Portal Lake.

4th, 5th and 6th Hiking Days: Retrace your steps, 17½ miles.

36 Wishon Reservoir to Crown Lake

TRIP

From Wishon Reservoir to Crown Lake (semiloop trip). Topo maps *Blackcap Mountain, Tehipite Dome.* Best early or mid season; 24 miles.

Grade	Trail/layover days	Total recom- mended days
Leisurely	4/1	5
Moderate	3/1	4
Strenuous	2/0	2

HILITES

Everybody wants to get off the beaten path, but if everybody goes to the same unused place, it will be beaten. This guidebook attempts to offer a number of selections for solitude, so that your chances of being alone, when you go to one of them, will be pretty good. This excursion touches a number of such places.

DESCRIPTION (Leisurely trip)

1st Hiking Day: Follow trip 34 to **Mooreboys Meadow**, 5½ miles.

2nd Hiking Day (**Mooreboys Meadow** to **Crown Lake**, 5 miles): Follow the 2nd hiking day of trip 32 to the junction of the Crown Lake Trail and turn right (south) on it.

From the junction, the trail descends steeply south to the large, lodgepole-ringed meadow of Crown Lake. Viewed from the pass, the lake does have a crownlike shape, but its west side, containing several small pools, can be quite marshy at times, and campsites are best on the east side of the lake, where the trail skirts it.

3rd Hiking Day (**Crown Lake** to **Indian Springs**, 6 miles): The trail becomes somewhat indistinct as it crosses the marshy south end below Crown Lake, but it can easily be located as it follows along the east side of the outlet creek. Here we descend easily in moderate forest, at first lodgepole, but later mixed with silver pine. Intermittent marshy patches interrupt the duff trail as it descends gently south, crossing the Crown Lake outlet about ¼ mile below the south tip of the lake. On the west side of this outlet, our trail descends easily past a junction with the Scepter Lake Trail and skirts above a large meadow through which the trail once ran. Just beyond this meadow the trail swings west of Scepter Creek, so that it is out of sight and sound, then returns to creekside at another meadow. Beyond this lovely meadow we cross another and then continue south up to a junction with the Chuck Pass Trail. After turning west on this level trail, we soon ford the sandy-bottomed, unnamed stream that drains Chuck Pass and then climb moderately up the southwest side of the little creek. The string of forest-bordered meadows along the creek's headwaters are, in the mountain springtime, narrow emerald ribbons interspersed with lush gardens— one of the finest series of meadows in the Sierra.

After topping out at Chuck Pass, our rocky trail leads down through heavy, parklike pine forest on a set of steep, dusty switchbacks. Soon the route passes above a rocky, snag-strewn meadow and then it descends to pass a series of sweeping green meadows, where the wildflower population boasts dozens of species. Descending gently, the trail reaches the vicinity of Indian Springs. It skirts the large meadow beside this label on the topo map and arrives at the good campsites just below the meadow on both sides of Woodchuck Creek. Nearby down the trail is a sign *Indian Springs,* but no springs.

4th Hiking Day: (**Indian Springs** to **Wishon Reservoir**, 7½ miles): The trail down the valley of Woodchuck Creek, often soft and muddy from the seepage of springs, penetrates a dense forest of lodgepole pine and reaches a junction with the Hoffman Mountain Trail. Here it veers north and immediately passes the ruins of an old cabin. This sandy forest path then dips west to meet the Wishon/Halfmoon Trail at a junction passed on the first hiking day. From here we retrace the steps of the first part of that hiking day to the roadend.

37   Little Rancheria Trailhead to Cabin Creek

TRIP   From Little Rancheria Trailhead to Cabin Creek (round trip). Topo map *Tehipite Dome.* Best early season, 9 miles.

Grade	Trail/layover days	Total recom- mended days
Leisurely	2/1	3
Moderate	2/0	2
Strenuous	day	....

HILITES   When the high country is still under snow, you can sample the Sierra springtime, with its millions of wildflowers, on this trip to a small but extremely attractive stream.

DESCRIPTION (Leisurely trip)

1st Hiking Day (**Little Rancheria Trailhead** to **Cabin Creek**, 4½ miles): From the end of the paved road, walk several hundred yards down the dirt road to Little Rancheria Creek. Cross the creek and find a duff trail leading up the opposite bank. This trail climbs steeply up the hillside in a dense red-fir forest. Then the grade becomes moderate as the trail winds along a ridge. One mile from your car this trail meets the Crown Valley Trail, at a point ⅓ mile east of Three Springs. The ascent eases off gradually before arriving at the Finger Rock Trail, and soon we reach the top of the flat ridge, where tiny tributaries repeatedly cross the trail. At the top of this climb is a lovely wildflower garden that includes lupine, monkey flower, golden brodiaea, currant, gooseberry and larkspur. As the trail turns one has limited views in the southeast of Spanish Mountain, Rodgers Ridge and the Obelisk. The duff trail then descends through a moderate-to-dense forest cover to a ford of a tributary of Cabin Creek. About ½ mile beyond, our trail arrives at the fair campsites on Cabin Creek (8240´). This creek is a tiny stream of water, but its diminutive size does not hide its irrepressible nature as it tumbles down with a riot of sound. Brook trout inhabit this little creek, but fishermen will find them generally very small. The better campsites are just upstream. Since many cattle graze in the area, treating the water is advised.

2nd Hiking Day: Retrace your steps, 5½ miles.

Shooting stars *Ron Felzer*

38 Little Rancheria Trailhead to Crown Creek

TRIP   From Little Rancheria Trailhead to Crown Creek
via Cabin Creek, Crown Valley (round trip). Topo
map *Tehipite Dome.* Best early to mid season; 21
miles.

Grade	Trail/layover days	Total recommended days
Leisurely	4/1	5
Moderate	3/0	3
Strenuous	2/0	2

HILITES   After a few miles in cowgrazing land, this trip
reaches the wilderness precincts of Crown Creek,
where it makes a detour off the main trail to an excellent campsite on this enchanting creek.

DESCRIPTION (Leisurely trip)

1st Hiking Day: Follow trip 37 to **Cabin Creek**, 4½ miles.

2nd Hiking Day (**Cabin Creek** to **Crown Creek**, 6 miles): Leaving
Cabin Creek, the trail climbs steeply and then crosses two easy
saddles and descends past the jeep road to a little meadow
where there is a junction with a trail to Chain Lakes and Hoffman Mountain. Our route then joins the jeep road and climbs
over another easy ridge, then traverses the slope above Cow
Meadow, leaves the jeep road, and soon comes to a junction
with the Statum Meadow Trail branching right. The red-fir-
and-lodgepole forest is dense as we pass Summit Meadow (in-
correctly labeled "Wet Meadow" on the topo map). Just beyond
a sandy flat we come to a junction with a trail to Fin Dome and
Geraldine Lake, branching right. Our duff-and-sand trail winds
through dense timber and passes a lateral on the right leading
to Spanish Lakes before it arrives at the uniquely constructed
Crown Valley Guard Station, where emergency services are
usually available. Turning somewhat north, the trail descends
to the lupine-infested and ghost-snagged west end of Crown
Valley meadows, where we cross a small creek. The trail then

winds around the fenced southern edge of the grassland, cross-ing several corduroy log bridges to arrive at a junction with the Tehipite Valley Trail. Just north of this junction are the half dozen or so buildings of the Crown Valley Ranch, a recently active guest ranch. About ⅓ mile beyond the ranch, where the trail to Mountain Meadow branches left, we pass a sign indi-cating our entrance into the John Muir Wilderness, in which the permanent works of man are barred.

From here the trail descends moderately, then steeply, into the drainage of Crown Creek. Occasional tree-shrouded views of Kettle Dome, Monarch Divide and Tombstone Ridge can be had on the upper part of this descent. About 1½ miles from the ranch our trail fords little Deer Creek and then Willow Creek. Then the trail climbs an easy ridge under a dense forest cover and drops down to the campsiteless ford of Bob Creek. Ahead, on the last, steep, sandy slope above Crown Creek is a junction signed *Campsite,* from where a lateral trail goes left, up-canyon, 3/4 mile and fords Crown Creek (difficult in high water) to arrive at an improved campground (7040'). This is a lovely site; anglers will delight in the good brook and rainbow fishing to be had along the creek, and naturalists will find the natural salt lick just above the ford a superlative spot for quiet wildlife watching.

3rd and 4th Hiking Days: Retrace your steps, 21 miles.

39 Little Rancheria Trailhead to Blue Canyon

TRIP
From Little Rancheria Trailhead to Blue Canyon via Cabin Creek, Crown Creek, Kettle Ridge (round trip). Topo maps *Tehipite Dome, Marion Peak, Mt. Goddard.* Best mid or late season; 37 miles.

Grade	Trail/layover days	Total recom- mended days
Leisurely	7/2	9
Moderate	6/1	7
Strenuous	4/1	5

HILITES
This trip winds through magnificent stands of fir and lodgepole before crossing lofty Kettle Ridge to Blue Canyon. Wildflowers abound around the many tributary crossings, and fishing is excellent.

DESCRIPTION (Leisurely trip)

1st 2 Hiking Days: Follow trip 38 to **Crown Creek**, 10½ miles):

3rd Hiking Day (**Crown Creek** to **Kettle Dome Campsite**, 4½ miles): Retrace your steps to the main trail, and turn left toward Crown Creek. After descending a few yards from this junction, the trail fords Crown Creek and continues eastward in fairly level fashion. As the trail nears the foot of Kettle Ridge, Kettle Dome comes into view as a granite finger. The trail crosses several small run-off streams (not all are indicated on the topo; fill your water bottle at the third stream), and at the Kings Canyon National Park boundary begins a steady climb. For those who are interested, the 7600-foot contour marks the best place to begin a side excursion to ascend Tehipite Dome. It is an interesting historical sidelight that Frank Dusy, a local sheepherder, around the turn of the century pursued a wounded grizzly bear approximately along this route. Further exploration by Dusy for grazing areas resulted in the blazing of this crossing of Kettle Ridge and the old Tunemah Trail (leading to Simpson Meadow). It is interesting to note that the lower slopes have some sugar pine, John Muir's favorite Sierra tree. The trail soon becomes very steep, with exceptionally few switchbacks, and this poor trail construction results in the trail's being heavily washed—a condition not helped by the heavy stock traffic it suffers. As the trail ascends, the forest cover thins somewhat, but still includes sugar pine, red fir, lodgepole and Jeffrey. The underbrush, for the most part, is manzanita and snowbrush. Eventually you reach the top of the ridge; it is time well spent to detour off to the right of the trail for the unsurpassed views of the Monarch Divide, Cirque Crest, the Middle Fork Kings River watershed, and a large part of eastern Kings Canyon National Park. The panorama of the Monarch Divide encompasses Goat Crest, Slide Peak, Kennedy Mountain and Hogback Peak. Slide Peak, with its clearly defined avalanche chutes, is particularly interesting, and above the canyon's blue haze one can trace the glacial paths on the far side that left the remarkable, unnamed, finlike ridge to the east-southeast. The trail then descends steeply from the top of the ridge, and this descent offers a different set of views, including Burnt Mountain, a little bit of Blue Canyon, Marion Peak, parts of Cirque Crest, Goat Crest and some of the Monarch Divide. The descent levels off in a meadowed bench containing a small tributary stream (unnamed), where there are several good primitive campsites around the meadow above the ford (8200'). These campsites are due east of Kettle Dome, and about 1000 feet above the Blue Canyon floor. The creek here, though small and isolated, has a fairly large population of rainbow trout.

4th Hiking Day (**Kettle Dome Campsite** to **Blue Canyon Cabinsite**, 3½ miles): The dusty and rocky trail descends by steady, steep switchbacks the remaining 1000 feet to the canyon floor. This descent meets the tributary on which the campsites for the previous hiking day were situated and then swings up-canyon as it nears Blue Canyon Creek. Ascending the rocky slopes of Blue Canyon, the trail alternates between steady and steep climbing through a moderate forest cover that includes white fir and Jeffrey pine, with manzanita and deerbrush underneath. Some cottonwoods appear along the creek, and as we climb higher some aspens, junipers and lodgepole pines join the forest's ranks. Looking back down Blue Canyon, one has **V**'d views across the Middle Fork Kings River to the "turrets" surrounding the Gorge of Despair.

Flowers along this ascent include Indian paintbrush, pennyroyal, Mariposa lily, pussy paws, scarlet gilia and larkspur. Just north of the large packer site, the trail crosses to the east side of the creek via a shallow wade-across ford, and then continues its steady climb. Above this ford, Blue Canyon Creek exhibits some interesting granite-bottomed chutes. The water slides down these chutes, which are up to several hundred feet long, and are marked at either end by cascades or waterfalls. At the head of one of these series, the trail emerges at Blue Canyon meadows. Here, in contrast to the white-water maelstrom below, Blue Canyon Creek winds docilely in typical meadow-meandering fashion, and immediately on the left one can see the old notched-log sheepherder cabin across the creek. Good campsites lie near the cabin, and angling for brook and rainbow (to 10") in Blue Canyon Creek is good. These campsites make a good base camp for angling and discovery side trips to the head of Blue Canyon basin.

5th, 6th, and 7th Hiking Days: Retrace your steps, 18½ miles.

Duck on glacial erratic

South Lake to Treasure Lakes

40

TRIP   From South Lake to Treasure Lakes (round trip). Topo map *Mt. Goddard.* Best mid or late season; 5 miles.

Grade	Trail/layover days	Total recom- mended days
Leisurely	2/0	2
Moderate	....	....
Strenuous	day	....

HILITES   This short trip is a fine "weekender." Touching the upper reaches of a tributary of South Fork Bishop Creek, it exposes the traveler to three life zones with a very limited expenditure of energy and time. As a bonus, the Treasure Lakes don't get the high use found just over the ridge along the Bishop Pass Trail.

DESCRIPTION (Leisurely trip)

1st Hiking Day (**South Lake** to **Treasure Lake**, 2½ miles): From the roadend (9760') the trail climbs steadily along the east side of South Lake. A moderate-to-dense forest cover of lodgepole pine lines the rocky route as it meets and turns onto the Treasure Lakes Trail. Mostly over duff and sand, the trail descends to ford a stream, ascends briefly, and then descends again to a bridge over Bishop Creek's South Fork. This stretch affords good views of Hurd Peak and the backgrounding, glacially topped peaks to the north. The trail then meanders over to the outlet from the Treasure Lakes, parallels it briefly downstream, and crosses it on a log. Beyond this ford we begin a moderate-to-steep ascent on a duff-and-sand trail. As the elevation increases, the forest cover shows increasing whitebark pine mixed with the lodgepoles, and there is an abundance of wildflowers lining the trail and clustered in the grassy patches that seam the granite. Although this trail does see some stock traffic, it is, for the most part, a hiker's trail. The ascent steepens, crosses an area of smoothed granite slabs dotted with glacial erratic boulders, and fords the outlet stream from Lake 10646 (difficult in early season). Then, in an easy ½ mile, we arrive at the good campsites on the northeast side of that lake, directly under dramatic, pointed Peak 12047. This lake, the largest in the Treasure Lakes basin (12 acres), affords fair-to-good fishing for golden (to 12"). Anglers who wish to spend a layover day here will find that, contrary to the usual rule of thumb, the fishing gets better as one tries the lakes of the upper basin.

2nd Hiking Day: Retrace your steps, 2½ miles.

Peak 12047 over Treasure Lake 10646

South Lake to Treasure Lakes

41

TRIP   From South Lake to Treasure Lakes, return via cross-country route to Long Lake (semiloop trip). Topo map *Mt. Goddard.* Best mid or late season; 8 miles.

Grade	Trail/layover days	Total recommended days
Leisurely	2/0	2
Moderate	....	....
Strenuous	day	....

HILITES   Like the previous trip, this two-day trek explores the Treasure Lakes chain, but, unlike the previous trip, it returns by an easy cross-country route to the Bishop Pass Trail. Views from the summit of the cross-country leg are more than worth the scramble.

DESCRIPTION (Leisurely trip)

1st Hiking Day: Follow trip 40 to **Treasure Lakes**, 2½ miles.

2nd Hiking Day (**Treasure Lakes** to **South Lake** via Long Lake, 5½ miles, part cross country): Following the faint fisherman's trail that ascends from the south end of the largest of the Treasure Lakes (10,646'), one follows a ridge east of the intervening stream to the cirque-basined three upper lakes. This ascent sees the timber cover thinning until, at the upper triad, all that remains is low-lying whitebark pine. Like the lower Treasure Lakes, these three lakes contain good populations of golden trout (to 15"). Trout were originally backpacked in by A. Parcher, son of the pioneer resort owner W. C. Parcher, and the spawn of that initial plant provide good fishing for today's anglers.

From the upper lake, our route crosses the outlet and ascends 500 vertical feet up moderate slopes to the saddle east of the lake. This ascent crosses easy ledges and some loose rock south of the gray fractured slopes of the northern outlier of Hurd Peak. Grand views from this saddle include Mts. Gilbert, Johnson and Goode to the west, and the spectacular comb ridge of the Inconsolable Range rimming the South Fork Bishop Creek drainage to the east.

From the saddle, the best route descends gently north-north-east about 100 yards, then veers over beside the little stream here, paralleling it momentarily beside a short waterfall. From there you scramble and stroll almost directly to Margaret Lake, visible down the valley. On the northwest side of this lovely lake you'll find a use trail that leads northeast to the southern-most point of Long Lake. A few steps up the inlet of this lake are places to ford the inlet, which is the South Fork of Bishop Creek. Then walk quickly past some incredibly overused camp-sites to find the Bishop Pass Trail, and turn left (north) on it.

After fording the willow-infested outlet of Ruwau Lake, your trail passes a lateral trail to that lake and then closely skirts the east shore of Long Lake. At the lake's north end you ford another inlet stream and pass the Chocolate Lakes Trail as you begin the long descent to the trailhead. The trail is dusty and overused, but it passes a number of charming pocket meadows and crosses dozens of runoff rills. Not far beyond the Mary Louise Lakes Trail we cross the outlet of those lakes on a small log bridge, and then reach the start of the Treasure Lakes Trail, from where we retrace the first mile of the first hiking day.

The Inconsolable Range (Mt. Agassiz at right)

South Lake to Dusy Basin

42

TRIP From South Lake to Dusy Basin via Bishop Pass (round trip). Topo map *Mt. Goddard*. Best mid or late season; 14 miles.

Grade	Trail/layover days	Total recommended days
Leisurely	....	....
Moderate	2/1	3
Strenuous	day	....

HILITES A popular route, the Bishop Pass Trail climbs the scenic course of South Fork Bishop Creek. At Bishop Pass, the trail enters King Canyon National Park, but, more significantly, it begins the adventure of the high, barren, granitoid country of Dusy Basin. Grand side-trip possibilities are sufficient reason for planning layover days on this trip.

DESCRIPTION (Moderate trip)

1st Hiking Day (**South Lake** to **Dusy Basin**, 7 miles): Starting from the roadend (9760')—about ¼ mile above the South Lake dam—the route ascends through a moderate-to-dense forest cover of lodgepole, fir and aspen on a somewhat rocky trail. This ascent traverses the moraine slope on the east side of South Lake, bearing toward Hurd Peak, and then passes a trail to the Treasure Lakes. After turning southeast, your trail soon crosses the Mary Louise Lakes outlet on a log bridge and then passes the trail to these lakes. Frequent patches of lupine, forget-me-nots, wallflowers and swamp onions delight the traveler as he fords streamlets and crosses swampy sections. Visible below on the right is small, clear Hurd Lake.

The trail then switchbacks up to a junction with the Bull-Chocolate Lakes Trail and levels off to reach the islet-dotted north end of Long Lake. After crossing this lake's inlet, it undulates along the east side of this popular lake (rainbow, brook and brown, to 17"). Near the lake's south end another trail goes east to Ruwau Lake, and then we cross the sparkling outlet stream from that lake to arrive in "tent city," the overused knolls above the south end of Long Lake.

The memorable vistas of the wooded and meadowed shores of Long Lake stay with the visitor as he ascends through sporadic subalpine tarn-dotted meadows. Sometimes steep, this steadily ascending trail climbs past spectacular Saddlerock Lake (rainbow to 10"), and the unmarked fisherman's spur trail to Bishop Lake (brook to 14").

Beyond Saddlerock Lake, the trail passes timberline and begins a series of steep switchbacks at the head of a spectacular cirque basin. Excellent views of Mt. Goode appear on the right, and the incredible comb spires of the Inconsolable Range on the left accompany the panting climber, making his breather stops unforgettable occasions. Glacially smoothed ledge granite and quarried blocks on every hand line this well-maintained trail. Occasional pockets of snow sometimes blanket the approach to Bishop Pass (11,972') late into the season, and care should be exercised in the final steep part of the ascent to the summit. Views from the pass are excellent of the Inconsolable Range to the north; Mt. Agassiz to the southeast; Dusy Basin immediately to the south, flanked by Columbine and Giraud peaks; and the Black Divide on the distant western skyline.

From the pass our route descends on a sometimes switchbacking southwestern traverse. This sandy descent contours over rock-bench systems some distance north of the basin's northernmost large lake (11,300'). Where the trail veers west, our route branches left, leaving the trail and crossing smooth granite and tundra to the fair campsites at the west end of this lake. Other fair campsites can be found a few yards to the southwest, along the outlet stream. Fishing for golden and brook trout on this northernmost lake is fair, but anglers should try the good-to-excellent golden and brook angling (to 22") at Lake 11393 and the lake just west of it, along with the connecting stream.

Alpine scenery from the above campsites is breathtaking in its vastness. One can see the Inconsolable Range as it rises behind Bishop Pass, and the climber's Mecca, the Palisade crest, fills the eastern skyline. Also to the east towers symmetrical Isosceles Peak. A very sparse forest cover of gnarled whitebark pine dots the granite landscape on all sides, and the fractures in the granite are filled with grassy, heather-lined pockets.

2nd Hiking Day: Retrace your steps, 7 miles.

South Lake to Chocolate Lakes   **43**

11 -
10 -
9 -

TRIP   From South Lake to Chocolate Lakes (round trip)
Topo map *Mt. Goddard.* Best mid season; 6 miles.

Grade	Trail/layover days	Total recom- mended days
Leisurely	2/0	2
Moderate	....	....
Strenuous	day	....

HILITES   The barren heights of the Inconsolable Range mir-
rored in the lakes of the Chocolate chain make this
trip one to be remembered. The good fishing on the
lakes is a bonus, and the package ties up as a grand
"warm-up" for the hiker starting his season late.

DESCRIPTION (Leisurely trip)

1st Hiking Day (**South Lake** to **Chocolate Lakes**, 3 miles): Proceed
to the Bull Lake Trail junction as described in the 1st hiking
day, trip 42. Here our route turns left, away from the Bishop
Pass Trail. Ascending moderately, the trail fords a tributary
of South Fork Bishop Creek, and arrives at sparsely timbered,
moderate-sized (10-acre) Bull Lake. Rock-encircled clumps of
willows alternate with grassy sections as the trail skirts the
north side of the lake. Fishermen may wish to sample this lake's
fair brook-trout fishing (to 9") before continuing up the lake's
inlet stream to the lower Chocolate Lakes.

This ascent crosses rocky talus stretches as it fords and refords the stream. Breather stops offer sweeping views back
across the South Fork Bishop Creek drainage to Mts. Goode,
Johnson, Gilbert and Thompson. Dominating all views to the
east are the barren, pinnacle-comb formations of the somber
Inconsolable Range. The granitic Chocolate Lakes chain
consists of three lakes that are progressively larger as one
ascends the basin. Necklaced together, they hang like sapphire
jewels around the northeast side of red-rocked Chocolate Peak.
The trail passes several good campsites at lower Chocolate
Lake. All these lakes have a fair fishery of brook (to 10"), and
the upper, larger lake (11,100') affords good campsites.

2nd Hiking Day: Retrace your steps, 3 miles.

44

South Lake to Palisade Basin

TRIP   From South Lake to Dusy Basin, Palisade Basin, Deer Meadow, Middle Fork Kings River, Bishop Pass (semiloop trip). Topo maps *Mt. Goddard, Big Pine.* Best mid or late season; 37½ miles.

Grade	Trail/layover days	Total recommended days
Leisurely	....	....
Moderate	6/2	8
Strenuous	5/2	7

HILITES   Those who yearn to go "high and light" will find this rugged route to their liking. For scenery the incomparable Palisade crest dominates the route, except along the section on the John Muir Trail down Palisade Creek and up LeConte Canyon.

DESCRIPTION (Moderate trip)

1st Hiking Day: Follow trip 42 to **Dusy Basin**, 7 miles.

2nd Hiking Day (**Dusy Basin** to **Glacier Creek**, 6 miles cross country): The backpacker can contemplate crossing to Palisade Basin via any one of three foot-walkers' passes: 1) Knapsack Pass; 2) the unnamed pass between Columbine Peak and Isosceles Peak; and 3) what has come to be known as "Thunderbolt Pass," just southwest of Thunderbolt Peak. Our route uses Knapsack Pass (11,673'). Leaving our campsite at the northernmost large lake of Dusy Basin, we descend on the trail and ford Dusy Branch at 10,900 feet, just above (north of) the lowest lakes of the basin. From here our cross-country route boulder-hops southeastward on a steady ascent. The footing is mostly rock, broken by occasional pockets of granite sand, and the forest "cover" consists of very sparse clumps of the five-needled, stunted whitebark pine. These lower lakes contain golden and brook trout (to 12").

Dusy Basin

The well-ducked, steady ascent over heavily fractured rock becomes steeper on the final climb to the pass. Impossible as it may seem, there are recorded visits to Palisade Basin via this pass with stock! Views from the pass include Black Giant, Mt. Powell and Mt. Thompson to the northwest, and the Palisade Basin and Crest to the east. From this vantage point, the vast expanses of Palisade Basin appear totally barren of life except for an isolated whitebark pine or a spiring snag, but a closer examination later in this hiking day will reveal much more. The continuing bracing views of the Palisade Crest, as our route descends from Knapsack Pass, stir the most blasé non-mountain climber. These peaks look, as one climber expressed it, "like mountain peaks are supposed to look." Precipitous faces composed of relatively unfractured granite, couloirs, buttresses and residual glaciers combine to make this crest one of the finer climbing areas in the Sierra Nevada.

Our well-ducked route keeps to the left as it descends over a moderate-to-steep ledge system to the westernmost lake of the Barrett chain. After passing around the south end of this rock-bound lake, this route crosses the easy saddle east of the lake to the largest lake of the chain, and follows a fisherman's trail around the north end. From this lake the sheer cliffs of the west face of North Palisade dominate the skyline, and our route continues east past several tiny, rockbound lakelets. In contrast to the granite of lower Dusy Basin, this granite looks "newer," since it shows much less fracturing and exfoliation, but both were formed at the same time.

After contouring around the head of the drainage at the east end of Palisade Basin, our route crosses the definite saddle between Point 12692 and the main Palisade Crest. Among climbers this saddle is called "Potluck Pass." Along with the continuing views of the Palisades, this vantage point also looks across the Palisade Creek watershed to Amphitheater Lake. To the southwest the glacially sculpted terrain has an appearance similar to the top of a meringue pie. The descent from Potluck Pass is a scramble over a steep, smoothed granite ledge system, keeping to the right. This downgrade continues over scree and then levels out at Lake 11672, and our route follows the west shore of the lake to the good campsites on that edge of the lake and along the outlet creek just below the lake. Fishing at this lake is poor-to-fair for golden (to 8"). Grassy sections around the sandy-bottomed lake provide a foothold for colorful alpine wildflowers, including yellow columbine, sturdy white heather, and blue sky pilot.

3rd Hiking Day **(Glacier Creek** to **Deer Meadow**, 5 miles, part cross country): After fording Glacier Creek, our route ascends the sloping basin east to a saddle overlooking the Palisade Lakes basin. Views from this saddle are good of Devils Crags and Mt. McDuffie to the west, North Palisade to the north and Middle Palisade to the east. Sometimes over snow, this route descends past several tiny glacial tarns across fractured granite as it veers westward. Part way down this moderate-to-steep grade, Palisade Lakes and the glacially smoothed bowl-like cirque surrounding the lakes come into view. Then, by route-finding down a ledge system, you will encounter sparse whitebark pine just before you meet the John Muir Trail just west of lower Palisade Lake.

Westward on the Muir Trail, the route descends by zigzagging switchbacks along the north side of Palisade Creek. The head of these switchbacks is an excellent vantage point from which to see the crest of Middle Palisade peak to the northeast, and, west beyond Deer Meadow lying immediately below, Devils Crags, Wheel Mountain and Mt. McDuffie. Slopes on both sides of this steep descent are dramatically glacially smoothed. As the trail reaches the head of the flats above Deer Meadow, it enters a moderate stand of lodgepole and silver pine. Abundant wildflowers, including western mountain aster, Douglas phlox, pennyroyal, red columbine and tiger lily, appear as the trail comes close to the creek, and red fir, juniper and aspen occasionally mingle with the predominant lodgepole forest cover. The trail then passes several good campsites before fording Glacier Creek via several step-across branchlets. There are excellent views across the Palisade Creek canyon to the cascading falls of Cataract Creek as they tumble down the steep south wall.

The trail soon reaches Deer Meadow, not really a meadow since it is overgrown with lodgepole pines. You are now two days' walk from any trailhead, and even though you are on the Muir Trail you may find considerably privacy. In June of 1976 here, we saw grass growing in the tread of the John Muir Trail! There are several good campsites (8870'), and fishing for golden and brook trout is excellent (to 12'').

4th Hiking Day (**Deer Meadow** to **Grouse Meadows**, 5 miles): About 100 yards below these campsites the trail fords the unnamed multibranched outlet of Palisade Basin, and then it descends moderately through a moderate-to-dense forest cover. This descent passes a packers' campsite about 1½ miles farther on, and then more campsites a short distance beyond that. Concentrations of wildflowers include Indian paintbrush, penstemon, white cinquefoil, Mariposa lily and goldenrod. The underfooting is mostly duff and sand, through alternating forest and meadow, where camping and fishing are good. Then the trail veers away from Palisade Creek, only to return, and, keeping to the north side of the creek, descends steadily over morainal debris to the Middle Fork Kings River Trail. Our route turns right, up the Middle Fork, and proceeds for a gentle uphill mile over an easy ridge to the campsites at the east side of Grouse Meadows. If these are full, back-track about ¼ mile.

5th and 6th Hiking Days: Follow trip 56, 5th and 6th hiking days. 14½ miles.

45   **South Lake to Courtright Reservoir**

TRIP   From South Lake to Courtright Reservoir, via
              Bishop Pass, Dusy Basin, John Muir Trail, Muir
              Pass, Evolution Valley, Goddard Canyon, Hell-for-
              Sure Pass, Rae Lake, Post Corral Meadows (shuttle
              trip). Topo maps *Mt. Goddard, Blackcap Mountain.*
              Best mid or late season; 58½ miles.

| | Trail/layover | Total recom- |
Grade	days	mended days
Leisurely	....	....
Moderate	8/2	10
Strenuous	6/1	7

HILITES   So much laudatory prose has been written about the
              famous Muir Trail that it seems redundant to add
              to it. Suffice it to say that this section of trail tours
              the essence of high country, and has the added fillip
              of finishing via the elegant forest stretches found
              west of Hell-for-Sure Pass.

DESCRIPTION (Moderate trip)

1st Hiking Day: Follow trip 42 to **Dusy Basin**, 7 miles.

2nd Hiking Day (**Dusy Basin** to **Little Pete Meadow**, 6 miles): The
trail from the northernmost lake of the Dusy Basin descends
over smooth granite ledges and tundra sections. Occasional
clumps of the flaky-barked, five-needled whitebark pine dot the
glacially scoured basin, and impressive Mts. Agassiz and Winchell and Thunderbolt Peak continue to make up the eastern
skyline. To the south the heavily fractured and less well defined
summits of Columbine and Giraud peaks occupy the skyline.
This moderate descent swings westward above the lowest lakes
of the Dusy Basin, and begins a series of steady switchbacks
along the north side of Dusy Branch creek. Wildflowers along

this descent include Indian paintbrush, pennyroyal, lupine, white cinquefoil, penstemon, shooting star and some yellow columbine. Just below a waterfall, a wooden bridge crosses to the creek's west side. Views of the U-shaped Middle Fork Kings River canyon are seen constantly during the zigzagging downgrade, and on the far side of the valley one can see the major peaks of the Black Divide, foregrounded by The Citadel and Langille Peak. As the trail descends, the very sparse forest cover of stunted whitebark seen in most of Dusy Basin gives way to the trees of lower altitudes, including silver pine, juniper, lodgepole, aspen and some red fir near the foot of the switchbacks. The trail recrosses Dusy Branch creek at the head of a stepladdering bench, and then makes the final 1½-mile switchbacking descent to a junction with the John Muir Trail in LeConte Canyon. Emergency services are usually available from the ranger station just a few yards northwest of the junction. Our route turns right, onto the famous Muir Trail, and ascends moderately over a duff trail through moderate-to-dense stands of lodgepole. Langille Peak dominates the views to the left, and its striking white, fractured granite face is a constant reminder of the massive forces expended by the river of ice that once filled this canyon. Abundant fields of wildflowers color the trail-

Palisade Crest from the air (looking west)   *E.P. Pister*

side, including corn lily, white mariposa, tiger lily, buckwheat, fireweed, larkspur, red heather, shooting star, paintbrush, cinquefoil, monkey flower, pennyroyal, penstemon, aster, gooseberry, currant, goldenrod and wallflower. As the trail approaches the south end of Little Pete Meadow, occasional hemlock will be found mixed with the lodgepole, and the view north at the edge of the meadow includes Mts. Powell and Thompson. There are good but heavily used campsites at Little Pete Meadow, and fishing for rainbow, golden and brook is good (to 13'').

3rd Hiking Day (**Little Pete Meadow** to **Wanda Lake, 9½** miles): The trail from Little Pete to Big Pete Meadow makes a moderate ascent on rock and sand through a sparse-to-moderate forest cover of lodgepole and occasional hemlock. Looking back over one's shoulder rewards one with fine views of LeConte Canyon, while ahead the granite walls where the canyon veers west show glacially smoothed, unfractured faces. Some quaking aspen can be seen as the trail ascends through Big Pete Meadow and passes the large area of campsites. As the trail turns westward, one has his first, excellent views of the darker rock of Black Giant, and a few yards beyond the turn the trail fords the stream draining the slopes of Mts. Johnson and Gilbert. Passing more campsites, the trail continues west on an easy-to-moderate ascent through grassy extensions of Big Pete Meadow. Most of the rock underfooting encountered to this point has been of the rounded morainal variety, but as soon as the trail leaves the westernmost fringes of Big Pete Meadow, the rock's sharp, fractured edges reflect its weathering origins. Over this talus, the trail ascends more steeply through a moderate forest cover of silver, lodgepole and whitebark pine and some hemlock. The meadowed flat where the trail jogs north toward the tiny, unnamed lake east of Helen Lake supports a sparse forest fringe of lodgepole, silver and some whitebark pine.

The ascent to Muir Pass starts with a steady climb over sand and rock through a sparse timber cover of whitebark pine. That timber cover soon disappears, giving way to low-lying heather. At the talus-bound, round, unnamed lake east of Helen Lake, the trail veers west, crossing and recrossing the trickling headwaters of Middle Fork Kings River. Excellent views to the southeast of the Palisades and Langille, Giraud and Columbine peaks make the breather stops welcome occasions. The trail becomes rocky and the slope more moderate as it passes the next unnamed lake and winds up the terminal shoulder of the Black Divide to Helen Lake. Rocks in colorful reds, yellows, blacks and whites that characterize this metamorphic divide

Mt. Goddard over Wanda Lake

are on every hand. The trail rounds the loose-rocked south end of this barren lake, and ascends steadily over a rocky slope that is often covered with snow throughout the summer. Looking back, one can see the striking meeting of the black metamorphic rock of the Black Divide and the white granite just east of Helen Lake.

Muir Pass (11,955') is marked by a sign and a unique stone shelter. This hut, erected by the Sierra Club in memoriam to John Muir, the Sierra's best-known and most-loved mountaineer, stands as a shelter for stormbound travelers. In a sense, it is a wilderness monument, and should be treated as such— leave nothing but your boottracks. (Even human waste has become a problem in the vicinity.) From this pass the views are magnificent. In the morning light, the somber crags to the north and south relieve the intense whites of the lighter granite to the east. Situated in a gigantic rock bowl to the west, Wanda Lake's emerald blue waters contrast sharply with its lower white edges, which, on the south side, merge into the darker rock of the Goddard Divide. The descent from the pass is moderate and then gentle over fragmented rock, and then it levels out, passing the southeast end of Lake McDermand. Skirting the east side of Wanda Lake, the trail affords excellent views of snow-and-ice necklaced Mt. Goddard, and then arrives at the fair if barren campsites near the lake's outlet. The expansive views from these campsites include Mt. Goddard and the Goddard Divide to the south, and Mts. Huxley, Spencer, Darwin and Mendel to the north.

4th Hiking Day (**Wanda Lake** to **Colby Meadow**, 6½ miles): Soon occasional wildflowers, including heather, wallflower and penstemon, can be seen as the trail descends over rock and sand. Below Wanda Lake the trail crosses Evolution Creek and stays on the west bank on a moderate descent that becomes switchbacks above Sapphire Lake. Fine views of the Sierra crest to the east make watching one's footing a difficult task. Sapphire Lake is indeed a high-country gem, fringed with green, marshy grass, and situated on a large glacial step, with some very large trout. Our route traverses its steeper west side, and, after a steady descent, refords Evolution Creek just above Evolution Lake (difficult ford in early or mid season). The trail crosses a meadowy section before winding the length of the lake's east shore. Glacial smoothing and some polish can be seen in the granite surrounding the lake, and on the abrupt walls on either side of the lake. After passing several campsites at the lower end of the lake, the trail makes a brief northward swing before switchbacking down to Evolution Valley. This northward swing passes the unsigned, ducked trail ascending to Darwin Canyon, and the route to the Darwin Glacier. The zigzagging downgrade over morainal debris re-enters forest cover and passes clumps of wildflowers that include penstemon, paintbrush, swamp onion, lupine, forget-me-not, cinquefoil, buckwheat and tiger lily. At the foot of the grade, where the trail fords the stream emptying Darwin Canyon, our route passes more campsites, and then continues for some distance on a relatively level course through moderate stands of lodgepole to the good campsites at Colby Meadow. Fishing for golden is fair (to 9") in nearby Evolution Creek.

5th Hiking Day (**Colby Meadow** to **Lower Goddard Canyon**, 5½ miles): From Colby Meadow the trail continues westward, passing McClure and Evolution meadows. The trail joining these meadows is a pathway that winds through moderate and dense stands of lodgepole, and, midway down McClure Meadow, passes a ranger station (emergency services usually available here). The friendly intimacy of the meadows has, over the past seventy years, made this valley a favorite camping site for backcountry travelers, and one which, with the subsequent establishment of the John Muir Trail, has subjected these delicate wild pastures to serious overuse. As our route winds past the campsites in McClure Meadow, the largest of the Evolution group, the traveler can see for himself the toll taken by the heavy traffic, both human and stock. Before controls were exerted upon grazing stock of large pack-train parties, the foraging animals trampled tender, young spring shoots of grass in such quantities as to change the meadow almost to a patchwork of barren hillocks. In the absence of grasses to hold back the water, serious erosion became a matter of concern, and today, to preserve these meadows, stock forage is necessarily limited, and the trail has been rerouted to skirt the meadows on the north side.

Our duff trail passes the drift fence below McClure Meadow on a moderate-to-steady descent that fords several tributaries draining the Glacier Divide. These fords are usually accomplished via footlogs or easy rock-hopping. Below Evolution Meadow the trail crosses Evolution Creek (on a log—difficult at high water) for the last time, and then continues west to the head of the switchbacks that drop down to South Fork San Joaquin River. Views before the dropoff are excellent of the cascades of the stream draining Emerald Peak, the falls and cascades of Evolution Creek below the ford, and the South Fork San Joaquin River drainage. Midway down the switchbacks, one has impressive views of Goddard Canyon, part of the route for the 6th hiking day. The forest cover along the zigzags is sparse-to-moderate lodgepole, juniper and some aspen, and flowers seen along the trail include pennyroyal, larkspur, penstemon, cinquefoil, currant, monkey flower, buckwheat and paintbrush. The switchbacking trail crosses glacial polish exhibiting some striations, and, at the bottom, passes a packer campsite and several good primitive sites as it passes through a heavy stand of lodgepole. Just beyond these campsites, our trail crosses the footbridge, meets the Goddard Canyon/Hell-for-Sure Pass Trail, and branches left. The forest cover of lodgepole, with large concentrations of quaking aspen, continues as the trail ascends moderately past a drift fence. About ½ mile above the drift fence, near a small meadow, the trail reaches several good-to-excellent campsites. Fishing on nearby South Fork San Joaquin is fair for rainbow, some golden and brook (to 10").

6th, 7th and 8th Hiking Days: Reverse the 3rd hiking day, trip 32, the 2nd hiking day, trip 27, and the 1st hiking day, trip 25, 24 miles.

46   South Lake to North Lake

TRIP   From South Lake to North Lake via Dusy Basin, LeConte Canyon, Muir Pass, Evolution Valley, Blaney Hot Springs, Piute Canyon and Piute Pass (shuttle trip). Topo maps *Mt. Goddard, Mt. Tom, Mt. Abbot, Blackcap Mountain.* Best mid or late season; 60 miles.

Grade	Trail/layover days	Total recommended days
Leisurely	10/2	12
Moderate	8/1	9
Strenuous	6/0	6

HILITES   The authors' policy is to have no trips consisting entirely of hiking days borrowed from other trips. This trip has been made the exception because it is the quintessential High Sierra hike. In between two crossings of the Sierra backbone, it visits beautiful and famous Evolution Valley, and spends a night at a campground by a hot-spring pool which beats all the hot tubs in Marin County. As a bonus, the nearness of the two trailheads to each other makes the shuttle almost short enough to walk.

DESCRIPTION Moderate trip)

1st 5 Hiking Days: Follow trip 45 to **Lower Goddard Canyon**, 34½ miles.

6th Hiking Day: Follow part of the 4th Hiking Day, trip 32, to **Blaney Hot Springs** (''a natural hot-spring pool'' in that days' description), 7 miles.

7th Hiking Day: Reverse part of the 3rd Hiking Day, trip 18, to **Hutchinson Meadow**, 8 miles.

8th Hiking Day: Reverse trip 17 to **North Lake**, 11 miles.

Taboose Creek Roadend to Bench Lake   **47**

TRIP   From Taboose Creek Roadend to Bench Lake (round trip). Topo maps *Big Pine, Mt. Pinchot.* Best mid or late season; 25 miles.

Grade	Trail/layover days	Total recommended days
Leisurely	....	....
Moderate	....	....
Strenuous	4/0	4

HILITES   The expansive views, the delightful flower-bedecked basin just over the pass, and the direct access via this route to the sparkling gem of Bench Lake make the great effort worthwhile *if* you are in top shape.

DESCRIPTION (Strenuous trip)

*1st Hiking Day (***Taboose Creek Roadend** to **Upper Taboose Creek**, 6½ miles): From the trailhead we cross a low lateral moraine and ascend gently westward over a sandy, sage-covered desert plain, with the awesome rampart of the Sierra just ahead. As we enter the broad portal of Taboose Creek canyon, the path veers left and rises steeply, staying above the rushing creek. After a while we drop momentarily alongside the willow-and-birch-lined creek, before climbing steeply up-canyon on footing alternately gravel and rock. The trail zigzags up a steep slope, then contours over to the creek, which we cross by boulders and logs, taking care not to slip.

From the ford, the trail switchbacks up through a mini forest of white fir and a few Jeffrey pines, crosses a bench, and climbs steadily west, once again in the open, through thickets of chinquapin, willow and other greenery. Looming high on the left are the red and white spurs of Goodale Mountain. The trail crosses the creek and climbs steeply up the north side of the canyon to a picturesque bench valley, shaded around the edges by gnarled whitebark pines and hemmed in between rust-colored cliffs, where there are several excellent campsites on the left (south) side of the bench.

2nd Hiking Day (**Upper Taboose Creek** to **Bench Lake**, 6 miles): After the trail crosses the creek for the fifth time, it switchbacks steeply up through very rocky terrain to a last bench just east of Taboose Pass. Though well above timberline, lush grasses and colorful wildflowers make the scene delightful. We wind up between granite outcroppings, passing several limpid tarns, and finally reach Taboose Pass, marked by a large sign announcing one's entry into Kings Canyon National Park. The scene that abruptly unfolds is breathtaking. Directly ahead is the deep crease of the Kings River's South Fork. Slightly to the left is beautiful Bench Lake, with the symmetrical spire of Arrow Peak as a backdrop. To the right is the ragged citadel of Mt. Ruskin.

From the pass, the trail drops southwest down a gradual slope, passing through sky gardens of buttercup, shooting star and senecio, carpeted with velvet green. In these gardens we ford a rivulet, pass just north of a rockbound tarn, and reach a hard-to-spot junction. After turning left here, we climb and then contour along a rocky slope, staying above the U-shaped bowl of the South Fork, to a junction with the John Muir Trail. Just 100 yards south on the Muir Trail is the lateral trail to Bench Lake, and we turn west onto this high, easy trail. Hikers will appreciate the short side trip to this sublime mountain lake, less than an hour's walk off the Muir Trail. The pathway leads west across a flower-bedecked meadow, descends a short distance, and then contours southwest along a granite bench under a canopy of lodgepole pines. We ford a shallow stream, pass two limpid tarns, and in 1½ miles from the John Muir Trail reach the northeast shore of Bench Lake. In the clarity of its waters and in its splendid setting amid granite peaks and spurs, this sparkling jewel has few peers in the High Sierra. The whitish pyramid of Arrow Peak, reflected in the lake's mirrorlike waters, is one of the classic views in the Sierra. Many fine campsites are among the lodgepoles along the north shore. (Halazone tablets are recommended.)

3rd and 4th Hiking Days: Retrace your steps, 12½ miles.

Taboose Creek Roadend to Twin Lakes   **48**

TRIP   From Taboose Creek Roadend to Twin Lakes
(round trip). Topo maps *Big Pine, Mt. Pinchot.* Best
mid or late season 40 miles.

Grade	Trail/layover days	Total recommended days
Leisurely	....	....
Moderate	....	....
Strenuous	5/1	6

HILITES   In addition to the attractions of the previous trip,
this route offers the alpine beauties of Lake Marjorie which has one of the most colorful settings in
the High Sierra. Off-the-beaten-path camping at
Twin Lakes is ample reward for the long hike to
them.

DESCRIPTION (Strenuous trip)

1st and 2nd Hiking Days: Follow trip 47 to **Bench Lake,** 12½ miles.

3rd Hiking Day (**Bench Lake** to **Twin Lakes,** 9 miles): After retracing the path to the John Muir Trail, this day's route turns south
and climbs through rocky meadows and clumps of lodgepole
and whitebark pine, passing above a shimmering lakelet on the
left, then another one on the right. Gnarled whitebark pines,
harbingers of approaching timberline, begin to replace the lodgepoles as the forest thins to scattered groves. After skirting
another rock-bound lake, the granite-paved trail climbs to the
north shore of magnificent Lake Marjorie. The setting here is
as richly colorful as any in the Sierra: to the right, ramparts of

steel-gray granite rise abruptly from the lake. South, above the lake's head, are slopes of black and ruddy brown. Just visible on the southeastern skyline is the dark notch of Pinchot Pass. To the left, rising above all, are the broken, multihued cliffs of Mt. Pinchot.

Amid this grandeur we pass above the east shore of Lake Marjorie and climb above the last, stunted whitebarks into a world of snow and bare rock. We ascend steadily over granite benches and through boulder fields, passing two stark lakelets. After fording an icy rivulet, the path traverses upward and then switchbacks steeply up over rocky terrain to 12,110-foot Pinchot Pass, on the divide that separates the waters of the Kings' South Fork from its tributary, Woods Creek. The views in both directions are inspiring. Far to the north, over Mather Pass, loom the black sentinels of the Palisades. South, beyond the serrated face of Mt. Cedric Wright, ridge after ridge fades into the distance.

From Pinchot Pass the pathway descends a steep talus slope, crosses a slight rise and drops into a high, open basin lush with grass and wildflowers. Particularly abundant are clusters of red heather and shooting star. Here we veer east, passing several placid tarns and fording the twin headwaters of Woods Creek, then turn south again and parallel the vibrant stream through alpine meadow country. As the trail descends toward 11,000 feet, clumps of whitebark pine welcome us back to timberline. The dominating round bulk of Mt. Cedric Wright looms up close by in the south, and the knifelike peak on the southern skyline is Mt. Clarence King, monarch of the Sixty Lake Basin. The trail drops steadily southward, passing a marshy lakelet on the right. Occasionally visible down to the left are Twin Lakes, nestled close under the spines of Mt. Cedric Wright. A quarter mile below the lower lake we meet the Twin Lakes Trail and turn northeast into it for $1/3$ mile to the good campsites along the west shore of the lower lake.

4th and 5th Hiking Days: Retrace your steps, omitting Bench Lake, 18½ miles.

Sawmill Creek Roadend to Sawmill Lake   **49**

TRIP   From Sawmill Creek Roadend to Sawmill Lake (round trip). Topo map *Mt. Pinchot.* Best early season; 16 miles.

Grade	Trail/layover days	Total recommended days
Leisurely	....	....
Moderate	....	....
Strenuous	2/0	2

HILITES   This strenuous trip up from hot Owens Valley to a lovely, cool lake at 10,000 feet gives one the satisfaction of getting high on his own sweat, and the thrill of strolling back down with next to no effort.

DESCRIPTION (Strenuous trip)

1st Hiking Day (**Sawmill Creek Roadend to Sawmill Lake,** 8 miles): To avoid the precipitous gorge of lower Sawmill Creek, the route up from Sawmill Creek roadend climbs the steep, hot, dry, sage-covered slope north of the creek. In early summer, this desert slope is splashed with flowering shrubs and blossoms of bright blue woolly gilia and yellow and white buckwheat. From the trail you look down on the Big Pine volcanic field, spotted with reddish cinder cones and black lava flows that erupted from the west side of Owens Valley. After a lengthy switchback, the trail rounds the ridge of Sawmill Point high above the waters of Sawmill Creek, visible as a white ribbon far below. The pathway descends slightly, then contours, and finally climbs along the precipitous north wall of Sawmill Creek canyon. As we near the sloping ridge known, appropriately, as The Hogsback, Jeffrey pines and white firs make a most welcome appearance. If one looks carefully at the lower end of The Hogsback, one can spot the remains of the Blackrock sawmill and flume, dating from the 1860s, after which Sawmill Creek and Sawmill Pass are named. For some distance above The Hogsback, one can occasionally see stumps, felled trees and logs used as "gliders" in this century-old operation to supply Owens Valley miners with lumber.

The trail climbs to meet a tributary stream north of The Hogsback, the first water on this hot climb. The trail fords this creek three times before crossing The Hogsback. Once over the top of this long, rounded ridge, the path veers south, contouring and climbing on a moderate grade, back into the main canyon, and reaches Sawmill Meadow, boggy and lush green in early summer, but drying considerably as the summer months progress. Beyond, the trail follows the creek, then zigzags steeply upward through Jeffrey pine and red fir to Mule Lake, perched on a small bench high up the canyon. After fording the creek, we climb through a jumbled mass of metamorphic rocks that are home for a large colony of grass-harvesting conies. After recrossing the creek, we finally arrive at the northeast shore of beautiful Sawmill Lake. Good campsites under clumps of foxtail pine are located here, and fishing for rainbow trout is fair to good.

Second Hiking Day: Retrace your steps, 8 miles.

Jim Jenkins at Sawmill Pass   *John W. Robinson*

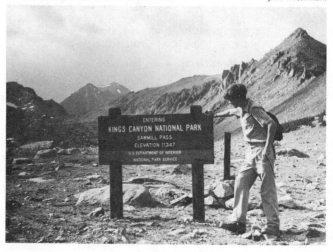

Sawmill Creek Roadend to Twin Lakes   **50**

TRIP   From Sawmill Creek Roadend to Twin Lakes (round trip). Topo map *Mt. Pinchot.* Best mid or late season; 28 miles.

Grade	Trail/layover days	Total recommended days
Leisurely	....	....
Moderate	....	....
Strenuous	4/0	4

HILITES   This trip proceeds by way of a horrendous ascent to Sawmill Pass and then takes you through the headwaters of Woods Creek, in a high basin clothed with whitebark pine, verdant meadows and multihued alpine flowers.

DESCRIPTION (Strenuous trip)

1st Hiking Day: Follow trip 49 to **Sawmill Lake**, 8 miles.

2nd Hiking Day (**Sawmill Lake** to **Twin Lakes**, 6 miles). Above Sawmill Lake the trail winds up through a thinning forest of foxtail and whitebark pine, passes a lakelet, crosses a small timberline basin, and climbs steeply upward to Sawmill Pass (11,347′), on the border of Kings Canyon National Park. From the pass you walk northwest across nearly level talus and sand, then drop into a resplendent lake-dotted alpine basin, the headwaters of Woods Creek. The trail winds westward, gradually descending as it passes just north of two small, nameless lakes. The largest body of water in the basin—Woods Lake—is a short cross-country jaunt south of the trail. Our route descends to the lower end of the basin, then turns abruptly north to climb and contour along the lower slopes of Mt. Cedric Wright. Finally, the trail drops to North Fork Woods Creek, goes north along its east bank a short distance, and then fords the creek to a junction with the John Muir Trail. A short half mile up this arterial route the Twin Lakes Trail turns off and leads northeast to the good campsites on the west shore of Lower Twin Lake.

3rd and 4th Hiking Days: Retrace your steps, 14 miles.

Sierra Crest near Independence

Sawmill Creek Roadend to Oak Creek   **51**

TRIP From Sawmill Creek Roadend to Oak Creek Roadend (shuttle trip): Topo map *Mt. Pinchot*. Best mid season; 33½ miles.

Grade	Trail/layover days	Total recommended days
Leisurely	....	....
Moderate	....	....
Strenuous	4/1	5

HILITES Another trip for those in top condition, this strenuous jaunt uses a small piece of the John Muir Trail to permit passage between two out of the way, lake-dotted alpine basins—the headwaters of Woods Creek and the Baxter Lakes basin.

DESCRIPTION (Strenuous trip)

1st Hiking Day: Follow trip 49 to **Sawmill Lake,** 8 miles.

2nd Hiking Day (**Sawmill Lake** to **Woods Creek Crossing,** 8½ miles): Follow the 2nd hiking day, trip 50, to the John Muir Trail and turn left (south) on it.

Your path veers southwest, ever dropping, following the U-shaped canyon cut by the glacier that flowed down Woods Creek. You pass another fine campsite on the left, and when you abruptly emerge from the forest, the great trough of Woods Creek opens in full grandeur ahead. For the next 3 miles, the trail descends through the gorge, sometimes alongside the joyous creek but more often well above it, through tangled thickets of dwarf aspen, willow and other greenery. Wildflowers add an abundant splash of color, and you may see paintbrush, lark-spur, purple aster, mountain violet, Bigelow sneezeweed, Labra-dor tea and yarrow. A ribbon of white water plunges from the dark cliffs high on the left. We cross several benches shaded by isolated clusters of lodgepoles, then ford the White Fork of Woods Creek (sometimes difficult in early season when the water runs high). Ahead is the great bend of Woods Creek, with the stupendous ramparts of King Spur as a backdrop. A descent over rocky terrain brings us back into the forest, now consisting of Jeffrey pine and gnarled junipers. The trail fords another side stream and drops alongside Woods Creek, its white froth spilling wildly over huge, inclined granite slabs. On the final descent to the canyon floor, manzanita provides a thick and thorny ground cover, with scattered Jeffrey pines for shade. At a major trail junction, the fork to the right is the Woods Creek Trail down to Paradise Valley; the Muir Trail goes left, and so do we. Where we re-reach Woods Creek, it is swollen to river proportions by the addition of its South Fork's waters, but a bridge is there. There are fair campsites, shaded by tall aspens and verdant white alders, on both sides of the creek. Fishing for brook and rainbow trout to 10 inches is fair to good.

3rd Hiking Day (**Woods Creek Crossing** to **Baxter Lakes**, 7 miles): After crossing the creek via a bridge, we turn southeast and begin the long climb up the South Fork. Juniper and red fir provide forest cover as we pass several adequate campsites on the left, along the creek. Also to the left, half-hidden by foliage, is one of Shorty Lovelace's pigmy log cabins. Shorty ran a trap line through this country during the years before Kings Canyon National Park was established. Remains of his other miniature cabins are located in Gardiner Basin and along Bubbs Creek.

Presently the trail rounds the base of King Spur and climbs well above the stream, through alternating stretches of lush greenery and patches of wildflowers, and sparse forest of aspen, red fir and lodgepole pine. We jump the rivulet that hurries down from Lake 10296 and enter an open, rocky area. Beyond, a wooden span provides an easy crossing of a boggy meadow. From the meadow, the trail climbs over a rocky ridge and fords the major creek descending from Sixty Lake Basin, passing through a gate in a drift fence. There are several small camp-sites here, under scattered pines. Across the canyon, Baxter Creek stitches a ribbon of white down the rock-ribbed slope. The trail climbs through rocky terrain, then approaches the main creek, passing a lodgepole-sheltered campsite on the left before again breaking into the open and ascending bouldery terrain. Ahead looms the peaked monolith of Fin Dome, heralding your approach to the beautiful Rae Lakes. To your right are the impressive steel-gray ramparts of King Spur. In contrast, the massive, sloping Sierra crest in the east is made up of dark metamorphic rocks. The long black striations that cross the face of Diamond Peak and the ridge north of it are metamorphosed lava, visual evidence of ancient volcanic activity.

Finally this long ascent climbs over a low, rounded spur and abruptly reaches the northernmost of the Rae Lakes chain, jewel-like Dollar Lake. The setting here is magnificent: lodgepoles crowd the shore amid granite outcroppings, and Fin Dome, along with some blackish spires beyond, provides a jagged backdrop for the mirroring blue waters of the lake. Good, though overused, campsites lie on the north and northwest shores. The unmarked Baxter Pass Trail takes off northeast from the north side of Dollar Lake. From this junction follow most of the 4th hiking day, trip 62.

4th Hiking Day: Follow the 5th hiking day, trip 62, 10 miles.

Fin Dome over Dollar Lake

52   Cedar Grove to Kennedy Lakes

TRIP   From Cedar Grove to Kennedy Lakes (round trip). Topo map *Marion Peak*. Best mid or late season; 20 miles.

Grade	Trail/layover days	Total recommended days
Leisurely	....	....
Moderate	4/1	5
Strenuous	3/0	3

HILITES   By going north instead of east out of Cedar Grove, this trip avoids the hordes of hikers bound for the John Muir Trail and instead brings the traveler to secluded little ponds in the meadows just over Kennedy Pass, which lie in a private cirque virtually on top of the Monarch Divide.

DESCRIPTION (Strenuous trip)

1st Hiking Day (**Cedar Grove** to **Frypan Meadow**, 6 miles): The trail starts at the Lewis Creek Trailhead, 1½ miles down-canyon (west) from the Cedar Grove Ranger Station, where there is a fair-sized parking lot on the river side of the road.

The trail starts climbing at once, rising quite steeply up the large eastern lateral moraine of Lewis Creek under a moderate forest cover of incense-cedar, ponderosa pine, black oak and canyon live oak, with manzanita and kit kit dizze growing underneath. About ¾ mile up the trail, a few open areas offer fine views across the Kings River Canyon to Sentinel Ridge, and the view up-canyon is humbling. About ¼ mile farther the grade levels off, and we meet the Hotel Creek Trail. Then our route crosses a lovely, unnamed stream which supports an exquisite flower garden all summer long. The trail now climbs steeply again, to stay high under an open forest of large trees. Occasional views of the peaks on the Monarch Divide in the north are seen from the open areas. Then the trail descends for a short distance to cross rainbow-trout-filled Comb Creek, near some poor campsites. When the stream is high, look for a footlog crossing either up or downstream.

Less ¾ mile past Comb Creek the trail crosses Lewis Creek just above a series of small waterfalls. (If needed there is a good footlog just upstream.) We then climb steeply up an open hillside, where we get excellent views of the Monarch Divide to the northeast, the Great Western Divide, the Sphinx Crest and Avalanche Peak to the southeast, and Sentinel Ridge to the south. After passing the Wildman Meadow Trail, we drop slightly and cross the lower end of Frypan Meadow, which is quite boggy until late summer. About 200 yards up the meadow is a large camp spot on a lovely stream, by the junction with the unmaintained trail to Grizzly Lakes. The flowers in the meadow bloom from early spring until fall, changing with the seasons but always making a large and beautiful garden.

2nd Hiking Day (**Frypan Meadow** to tarns, **upper Kennedy Creek canyon**, 4 miles): The sign at the top of the meadow reads *Kennedy Pass 4 mi.* but one should remember that it goes from 7800 to 10,800 feet in elevation, a strenuous climb for anyone not in top physical condition. From the Grizzly lakes trail junction at the top of the meadow, the trail undulates eastward past 4 small creeks and then fords Lewis Creek. Beyond this ford, just above a lovely waterfall, the trail climbs steeply under a dense cover of Jeffrey pine and white fir. As the route rounds the south ridge of Kennedy Mountain, the forest cover fades, and we can more easily enjoy the excellent views of the Monarch Divide, the Great Western Divide, and the Kaweah Peaks Ridge far to the south. An extensive grove of aspens is traversed as the trail heads into upper East Fork Lewis Creek canyon, and we can see Kennedy Pass far above. The grade levels momentarily where a flower-lined creek provides the last water on this side of the pass.

The route now climbs the last, steep, switchbacked grade to Kennedy Pass. As we climb, silver pine, Jeffrey pine and red fir disappear, and at the pass there are only a few weathered whitebark pines. From the pass (10,800′) views to the north are outstanding of the Black Divide and northern Kings Canyon National Park. In the foreground, just below Kennedy Pass, are several small tarns surrounded by brilliant green, grassy meadows. These meadows provide campsites of rare beauty, deserving the effort that is required to reach them. (The steep descent from the pass may be difficult in early season because of snow.) One of the most extensive views in the entire range is attained from the nearby summit of Kennedy Mountain, which is easily reached by following the ridge from Kennedy Pass. Keep to the left side of the ridge.

3rd and 4th Hiking Days: Retrace your steps, 10 miles.

Margaret Lake

Cedar Grove to Volcanic Lakes

53

TRIP From Cedar Grove to Kennedy Pass, cross-country to Volcanic Lakes, return via Granite Pass, Granite Lakes (shuttle trip). Topo map *Marion Peak.* Best mid or late season; 24 miles.

Grade	Trail/layover days	Total recommended days
Leisurely	....	....
Moderate	5/1	6
Strenuous	4/0	4

HILITES The little-traveled divide that separates the gigantic gashes of the south and middle forks of the Kings River, the Monarch Divide, is the setting for this loop trip through high, wild, dramatic country dotted with dozens of lakes, named and unnamed, on-trail and off-trail.

DESCRIPTION (Strenuous trip)

1st 2 Hiking Days: Follow trip 52 to **tarns, upper Kennedy Creek canyon,** 10 miles.

3rd Hiking Day (**tarns, upper Kennedy Creek canyon,** to **Granite Lake,** part cross-country, 5½ miles): The cross-country route to Granite Pass is short, but one can easily spend a whole day exploring the mostly treeless upper Volcanic Lakes basin. From the tarns near Kennedy Pass follow the switchbacking trail toward Kennedy Creek until you are just above a little lake on your right. Turn right and go straight up the hill past the left side of the lake to the northwest shore of East Kennedy Lake (poor campsites). Our route goes up the tree-dotted slope on the east to the little forested area at the top of the slope. Beginning at the outlet of East Kennedy Lake, we skirt the north shore for a few hundred feet and then head uphill. Staying on the left side of the slope, our route passes through the little forested area and arrives at the top of the ridge. A little to the left of the shallow saddle is an excellent viewpoint, Point 10979 on the topo map. From it we can see Mt. Gardiner and the Kings-Kern Divide above the Monarch Divide, Arrow Peak, the Palisades, the Black Divide, Mt. Goddard, and the Sierra crest beyond.

From about 50 feet south of this point the route descends down a grassy gully that leads toward the head of the largest of the Volcanic Lakes. Near the lake, the slabs can be avoided by walking several dozen yards to the right. From the head of the lake, follow the inlet stream toward the highest two Volcanic Lakes, where there are rainbow and golden trout (to 16"). Walk around the rocky north side of the first lake and cross the low saddle to the northeast. It's worthwhile strolling up to the highest lake: nestled under the Monarch Divide, this lake presents a scene of alpine splendor at its finest. Just below the saddle is a fishless lake. Descend to its south shore and walk around the east side to where two points of rock jut into the lake. From here a grassy gully angles up, right, to the top of the ridge on the east. From this ridgetop contour east to Granite Pass (10673'). Then from the pass, the rocky-sandy trail descends, steeply at times, to a small meadow filled with lavender shooting stars in early season, where there are several good campsites. Our trail then descends moderately through lodgepole forest to a junction with the spur trail to Granite Lake (10,100'). Here we turn right (west) and skirt the north side of a meadow to the fair campsites on that lake, where fishing is fair-to-good for brook trout (to 10").

4th Hiking Day (**Granite Lake** to **Cedar Grove Roadend**, 8½ miles): Reverse the steps of the 1st hiking day, trip 54.

Cedar Grove to Granite Lake   **54**

TRIP From Cedar Grove Roadend to Granite Lake (round trip). Topo map *Marion Peak*. Best early or late season; 17 miles.

Grade	Trail/layover days	Total recom-mended days
Leisurely	....	....
Moderate	3/1	4
Strenuous	2/0	2

HILITES "The first day is always the toughest" is an old adage to the backpacker. And this old saw added to the 5000-foot-plus elevation gain should warn the hiker that this "weekender" is one to be undertaken only after some conditioning. However, it should also be noted that the fine views and the good alpine campsite at the end of the trek compensate for the effort.

DESCRIPTION (Strenuous trip)

1st Hiking Day (**Cedar Grove Roadend** to **Granite Lake,** 8½ miles): The extreme elevation change encountered in the course of this trip (over 5000 feet), necessarily removes it from the "Leisurely" grade, but it makes a fine weekender for anyone in good physical condition. Starting at the north side of the parking loop (5035´), the Copper Creek Trail winds through a mature stand of ponderosa, incense-cedar, sugar pine and black oak. As the traveler begins this trip, he might contemplate the historic usage of this trailhead. Evidence from archeological excavations nearby indicate that Zumwalt Meadows was a permanent base camp for Indian hunting parties for a period of time ranging from (in white man's terms) Magna Carta to the Declaration of Independence. Mortar rocks, pestles and manos found in the yard-deep midden piles in this vicinity indicate that the acorn of the plentiful black oak was one of the main staples of the Indian's diet. It is also possible that these grinding implements were used to grind the pine nut (occasional piñon trees are found in the canyon). But also found in the excavation sites were bones of deer and various rodents, indicating that foraging parties took to the higher country—and arrowheads found in the country of the Monarch Divide indicate that these parties frequently used this same trail.

The flats of Zumwalt Meadows soon fall behind, and the trail ascends above the dense forest cover to a moderate forest cover of scrub oak. The trail begins steadily rising up switchbacks through dense thickets of oak and manzanita, as glacially smoothed Grand Sentinel and the Sphinx dominate views of the canyon's south wall. The first set of hot, tedious switchbacks terminates just east of North Dome, and the grade abates to a moderate-to-steady ascent through a mixed forest cover of sugar pine, ponderosa pine, incense-cedar and black oak. Looking back over one's right shoulder, to the southeast, one has a fine view of a beautifully formed avalanche chute on the northwest face of The Sphinx. The trail then fords several trickling tributaries of Copper Creek, as it climbs steadily to the several campsites sheltered in groves of white fir and aspen by the creek ford, in the area called Lower Tent Meadow.

From Lower Tent Meadow the trail climbs steadily to the poor campsites of Upper Tent Meadow, in the red-fir belt. From here one can look up the long, wide, treeless slope which is frequently swept by avalanches, leaving only lush, low-lying bushes. The trail swings close to the creek that runs down this avalanche-swept hillside before beginning a series of long switchbacks. Fill your water bottle here. Far up this shady ascent the dense red-fir forest changes to a more moderate forest of mostly silver pine. From the top of the ridge between Copper Creek and Granite Creek, views to the east are excellent, the two prominent peaks being Mts. Gardiner and Clarence King. For those who prefer an isolated campsite, Grouse Lake can be reached via cross-country by leaving the trail just before it descends into Granite Basin. Contour down and right until you reach Copper Creek, then follow it up either bank to the good campsites on the south side of secluded Grouse Lake (fishless).

From the viewful ridgetop, the trail makes an undulating descent into aptly named Granite Basin. Then we make a gentle, rolling ascent through Granite Basin before skirting an alpine meadow, beyond which we reach the Granite Lakes lateral trail. Our route turns left onto it and ascends an easy slope to the north side of scenic Granite Lake (10,100′). The fair campsites here are mostly on the north side of the lake. A more secluded campsite is in the grove on the peninsula jutting out from the west shore. Views of the Comb Spur are excellent, and the camper may soon establish a vocal relationship with the many noisy marmots that share this private cirque. Fishing for brook trout is fair-to-good (to 10″).

2nd Hiking Day: Retrace your steps, 8½ miles.

The Sphinx from the Copper Creek Trail

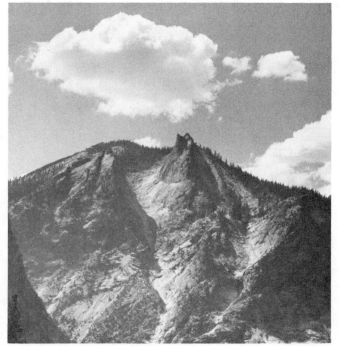

55

Cedar Grove to State Lakes

TRIP   From Cedar Grove Roadend to State Lakes via
              Granite Basin, Granite Pass (round trip). Topo map
              Marion Peak. Best early or late season; 31 miles.

Grade	Trail/layover days	Total recommended days
Leisurely	....	....
Moderate	5/2	7
Strenuous	4/2	6

HILITES   Once past the initial, tough 5000-foot climb, this
              exciting route has all the aspects of a glorious fish-
              ing trip. Beneath the peaks of the Monarch Divide,
              this trail visits the excellent fishing lakes of the
              State Lakes chain, and offers fine side trips for
              those who would linger.

DESCRIPTION (Strenuous trip)

1st Hiking Day: Follow trip 54 to **Granite Lake**, 8½ miles).

2nd Hiking Day (**Granite Lake** to **State Lakes**, 7 miles): We begin
this hiking day by retracing our steps to the Granite Pass Trail,
where our route turns left toward Granite Pass. The ascent
starts moderately, but soon steepens over rocky underfooting.
After passing a tiny meadow with several campsites, the trail
climbs again, and arrives at Granite Pass (10,673′). This summit
marks the divide between the immense canyons of the Middle
and South Forks of the Kings River. Views from the pass are
extensive and excellent. From the pass, the trail descends
moderately through a granite-walled ravine. Probably following
a fault line, the ravine is deep-cut, and exhibits fine examples
of mirrorlike glacial polish. Through a sparse cover of lodgepole

and whitebark, the trail has been rerouted around a marshy area, and then we pass a drift fence. The trail descends into another level area, and there is an excellent campsite across the creek from a second drift fence. The trail now descends steeply via short switchbacks into the canyon of Middle Fork Daugherty Creek, where the going is more level through a denser lodgepole-pine cover. After crossing the creek three times, our route passes the Volcanic Lakes Trail. At a ford of the small, golden-trout-filled outlet from the western two Glacier Lakes, a short spur trail leads up the east side of the creek to an improved campsite in dense lodgepole forest. From this ford, our trail climbs over a small ridge, at the top of which we pass a drift fence, and then descends gently into the East Fork Daugherty Creek canyon. Our route passes the trail to Simpson Meadow and soon climbs over a large shoulder to a ford of East Fork Daugherty Creek. Although not abundant, the wildflowers along the trail are of many species, and one is sure to encounter wallflower, shooting star, penstemon, currant and cinquefoil. Near the ford there are excellent views up Glacier Valley to the Glacier Lakes cirque, and the sheer face of Goat Crest. After the ford, the trail ascends moderately to the excellent campsites on the north and northwest sides of the westernmost lake (10,300') of the State Lakes group. Here, fishing for golden (to 16") is excellent; and excursionary side-trip possibilities are magnificent. Although the next State Lake to the northeast is fishless, anglers will want to try the waters of Glacier Lakes and Horseshoe Lakes. Climbers looking for challenge will find the Cirque Crest peaks more than adequate.

3rd and 4th Hiking Days: Retrace your steps, 15½ miles.

56   Cedar Grove to South Lake

	Grade	Trail/layover days	Total recommended days
TRIP	Leisurely	....	....
	Moderate	7/3	10
	Strenuous	6/3	9

TRIP   From Cedar Grove Roadend to South Lake via Granite Basin, Granite Pass, State Lakes, Simpson Meadow, Middle Fork Kings River, Dusy Basin, Bishop Pass (shuttle trip). Topo maps *Marion Peak, Mt. Goddard.* Best mid or late season; 48 miles.

HILITES   This trans-Sierra route is relatively little used from Cedar Grove Roadend to the junction with the Muir Trail, and the hiker can count on a measure of solitude. Fine angling and magnificent panoramas are expectations to be realized, and the sweeping variety of flora and fauna encountered on this trail knows no equal in Sierra trips.

DESCRIPTION (Strenuous trip)

1st and 2nd Hiking Days: Follow trip 55 to **State Lakes**, 15½ miles.

3rd Hiking Day (**State Lakes** to **Simpson Meadow**, 8 miles): Our ducked trail starts northward on the north side of the meadow at the northwest end of the lake. Wildflower fanciers will find the area around the State Lakes visited by the trail a plethora of color. Rank fields of false solomon's seal cover the open flats, and lush-foliaged shooting stars wave above dense mats of moss and low-lying fern in the damp grottos along the streams. In the drier stretches along the trail that continues northward to the next of the State Lakes group, one will find the supine pussy paws, prim Douglas phlox, taller lupine, and tall, stately bluebells. The grassy fringes of this next lake offer good campsites on the west side where the trail fords the outlet stream. (A warning note: this stream marks the last reliable water until Middle Fork Kings River.) Beyond State Lakes the trail turns west, going moderately down and then up, past a lateral to enchanting Horseshoe Lakes and then past the sandy junction with the Dougherty Meadow Trail. Beyond the divide ridge, our route descends moderately and then steeply. Across the canyon of Middle Fork Kings River, the heights of Tunemah Peak and the White Divide come into view, and from several vantage points one can see up rocky Goddard Creek and Enchanted Gorge to the Black Divide.

The rapidly descending route continues down via steep, eroded switchbacks through three life zones. Lodgepole, the predominant tree of the higher elevations, shows growing inclusions of juniper, silver pine, sugar pine and incense-cedar. The mixed forest cover drops behind as the trail zigzags its final drop to the canyon floor. There the trail passes a drift fence and, winding through lush vegetation, meets the Middle Fork Trail. At this junction, our route turns right into Simpson Meadow. Used first by the Yokuts Indians, and then by sheepmen and cattlemen, this meadow is presently nearly forgotten. Its remoteness and difficulty of access have made it one of the least-visited meadows in this part of the Sierra, and today it is usually visited only by the wilderness traveler who seeks solitude and is not alarmed by the sight of an occasional rattlesnake.

Our route passes a sometimes-manned ranger station about 200 yards above the junction on a gently ascending, very rough trail, and arrives at the fair packer and primitive campsites on nearby Horseshoe Creek (5910′). Alternative primitive sites can be found along the river upstream. Travelers with two layover days and an inclination to a lengthy side trip may wish to visit Tehipite Valley 12 miles downstream, there to see the magnificently polished granite facade of Tehipite Dome, and the adjacent impressive falls. Rattlesnakes are commonly encountered enroute and at Tehipite Valley. Fishing on Middle Fork Kings River is good-to-excellent for rainbow (to 14″).

4th Hiking Day (**Simpson Meadow** to **Grouse Meadows**, 10 miles): Ascending gently, the poorly maintained trail continues northeast through alternating meadow and moderate forest of white fir, incense-cedar, Jeffrey pine and quaking aspen. Sagebrush frequently overhangs the trail, making footing sometimes difficult, and in the wetter sections the eroded trail is obliterated. As the trail rounds the talus-ridden slopes of Windy Peak, it offers good views of Goddard Creek canyon, and the evidence of a fire that swept unchecked up Middle Fork Kings River and Goddard Creek canyons is painfully evident in their brush-choked, black-stumped slopes, Still ascending gently, the sandy trail swings somewhat more eastward as it fords multibranched Windy Canyon Creek. To the northeast, the east canyon wall shows the break carved there by the feeder glacier emanating from the upper reaches of Cartridge Creek.

Just beyond the ford of Windy Canyon Creek, the trail turns north, and the canyon walls narrow dramatically. The trail then crosses Cartridge Creek by a substantial bridge, and passes the Cartridge Creek Trail, branching right from the packer's campsite. Ascending more steeply now, the trail crosses rocky stretches broken by pockets of timber cover, and the visible waters of the Middle Fork are white with rapids and cascades. The trail keeps to the canyon walls, usually 50 to 100 feet above the stream, and the drop to the river's waters is frequently a sheer face of polished granite. Flowers seen along this stretch are generally of the dry-country variety, including paintbrush, penstemon, Collinsia, forget-me-not, lupine and fleabane. The trail climbs steeply to the flats just below Devils Washbowl. To the right, the east canyon walls provide a fascinating study in convoluted glacial polish, and the views to the west and northwest of the Great Cliffs and the heavily fractured rock of Devils Crags portend later, equally exciting views of the Black Divide. The trial touches the river briefly near some sandy campsites, and then switchbacks up to awesome Devils Washbowl, a wild, spectacular falls and cataract in a granite gorge setting. Leaving the tumult of the water behind, the trail continues to ascend over rock to the innocuous-looking but treacherous ford of the unnamed creek draining Windy Cliff to the southeast. The flora around these tributary fords deserves the traveler's attention because of both its lushness and the presence of the very rare copper birch. Among the wildflowers one is sure to find at stream crossings are paintbrush, penstemon, pennyroyal, white Mariposa, cinquefoil, tiger lily, lupine, columbine and elderberry.

Ascending and descending steeply, the vacillating trail is sometimes at river's edge, and other times 200 feet above. The underfooting is very rocky and treacherous until we near the Palisade Creek crossing. This crossing is preceded by a re-acquaintance with a timber cover of Jeffrey, lodgepole and silver pine and white fir. Just after the steel bridge crossing of Palisade Creek, our route meets and turns left onto the John Muir Trail and passes several excellent campsites. Continuing north, the trail crosses an easy ridge, fords the unnamed tributary draining the west slopes of Giraud Peak, and arrives at the excellent campsites at the east side of Grouse Meadows. The intimate views are excellent of the lush meadows, and the quiet waters of the meandering river. Fishing for rainbow, some golden and brook (to 13") is good.

5th Hiking Day (**Grouse Meadows** to **Dusy Basin**, 7½ miles): Leaving the pleasant grasslands of Grouse Meadows behind, the trail continues its gentle but steady ascent. On the left, the river foregoes the placid temperament of its winding meadow course and resumes its mad, white-water plunge. Beyond the river to the west, The Citadel's granite face stands guard over the south side of an obvious hanging valley, and the early-morning traveler is often treated to a burst of reflected sunlight from glacially polished surfaces high on the canyon's west wall north of that valley. The trail undulates up and down the east wall, sometimes 80 to 100 feet above the river, sometimes right alongside it. The thin lodgepole forest cover occurs mostly in stands, with

Grouse Meadows on the Middle Kings River   *Esther Higgins*

intermittent stretches of grassy pockets, and the underfooting is mostly rocky. Ahead, the canyon narrows, and the trail crosses Dusy Branch via a substantial steel footbridge to meet the Bishop Pass Trail. A few yards north of this junction is the LeConte Ranger Station (emergency services usually available).

Our route turns right (east) and begins the steep, switchbacking ascent of the east canyon wall. This ascent is broken into two distinct steps that gain 2000 feet in about 2 miles, but the steepness of the slope is tamed by the well-graded switchbacks. Touching the creek at strategic intervals (a cold drink on this climb is always welcome), the trail offers magnificent views of the monolithic granite structures on the far side of the canyon. Near the creek, the wildflower lover will find lush shooting star, fireweed, penstemon, pennyroyal and some yellow columbine nestling next to damp, moss-covered rocky grottos. Along the switchbacks, occasional lodgepole and juniper break the monotony of the slab granite, and one particular juniper stands out with a near record girth. Like a bettle-browed sentinel this ancient specimen guards one of the switchbacks near the top of the first climb. Views of the chutes and cascades of Dusy Branch reward the dusty trail-pounder as he finishes the first climb and enters a cooling bower of a mixed stand of lodgepole and aspen. The trail crosses the creek on a bridge and then returns over another as it continues the switchbacking up through a sparse cover of aspen. This ascent levels out near the lowest of the Dusy Basin lake chain, and emerges to open, breathtaking views of Mt. Winchell, Mt. Agassiz, Thunderbolt Peak, and Columbine Peak. Rounding the north side of the lower Dusy Basin lake chain, the trail turns north and climbs a series of grass-topped ledges. A short, well-worn spur trail branches right, leading to campsites situated both alongside Dusy Branch and on the middle lakes of the Dusy Basin chain (10,734′).

Our route veers away from the creek, climbing above it, and where it rejoins the creek while on an eastward jog, our route turns right a short cross-country distance and descends through an alpine fell field to the fair campsites near the west side of the northernmost large lake in the basin. Fishing for golden and golden hybrids is good (to 8″). This campsite offers the camper a fine base for further explorations of Dusy and Palisades basins, and a granite outcropping just east of the lake provides the finest panoramic viewpoint in the entire basin. Those with a bent for angling will find the fishing on the outlet of the large lake to the east rewarding (golden and golden hybrids to 23″).

6th Hiking Day (**Dusy Basin** to **South Lake**, 7 miles): Reverse the 1st hiking day, trip 40.

Cedar Grove to Vidette Meadow   **57**

TRIP   From Cedar Grove Roadend to Vidette Meadow
(round trip). Topo maps *Marion Peak, Mt. Pinchot.*
Best early-to-mid season; 26 miles.

Grade	Trail/layover days	Total recom-mended days
Leisurely	4/1	5
Moderate	3/0	3
Strenuous	2/0	2

HILITES   Climbing 4000 feet, this trip follows an old Indian
trade route paralleling Bubbs Creek. Beyond the
realm of the Park's dayhiker, the trail climbs the
path of an old glacier to beautiful Vidette Meadow,
a "high country crossroads." Here in the shadow of
the spectacular Kearsarge Pinnacles this route
meets the famous John Muir Trail.

DESCRIPTION (Moderate trip)

1st Hiking Day (**Cedar Grove Roadend** to **Charlotte Creek**, 7½ miles):
From the paved roadend loop (5035′) the wide, sandy trail heads
east through a mixed forest of ponderosa pine, incense-cedar,
black oak, sugar pine and white fir. But soon the shade is left
behind, and there is only a sparse cover of ponderosas. The
balmy climate usually characteristic of the gently sloping canyon floor made this area a favorite of the Indians, who had
their summer hunting camps here. Foraging parties of Indians
made their "spur" camps along Bubbs Creek at many of the
same spots chosen by today's backcountry travelers.

Soon our trail enters a cool, dense forest of alder, white fir
and ponderosa and sugar pine, and we pass the Paradise Valley/
Woods Creek Trail branching north just before crossing a large
steel bridge over the South Fork. We then pass a trail heading
down-canyon and turn east to cross four branches of Bubbs

Creek on expertly constructed log-and-plank bridges. The last bridge crossing marks the beginning of a series of steady switchbacks. This climb is hot and dry, so try to get an early start. Along this climb we find some rare (for this side of the Sierra) piñon pines. This tree, whose fruit provides the delicious pine nut, is of the single-needle group, and may be identified by either its single needle or its distinctive spherical cone. Most noticeable about the cone is its very thick, blunt, four-sided scale. This ascent offers fine views back into the dramatic U-shaped South Fork Kings River canyon. On the south side of the Bubbs Creek canyon the dominating landmark is the pronounced granite point known as The Sphinx. To the east its namesake stream cuts a sharp-lipped defile on the peak's east shoulder.

Above the switchbacks, as we angle toward tumbling Bubbs Creek, we re-enter the cool shade of tall conifers and climb past a drift fence, but the shade does not last long because at the junction with the Sphinx Creek Trail begins the section of Bubbs Creek canyon that was ravaged by fire in 1976. The burnt area extends all the way to Charlotte Creek, and the fire killed most of the trees, so the several miles to Charlotte Creek are hot and dusty. The extent of this destruction is realized when we note how far the fire burned up the slopes on both sides of the canyon. Before the fire this section of Bubbs Creek was one of the loveliest areas in the Sierra, and its loss is indeed tragic. The hiker is not the only one who feels the effects of more sun: with so little shade, the ground-cover species have become prolific, and there are large patches of fern, wild pea and stinging nettle. Eventually we reach Charlotte Creek, and living, healthy forest. There are several good campsites several hundred feet beyond the ford under tall white firs.

2nd Hiking Day (**Charlotte Creek** to **Vidette Meadow**, 5½ miles); From Charlotte Creek the grade becomes steep, rocky and dusty. The steep southern rampart of Mt. Bago is up to the left as we arrive at the campsites at the west end of Junction Meadow, where there is one of the several bear cables erected in places of heavy use in this national park. At the east end of the meadow our route passes the East Lake Trail. (This meadow is closed to grazing.) The trail then begins a steady, rocky climb and soon emerges onto a sparsely forested hillside. Bubbs Creek, on the right, flows down through a steep, narrow gorge, and it is worthwhile to walk over a few yards at one of the right-hand switchbacks to look at the spectacular cascades and waterfalls.

Southern rampart of Mt. Bago

The steepest part of the climb ends at the top of these switchbacks, and then the trail proceeds on a moderate ascent past a drift fence under an old, weathered foxtail pine. Looking back, one has fine views of the avalanche-scarred north face of West Spur. The ascent is gentle now, and we soon arrive at a junction with the John Muir Trail. Here our route turns right, fords the outlet creek from Bullfrog Lake, and arrives at the good campsites (9600′) above beautiful Vidette Meadow, scattered along Bubbs Creek. Fishing for brook and rainbow trout (to 8″) is fair. Because of the area's heavy use, a toilet pit is located several dozen yards down-canyon from the trail junction, just uphill from the Bubbs Creek Trail.

3rd Hiking Day: Retrace your steps, 13 miles.

58

Cedar Grove to Charlotte Lake

TRIP From Cedar Grove Roadend to Charlotte Lake (round trip). Topo maps *Marion Peak, Mt. Pinchot.* Best mid or late season; 33 miles.

Grade	Trail/layover days	Total recommended days
Leisurely	5/1	6
Moderate	4/1	5
Strenuous	2/1	3

HILITES Striking right into the heart of the high country, this route ascends a lengthy stretch of the Bubbs Creek drainage to the charming meadows at the foot of the Kearsarge Pinnacles and Videttes. The terminus of this trip, Charlotte Lake, is an exciting base camp location for trips to four major lake basins.

DESCRIPTION (Leisurely trip)

1st and 3nd Hiking Days: Follow trip 57 to **Vidette Meadow**, 13 miles.

3rd Hiking Day (**Vidette Meadow** to **Charlotte Lake**, 3½ miles): First, retrace your steps to the junction of the John Muir Trail and the Bubbs Creek Trail. Following the Muir Trail as it switchbacks up the steep north side of the canyon, the traveler is treated to breathtaking views of the Kearsarge Pinnacles to the east, and the Videttes and snow-necklaced Deerhorn Mountain to the south. It is easy, while viewing this spectacle, to understand the popularity of the Muir Trail, and it is with a sense of loss that one leaves the Bubbs Creek valley and crosses the lip of the Bullfrog Lake basin. Our route crosses a small creek twice, bypasses the first of several laterals to Bullfrog Lake and continues northwest on a series of switchbacks to a junction with the Charlotte Lake Trail. This trail leaves the Muir Trail at an **X** junction in a sandy saddle and, after providing one last look back to the Bubbs Creek drainage and far south into Center Basin, with the Kings-Kern Divide in the background, zigzags down to Charlotte Lake. High on the left of the switchbacks tower the several summits of red-rocked Mt. Bago. Good campsites may be found along the north side of the lake (10370′). Emergency services are usually available from a resident summer ranger. Fishing for rainbow and brook trout (to 10″) is good.

4th Hiking Day (**Charlotte Lake** to **Junction Meadow,** 5 miles): Retrace the steps of the 3rd and part of the 2nd hiking day.

5th Hiking Day (**Junction Meadow** to **Cedar Grove Roadend,** 11½ miles): Retrace the steps of part of the 2nd and all of the 1st hiking day.

Tarn on Bullfrog Lake's outlet stream

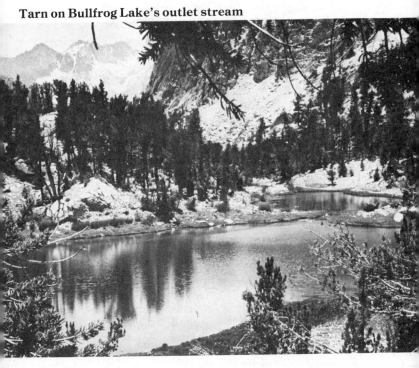

59   **Cedar Grove to Gardiner Basin**

TRIP

From Cedar Grove Roadend to Gardiner Basin (round trip). Topo maps *Marion Peak, Mt. Pinchot.* Best mid or late season; 50 miles.

Grade	Trail/layover days	Total recommended days
Leisurely	7/2	9
Moderate	6/1	7
Strenuous	5/0	5

HILITES

The hiker who values serenity and seclusion amid true alpine surroundings, and is tired of encountering the swarms of hikers and campers who crowd the Muir Trail and other popular routes in the Sierra, will appreciate Gardiner Basin. This hidden sanctuary, forested in its lower reaches and spotted with sparkling lakes, ringed on three sides by granite ridges and sharp peaks, will satisfy a longing for a genuine wilderness experience.

DESCRIPTION (Leisurely trip)

1st 3 Hiking Days: Follow trip 58 to **Charlotte Lake**, 16½ miles.

4th Hiking Day (**Charlotte Lake** to **Gardiner Basin**, 8½ miles): From the west end of Charlotte Lake, the trail fords Charlotte Creek, skirts the south edge of a grassy clearing, and crosses again to the north side of the creek. Beyond here, the trail is infrequently maintained. We cross a maze of avalanche-downed trees and descend westward, above the stream, through scattered aspens, lodgepole pines and junipers interspersed with large areas of manzanita which often obstruct the hot, dry trail. The trail drops gradually along the south slope of Gardiner Ridge, leaving the rapidly descending creek far below. Ahead is the Yosemitelike monolith of Charlotte Dome, unnamed on the map but strikingly prominent. Finally we begin climbing through open forest, cross a low rocky spur, and reach bubbling North Fork Charlotte Creek. The trail recrosses the creek twice, traverses a small meadow, and commences the long climb to Gardiner Pass. On this lengthy ascent, the trail makes numerous switchbacks through a fine forest of lodgepole pine, until tall foxtail pines become predominant near 11,000 feet. From the 11,200-foot pass—one of the few forested passes higher than 11,000 feet in the Sierra—one has breathtaking panoramas. To the south, the high, rugged summits of the Kings-Kern Divide lace the sky. Northward, one can look over the deep trench of Gardiner Basin to peaks as far north as Mt. Goddard.

From Gardiner Pass the trail zigzags down steep talus into the glaciated head of Gardiner Creek's South Fork, fords the icy creek, and reaches an unnamed lake. For the next 2 miles, we descend from granite bench to granite bench, arranged like progressive stepping-stones, several of them containing tarns or marshy lakes. The forest cover becomes exclusively lodgepole, interspaced with verdant clearings laced with colorful wildflowers. The trail passes 50 feet above the east edge of the large lower lake, then drops to large, well-used campsites along the northeast shore. From here, you cross a low rise, then abruptly drop in unbelievably steep zigzags to the floor of Gardiner Creek's main basin. To your left, hidden in forest and brush on a small flat 200 yards south of the creek, is the remains of one of Shorty Lovelace's pigmy cabins, built in the years when Shorty ran a trap line before the establishment of King Canyon National Park. Beyond this point, the topo map shows a footpath ascending east into upper Gardiner Basin. It is nothing but a ducked route, with occasional semblances of trail.

5th Hiking Day: Reverse the 4th hiking day, 8½ miles.

6th and 7th Hiking Days: Reverse the 5th and 4th hiking days, trip 58, 16½ miles.

60 Cedar Grove to Rae Lakes

TRIP From Cedar Grove Roadend to Rae Lakes via Vidette Meadow, Glen Pass (round trip). Topo maps *Marion Peak, Mt. Pinchot.* Best late season; 42 miles.

Grade	Trail/layover days	Total recommended days
Leisurely	6/2	8
Moderate	5/1	6
Strenuous	4/1	5

HILITES Rae Lakes have long been a favorite of the highcountry hiker and photographer—and with good cause. Situated beyond Glen Pass, and between the Sierra crest and the King Spur, these lakes are a scenic paradise. Because of this, and because of the central location, anyone contemplating this trip should plan on spending some days exploring the Sixty Lake Basin.

DESCRIPTION (Moderate trip)

1st 2 Hiking Days: Follow trip 57 to **Vidette Meadow**, 13 miles.

3rd Hiking Day (**Vidette Meadow** to **Rae Lakes**, 8 miles): From Vidette Meadow our route follows the John Muir Trail north as it climbs out of Bubbs Creek canyon. This climb parallels and sometimes crosses a tributary stream in a series of switchbacks. Excellent views of the Kearsarge Pinnacles to the east complement the view of the Videttes to the south. Beyond the Videttes tower the peaks of the Kings-Kern Divide, foregrounded by the barren granite of Center Basin. The peaks of the main Sierra crest appear to the northeast, and although mostly white granite, some of the higher peaks reveal more ancient sedimentary and metamorphic rocks.

Our route, on the John Muir Trail, passes a trail lateral to Bullfrog Lake and, at the top of the climb, a lateral to Charlotte Lake and a trail to Kearsarge Pass (most of which is not on the topo map). Because of the heavy traffic and camping impact from the Muir Trail and the Kearsarge Pass lateral, Bullfrog Lake is closed to camping. From the Charlotte Lake Trail, our route turns north on a long, steady ascent that rounds a granite promontory; then it descends slightly, veers east, and passes another trail to Charlotte Lake. As the headwall of Glen Pass comes into view, it is hard to see where a passable trail could go up it. And indeed the last 500 feet up to the top are steeply switchbacking—but never on the edge of a cliff. This trail section offers good views of Charlotte Lake, the Charlotte Creek canyon, Charlotte Dome and Mt. Brewer. At the pass (11,978′), one can look north down on the unnamed glacier lakes immediately to the north, and several of the Rae Lakes below. Beyond them in the north are Mt. Cotter, Mt. Clarence King, Mt. Pinchot, Dragon Peak, Black Mountain, and, far north, the 14,000-foot Palisades.

The descent from the pass is by zigzagging, rocky switchbacks down to the granite bench holding the unnamed lakes seen from the pass. (The bad underfooting here requires care in placing one's feet.) After crossing the outlet stream of these lakes, the trail resumes its switchbacking descent, re-enters a pine forest cover and skirts the west shore of upper Rae Lake. Just before the trail crosses the narrow isthmus separating the upper lake from the rest of the chain, we pass a spur trail branching west to Sixty Lake Basin. After crossing the sparsely timbered isthmus, the route swings north, passes the short lateral to Dragon Lake, and arrives at the many good campsites near the east shores of middle and lower Rae Lakes (10,560′) Fishing is good for brook trout and some rainbow (to 16″). Views from the campsites across the beryl-green lake waters to dramatically exfoliating Fin Dome and the King Spur beyond are among the best and longest remembered of the trip, along with sun-up views of Painted Lady in the south. A summer ranger is stationed on the east shore of the middle lake.

4th and 5th Hiking Days: Retrace your steps, 21 miles.

61   Cedar Grove to Rae Lakes

TRIP   From Cedar Grove Roadend to Rae Lakes, return via South Fork Woods Creek, Paradise Valley (loop trip). Topo maps *Marion Peak, Mt. Pinchot.* Best late season; 41½ miles.

Grade	Trail/layover days	Total recommended days
Leisurely	7/2	9
Moderate	6/1	7
Strenuous	4/1	5

HILITES   Known as the "Rae Lakes Loop," this fine trip circles the King Spur. The landscape viewed en route is dramatic enough to challenge the most accomplished photographer or artist as the route circles beneath the Videttes and the Kearsarge Pinnacles and traverses a lengthy stretch of the Sierra crest.

DESCRIPTION (Moderate trip)

1st 3 Hiking Days: Follow trip 60 to **Rae Lakes,** 21 miles.

4th Hiking Day (**Rae Lakes** to **Woods Creek Crossing,** 6½ miles): The trail covered in this hiking day is an easy downhill stretch that traces the length of South Fork Woods Creek. Beginning from the campsites on the east side of Rae Lakes, the trail continues along the east side of the lake chain and the intervening stream on a moderate descent. Fin Dome drops behind, and the outstanding landmark is then Diamond Peak to the east. The long black striations seen along the face of Diamond Peak and the continuing ridge to the north are metamorphosed lava, one of the few remaining bits of volcanic evidence to be found in this area. Just west of Diamond Peak the trail fords South Fork Woods Creek and skirts the west side of the lowest lake of the Rae Lakes chain. At the outlet our route passes the turnoff to Baxter Pass, and then descends more sharply over rocky stretches that are interrupted by pockets of alluvial sand. The valley floor is relatively open as the trail descends and crosses the stream draining Sixty Lake Basin (difficult ford in early season) and the stream draining Lake 10296.

Rounding the northernmost prominence of the King Spur, the trail veers west, and its moderate descent levels off as it approaches the Woods Creek Crossing. A few yards above this crossing the traveler should keep an eye peeled for one of this region's most interesting historic landmarks, one of Shorty Lovelace's unusual line cabins, which still stands on the west side of the creek. Those who take time out to examine this structure will soon discern its unique character. Appearing to be almost a miniature replica of the real article, it was erected to suit the needs of its builder, and it would scarcely accommodate the average person—standing or sleeping. It was from this cabin and several others in this general area that Shorty worked his trap line before it was included within the Park's boundaries. The trail crosses just below the confluence of the South and North forks of Woods Creek via a bridge (8492'). Fair campsites may be found near the crossing. Fishing in the creek is good for brook and rainbow (to 10").

5th Hiking Day (**Woods Creek Crossing** to **Paradise Valley**, 7 miles): Leaving the John Muir Trail our route turns west, staying on the north side of Woods Creek. The underfooting is alternately sandy and rocky as the trail descends gently between the narrowing canyon walls. The forest cover, still predominantly lodgepole, shows inclusions of red fir as the altitude lessens, and clumps of the water-loving quaking aspen dot the stream banks. This smooth-barked, whispering tree is the most conspicuous member of the deciduous group found in the high country. Always found near running water or at the edge of porous seepage areas (lava, talus, gravel), it acts as a native water locator, and its ghostly white trunk can be seen for great distances. Hikers who have camped in a grove of aspen will always remember the tree's gentle rustling sound as the leaves, responding to the slightest breeze, tremble against one another.

Soon the trail passes a burn scar and winds through Castle Domes Meadow, named for the obvious landmarks to the north.

Undulating up and down the north canyon wall, the trail descends on a moderate grade, fords two unnamed right-bank tributaries, and then descends more steeply to a ford of South Fork Kings River. In late season the ford of the South Fork, which is in two channels here, is not difficult. The first channel is forded by proceeding down from where the trail meets the river for about 75 yards to a log jam, and then the next channel can be boulder-hopped. In early and mid season this is not possible. About 100 yards east of where the trail meets the river there is a trail leading up the east bank of the South Fork to an area above the divergence of the two channels. Above this there are two footlogs. One, which is fairly old, rests on the west side of the river on top of a huge granite block. Cross one of these logs and follow the west bank down to the point where the trail fords the South Fork by its confluence with Woods Creek. After the ford, the trail turns southwest and descends gently past a drift fence to the open expanses of Paradise Valley (6640'). Good campsites are near the stream, and fishing for rainbow and some brown is fair (to 8").

6th Hiking Day (**Paradise Valley** to **Cedar Grove Roadend**, 7 miles): On a gentle descent through a mixed forest cover of lodgepole, red fir, white fir, Jeffrey pine and some juniper and aspen, the trail continues southwest. At the lower end of Paradise Valley, the descent steepens, and the smooth, serpentining South Fork Kings River straightens out and dashes down the canyon. Views during this descent include the already familiar landmark, The Sphinx. Midway down this stretch the trail pauses in its descent near Mist Falls, a cascade that deserves its name only during times of high water, because by midsummer this white-water tumble becomes sedate and subdued. Beyond Mist Falls the grade eases before leveling out in the area above the confluence of South Fork Kings River and Bubbs Creek. A short distance farther on, our route meets and joins the Bubbs Creek Trail, and returns over the short 2-mile stretch described in the 1st hiking day.

Cedar Grove to Oak Creek Roadend **62**

TRIP

From Cedar Grove Roadend to Oak Creek Roadend via Bubbs Creek, Glen Pass, Rae Lakes, Baxter Pass (shuttle trip). Topo maps *Marion Peak, Mt. Pinchot.* Best late season; 36½ miles.

Grade	Trail/layover days	Total recommended days
Leisurely	7/2	9
Moderate	5/2	7
Strenuous	4/1	5

HILITES

This trans-Sierra crossing makes a delightful **S**-curve as it journeys north from Bubbs Creek canyon over Glen Pass to Rae Lakes and then emerges on the east side via little-used Baxter Pass. The scenic lakes and towering, Alp-like peaks of this route make this a fine route for photography.

DESCRIPTION (Moderate trip)

1st 3 Hiking Days: Follow trip 60 to **Rae Lakes,** 21 miles.

4th Hiking Day (**Rae Lakes** to **Baxter Lakes,** 5½ miles): The first 2½ miles of this day's hike follow the gentle-to-moderate descent of South Fork Woods Creek. From Rae Lakes the trail passes through granite slab areas broken by stands of dwarfed lodgepole as it skirts the east side of the lower lakes of the Rae Lakes chain. Anglers will want to try their luck for the good brook trout fishing on some of these lakes and the stream flowing between them. The route fords the stream between the lowest and next to lowest lakes, and circles the west side of the lowest lake before leaving the John Muir Trail at the outlet of this lake, sometimes called Dollar Lake. We cross the outlet on logs and pick up a faint, unsigned, sometimes ducked trail that diagonals up the east wall of the valley. This ascent makes a long northward traverse, and from it we have fine views down the canyon of the South Fork. On the far side, a very evident line is the John Muir Trail, and most likely we will see a number of hikers on this wilderness boulevard. After a mile of ascent, the trail descends down into the Baxter Creek drainage, into a handsome grove of foxtail pines that give welcome shade. Then it swings east to continue the steep ascent to the Baxter Lakes. The trail here is ducked but sometimes hard to see as it follows the course shown on the topo map. The sparse forest cover thins as the route fords Baxter Creek and passes several tiny lakelets. Fair campsites may be found in a grove of whitebark pines below the treeless highest lake (11,150′), where fishing for brook trout (to 12″) is good.

5th Hiking Day (**Baxter Lakes** to **Oak Creek Roadend**, 10 miles): After rounding the north side of the highest and largest lake of the basin, the trail turns south as it ascends the steep granite scoop above the lake. Excellent views of Mt. Baxter and Acrodectes Peak to the north accompany the climb, and rockhounds can marvel at the dramatic striping on some of the peaks, known as mafic diking. These dikes, glaciated remnants of ancient magma intrusions, are evidence of the substantial igneous action that played a part in the petrology of the area.

Our rocky footpath ascends southwest, mostly on a moderate grade, and then descends momentarily across a snowfield. Even in this high, mineral world the vegetable kingdom stays alive, in the form of small specimens of alpine sorrel, Davidson's penstemon and Sierra primrose. Finally, the trail switchbacks up to scree-laden Baxter Pass (12,320′), where one has fine views of the Sierra crest, including multistriped Diamond Peak to the southwest, the North Fork Oak Creek canyon to the south, looking like a vertical-sided, giant gash, and even the town of Independence, far below in Owens Valley. The trail is over loose rock as it descends to Summit Meadow, where one can enjoy the russet and copper colors of the nearby rocks. The trail stays mostly well above the tumbling waters of North Fork Oak Creek, undulating down through many fields of very colorful wildflowers that include monkey flower, arnica, milfoil, cinquefoil, pennyroyal, buckwheat, spiraea, gilia, penstemon, Queen Anne's Lace, shooting star, paintbrush and buttercup.

As the trail follows the sharply cut defile of the stream one can see the heavy concentrations of metavolcanic rock which vented nearby and which characterizes the remaining descent onto the alluvial apron below. Midway down this long, flowery descent we ford the creek (difficult at high water) in the middle of a mixed forest cover, and soon embark on another long set of zigzags. These are succeeded by a gentle sandy descent to end with a few more quick switchbacks down to the last crossing of the creek. As the trail drops to the creek, one encounters a good sampling of typical east-side Sierra flora including rabbit brush, bitter brush, sagebrush, juniper, and mountain mahogany. Beyond a log over North Fork Oak Creek we leave the John Muir Wilderness, boulder-hop a side stream, and arrive at a dirt road west of Oak Creek Campground.

Mist Falls on the South Fork Kings River

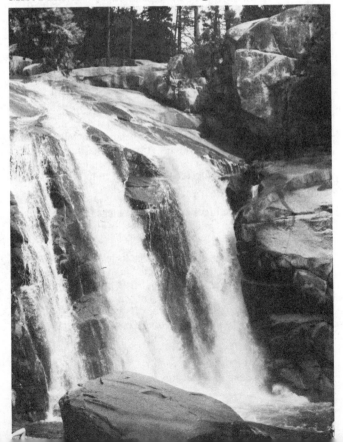

Cedar Grove to Lake Reflection

TRIP   From Cedar Grove Roadend to Lake Reflection
(round trip). Topo maps *Marion Peak, Mt. Pinchot,
Mt. Whitney.* Best mid or late season; 30 miles.

Grade	Trail/layover days	Total recommended days
Leisurely	6/1	7
Moderate	4/1	5
Strenuous	3/1	4

HILITES   Those who appreciate the serenity of high, alpine
lake basins will find this trip to the upper reaches
of East Creek a rewarding choice. Excellent fishing
amidst spellbinding surroundings makes this a
fine angling trip, and if one doesn't fish, it is time
well spent just "soaking up the country."

DESCRIPTION (Moderate trip)

1st Hiking Day (**Cedar Grove Roadend** to **Charlotte Creek**, 7½ miles):
Proceed to Charlotte Creek as described in the 1st hiking day,
trip 57.

2nd Hiking Day (**Charlotte Creek** to **Lake Reflection**, 8 miles): Proceed to Junction Meadow, as described in part of the 2nd hiking
day, trip 57. At Junction Meadow our trail branches right, fords
Bubbs Creek by a log, and starts to ascend East Creek canyon.
This ascent is accomplished via rocky switchbacks that zigzag
through a sparse-to-moderate forest cover of lodgepole, fir,
silver pine and some aspen. The view back to the north is dominated by the red metamorphic rocks of Mt. Bago, with Mt.
Gardiner coming into view beyond it. As one tops the first rise
of the ascent, peaks of the Kings-Kern Divide come into view.

Anglers trying their luck along East Creek will find rainbow and brook trout (to 8″), but the trout are somewhat larger in East Lake.

After a brief stretch of moderate uphill going the trail crosses East Creek via a log-and-plank bridge and then climbs steadily along the creek's east bank. The grade steepens and our route enters a forest of pines and firs. After the ford of an unnamed, fern-lined creek, our trail levels off near the outlet of East Lake. One's first view of these picturesque waters with their grassy fringes may be accompanied by a sighting of one of the many mule deer that frequent the canyon. The trail rounds the lake's east side to the fair-to-good campsites in dense forest at the head of the lake. The barren, unjointed granite walls that rise on either side—especially Mt. Brewer on the west—are an impressive backdrop for leisure moments spent on the shores of this mountain gem, and it is always with some reluctance that visitors move on. Beyond the head of East Lake the trail climbs steadily past a drift fence through rock-broken stands of lodgepole and foxtail pine. Just before crossing a 50-yard-wide talus slope, we pass the unmarked start of the Harrison Pass Trail. Beyond the talus slope, the easy grade traverses many wet areas along the east side of East Creek to the good campsites beside the little lake below Lake Reflection and at the northeast end of Lake Reflection (10,005′). The angler will find good fishing for golden, rainbow and hybrids (to 16″). When a breeze is not stirring the waters of this lake, the tableau of peaks reflected in their depths is a memorable scene of a scope seldom matched in the Sierra. At the head of the cirque basin, all side excursions are up, but the expenditure of sweat and effort required to explore the surrounding lakes and lakelets is repaid by great views and a sense of achievement that has been shared by many mountaineers since the Brewer Party first ascended these heights.

3rd and 4th Hiking Days: Retrace your steps, 15 miles.

64   **Cedar Grove to Upper Kern River**

TRIP   From Cedar Grove Roadend to Upper Kern River
                 via Bubbs Creek, Forester Pass, return by Harrison
                 Pass, East Lake (semiloop trip). Topo maps *Marion
                 Peak, Mt. Pinchot, Mt. Whitney.* Best late season;
                 49 miles.

Grade	Trail/layover days	Total recommended days
Leisurely	....	....
Moderate	7/3	10
Strenuous	6/2	8

HILITES   Crossing two high passes, this trip explores the
                 glaciated upper reaches of the Kern Trench and
                 circumnavigates a good piece of the Kings-Kern
                 and Great Western divides. This is a long and
                 rugged route that is recommended for the hearty
                 backcountry traveler possessed of a sense of adven-
                 ture and a liking for high, barren surroundings.

DESCRIPTION (Strenuous trip)

1st Hiking Day: (**Cedar Grove Roadend** to **Junction Meadow**, 10
miles): Proceed to Junction Meadow as described in the 1st and
part of the 2nd hiking day, trip 57.

2nd Hiking Day (**Junction Meadow** to **Upper Bubbs Creek**, 6½
miles): Follow the 2nd hiking day, trip 57, to Vidette Meadow,
where our route joins the John Muir Trail and turns southeast,

ascending beside Bubbs Creek. About ½ mile above Vidette Meadow our route passes an old trapper's cabin. Shorty Lovelace trapped this country until it was made into a national park, and a network of his cabins remains to remind today's travelers of an era of the not-too-distant past. After the initial steep ascent above Vidette Meadow, the trail levels out to a moderate but steady ascent along the east bank of the creek through a moderate forest cover of lodgepole and occasional hemlock. Several campsites line Bubbs Creek, and those at 10,200 feet offer fine views of University Peak to the east, Center Peak to the southeast, and East Vidette and East Spur to the west. However, to be nearer Forester Pass, we continue to the good campsites near the junction with the Center Basin/Junction Pass Trail. Fishing for brook trout (to 7") is good. Side excursions for golden-trout fishing or mere pleasure can be made via the old Muir Trail route to Center Basin.

3rd Hiking Day (**Upper Bubbs Creek** to **Outlet Stream of Lake 11440**, 9 miles): From these campsites the trail ascends more steeply over the barren granite west of Center Peak. This climb takes one above timberline as it winds back and forth over the tributary that drains Lake 12248, and over one's shoulder the peaks of the Sierra crest march away on the northern horizon. After fording the outlet of Lake 12248, the trail climbs the west wall of the canyon and then switchbacks steeply up to the narrow notch in the Kings-Kern Divide that is Forester Pass (13180'). Views from the pass to the northeast include Mt. Pinchot, University Peak, Mt. Bradley and Mt. Keith. To the south are Mt. Kaweah, the Kaweah Peaks Ridge, the Red Spur, Kern Point and Black Kaweah. Close by, Caltech Peak is to the west and Junction Peak to the east. You can climb Junction Peak and be back in an hour, if you hurry.

Leaving this windy orientation point behind, the trail descends steeply by numerous, short switchbacks, some of which are mere shelves carved into the steep face of the Junction Peak ridge. A few hardy polemonium and some yellow hulsea share the high slope with scurrying conies, and the traveler who lifts his eyes is sometimes treated to a sighting of a golden eagle soaring high above the granite steeples. After the trail levels off somewhat, the rocky route winds among a number of unnamed lakes that make up the headwaters of this branch of Tyndall Creek. To the east the unusual formation called Diamond Mesa appears as a sheer-walled, flat-topped ridge dangling from the jumbled heights of Junction Peak. Here, the trail passes through "marmot land," and the traveling human intruder is looked upon indulgently as a seasonal part of the scenery—accepted, at a respectful distance. Near timberline, our route intersects the signed Lake South America/Milestone Creek Trail and turns right onto it. This trail soon turns west, and then ascends gently at timberline for ½ mile to another signed junction, where the Lake South America Trail turns north and our route veers southwest. At the outlet stream of Lake 11440, the hiker should turn left and descend cross country to the good campsite (11,220') in foxtail pines at the edge of the meadow ¼ mile south.

4th Hiking Day (**Outlet Stream of Lake 11440** to **East Lake**, 10 miles, part cross country): Retrace the steps of the previous hiking day to the Lake South America/Milestone Creek Trail junction, where this day's route turns north and ascends gently up the east side of a long, boulder-strewn meadow. At the head of this ascent, the trail becomes steeper and switchbacks up 500 feet of barren, broken granite to a saddle which give access to the large cirque basin at the head of the Kern River. Beside a charming little lake that feeds the Kern River our route meets a trail coming up from the river and turns right, toward Lake South America (so called from its shape), where the angler may wish to try the good fishing for golden to 12″.

From here the trail is ducked as it climbs toward Harrison Pass. Ahead, locating the pass by visual sighting is difficult, as the lowest point on the headwall of the canyon is nearer Mt. Ericsson than the actual pass is. Our ducked route veers eastward, toward Mt. Stanford, where the best descent on the north side may be had. This descent is often snow-choked until late summer. Views from Harrison Pass to the south include Mt. Kaweah, Kaweah Peaks Ridge, Milestone Mountain and Mt. Guyot. Looking north, Deerhorn Mountain with its avalanche chutes and talus fans stands athwart the view, but Mt. Goddard can be seen far in the distance to the left of it, and Middle Palisade in the distance to its right. From the pass, the route leads north down the talus (sometimes over snow).

We carefully pick our way downward, toward the first lake visible on the cirque floor. Then we cross its outlet and veer west to ford the stream connecting the second and third lakes in the cirque. From here the ducked route ascends somewhat and then drops to the outlet of the third lake, passing close under the buff and tan granite cliffs of soaring Ericsson Crags. In the canyon below the third lake we encounter timber, and also achieve our first view of Mt. Brewer, due west across the canyon of East Creek. The route then levels off briefly in a meadow and fords the crystal stream to the north side. The white color of the trumpet-shaped flowers of alpine gentian in this

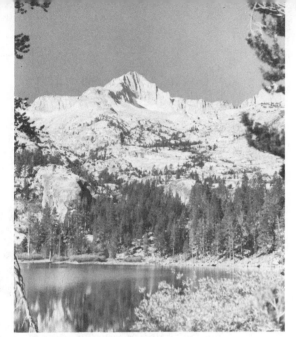

Mt. Brewer over East Lake

meadow tells us we are still quite high; blue gentians lie below. After passing several lovely tarns not shown on the topo map, the ducked and sometimes blazed trail easily crosses a little divide on a southbound course and traverse down to Golden Lake (not named on the map), where there is one excellent campsite. From the lake we have a direct view of Lucys Foot Pass, on the Kings-Kern Divide. This pass is Class 3 in places and it is not advised for ordinary backpacking or for inexperienced mountaineers. Due to all the loose "garbage" on the north side, the best passage is south-to-north.

From Golden Lake the route has a short level segment and then it descends steeply on a rocky-dusty, ill-maintained trail down poorly built switchbacks to the East Creek Trail, meeting it at an unsigned junction a few yards north of a talus rockslide. Here we turn right (north) and descend gently, sometimes moderately, for 1 mile to the good campsites at the north and south ends of East Lake, described in the 2nd hiking day, trip 63.

5th Hiking Day (**East Lake** to **Charlotte Creek**, 6½ miles): Descend to Junction Meadow, reversing part of the 2nd hiking day, trip 63, then retrace your steps to Charlotte Creek.

6th Hiking Day (**Charlotte Creek** to **Cedar Grove Roadend**, 7 miles): Reverse part of the 2nd hiking day and all of the 1st hiking day, trip 57.

65   Cedar Grove to East Lake

TRIP From Cedar Grove Roadend to Upper Kern River and East Lake via Colby Pass and Harrison Pass (semiloop trip). Topo maps *Marion Peak, Mt. Pinchot, Mt. Whitney, Triple Divide Peak.* Best mid to late season; 69½ miles.

Grade	Trail/layover days	Total recom-mended days
Leisurely	....	....
Moderate	9/4	13
Strenuous	7/2	9

HILITES Few trips that do not involve shuttling cars offer the variety of this loop around the major portion of the Great Western Divide. This is a trip for experienced backpackers, whose rewards for much effort will include almost continuous views of the highest High Sierra and great stretches of wilderness solitude.

DESCRIPTION (Moderate trip)

1st through 4th Hiking Days: Reverse the 8th through the 5th hiking days, trip 71, 30 miles.

5th Hiking Day (**Kern-Kaweah River** to **Upper Kern River**, 7 miles): Reverse the 4th and part of the 3rd hiking day, trip 76 to the junction of the Kern River Trail and the High Sierra Trail. One half mile up the canyon from the junction is a roofless cabin that was a powder magazine used by crews constructing trails in this region. Beginning here there are several good campsites along the river, where fishing is good for rainbow and golden trout (to 10″).

6th Hiking Day (**Upper Kern River** to **Outlet Stream of Lake 11440,** 9 miles): Reverse most of the 3rd hiking day, trip 70. At Lake 10650 our route turns right up a short, steep ascent through a cover of moderate lodgepole and foxtail. After half a mile the trail passes a picturebook lake which is fast (geologically speaking) becoming a meadow. The trial continues eastward up a moderate ascent through alternating rocky and meadowy sections, where the Oregon junco is likely to be seen flitting among the willows. Careful study of the ground as one walks along may discover a junco nest under the overhang of a boulder, a fallen log or a tree bole. This route climbs above timberline and crosses the ridge coming down from Point 12223, where there are good views back to the west of Mt. Jordan, Thunder Mountain, Milestone Mountain, Midway Mountain, Kern Ridge and the Red Spur. Beyond this point the trail descends slightly and skirts the north side of a small, unnamed lake. Just beyond this lake the trail meets the outlet stream of Lake 11440. Here the hiker should turn right and descend cross country to the good campsite at the edge of the meadow ¼ mile south.

7th, 8th and 9th Hiking Days: Follow the 4th through the 6th hiking days, trip 64, 23½ miles.

Milestone Mountain

66   **Onion Valley to Flower Lake**

| **TRIP** | From Onion Valley to Flower Lake (round trip). Topo Map *Mt. Pinchot.* Best early or mid season; 5 miles. |

Grade	Trail/layover days	Total recom- mended days
Leisurely	2/0	2
Moderate	....	....
Strenuous	day	....

HILITES Employing one of the "easiest" east-side entries, this trip climbs to the friendly lakes making up the headwaters of Independence Creek. The ample opportunities for good angling and the exciting alpine scenery occupy one's weekend time in grand style.

DESCRIPTION (Leisurely trip)

1st Hiking Day (**Onion Valley** to **Flower Lake**, 2½ miles): The trail leaves the road a few yards north of the Onion Valley campground and switchbacks up a dry, manzanita-covered slope. Switchbacks always seem to come in bunches, and this ascent is no exception. The first set of switchbacks is relatively open and exposed, offering fine views back on Onion Valley and south to the heavily diked summit of Independence Peak. After about ⅓ mile there is short level stretch where one may study the distinctive shapes of the large foxtail pines nearby. Then the trail enters the John Muir Wilderness and switchbacks steadily again, until after a mile it comes close enough to tumbling Independence Creek that only a few steps are needed to reach the wildflower-lined stream bank and slake one's thirst.

After this draught, on a more gradual slope, our path crosses many runoff rills in early and mid season, where a neophyte botanist may identify specimens of Queen Anne's lace, paintbrush, wallflower, tiger lily, columbine, shooting star and whorled penstemon. At the top of this gentle grade is Little Pothole Lake, not much for camping, but boasting two beautiful, willow-lined cascades pouring into its south and west bays. After another set of rocky switchbacks, the trail levels off in a slightly ascending groove across a glacial moraine and then reaches small, round Gilbert Lake (10,930'). Poor-from-overuse camp-sites dot the shores of this fine swimming lake, and fishing for rainbow and brook trout is good in early season. This small lake absorbs much of the day-hiking impact from people camp-ing at Onion Valley, as does Flower Lake, at the top of the next set of switchbacks. Less used and more scenic are Matlock and Slim lakes, the first reached by a trail that leads south from the east side of Flower Lake, and the second, cross country west from the first. There are many highly used campsites along the north and east sides of this shallow lake (10,450'). Fishing for rainbow and some brook trout is fair on this small lake, but serious anglers will hike to the more distant lakes in the tim-bered cirque basin to the south.

2nd Hiking Day: Retrace your steps, 2½ miles.

Lake Reflection

67 Onion Valley to Cedar Grove

TRIP   From Onion Valley to Cedar Grove Roadend via Kearsarge Pass, Charlotte Lake, Glen Pass, Rae Lakes, South Fork Woods Creek, Paradise Valley (shuttle trip). Topo maps *Mt. Pinchot, Marion Peak.* Best mid or late season; 34 miles.

Grade	Trail/layover days	Total recom- mended days
Leisurely	6/2	8
Moderate	5/2	7
Strenuous	4/2	6

HILITES   Kearsarge Pass, because of its relatively low elevation and its proximity to an east-side roadend, is a popular way to reach the John Muir Trail. Because of this popularity, many of the lakes and meadows en route have been overrun, and Park officials have felt it necessary to close these "impacted" areas to grazing and camping. Despite these restrictions, the country retains its popularity, and anyone planning to tramp the Muir Trail in the vicinity of this pass should expect company.

DESCRIPTION (Leisurely trip)

1st Hiking Day: Follow trip 66 to **Flower Lake**, 2½ miles.

2nd Hiking Day (**Flower Lake** to **Charlotte Lake**, 5½ miles): At Flower Lake the Kearsarge Pass Trail turns north and ascends steeply to a viewpoint overlooking Heart Lake. From this point the trail switchbacks up to another overlook—this time the lake is the nearly perfect blue oval of Big Pothole Lake. From the trail high above the water, the lake, with its backgrounding granite finger, is particularly photogenic. From the switchbacks on, the trail rises above timber, except for a few hardy whitebark specimens, and then makes two long-legged traverses across an exposed shaley slope to the low saddle of Kearsarge Pass (11,823´). To the west, the view is impressive, as it includes the Kearsarge Lakes, Bullfrog Lake and the serrated spires of the Kearsarge Pinnacles.

On the west side of the pass our route drops down on a traverse that later resolves into the inevitable switchbacks. After passing a spur trail branching left to the Kearsarge Lakes and Bullfrog Lake (no camping), the route continues westward on a gentle descent into sparse timber. Crossing several small runoff streams in early season, the rocky-sandy trail contours high on the viewful slopes above Bullfrog Lake.

Now descending steadily through sparse-to-moderate whitebark and foxtail pine, the trail offers fine views south to Center Peak and Junction Peak. We meet the topo-map trail that leads northwest from Bullfrog Lake and follow it past a junction where a shortcut trail leads right to the Muir Trail. Then our route descends gently onto a sandy flat in a broad saddle overlooking Charlotte Lake, where at an **X** junction we take a signed trail that switchbacks down moderately-to-steeply for a short mile to Charlotte Lake (10,370´). Good campsites line the north shore, and fishing for rainbow and brook trout (to 10˝) is fair. Emergency services are usually available from the resident summer ranger on the north shore.

3rd Hiking Day (**Charlotte Lake** to **Rae Lakes**, 5½ miles): Retrace your steps to the John Muir Trail and then proceed as in the 3rd hiking day, trip 60.

4th, 5th and 6th Hiking Days: Follow the 4th, 5th and 6th hiking days, trip 61, 20½ miles.

Bubbs Creek to Lower Kern

This stretch of country composes the least visited, least known, and least trampled region in the southern Sierra. It owes its integrity not to its lack of scenic or recreational potential, but rather to the presence of a fortuitously placed series of natural barriers—the Great Western Divide, the Kings-Kern Divide, and the Sierra crest. Joined together in an upside-down **U**, they protect the first 24 miles of the Kern River watershed with a wall of mountains crossed only by 1) people who have business here (rangers, packers, etc.), 2) people who have a love for the high country, and 3) people who fly over in airplanes. There are those among us who would restrict the third category because of the objectionable sonic booms.

The one area described in this region that sits outside this protective cup of divides and ranges is the Roaring River Country. Remoteness from roads and a convoluted terrain guarantee its sanctuary. And sanctuary it is, for in the remote headwaters of Roaring River a hiker can walk for one, two, or even three days without seeing a soul.

This high region has a delicate balance between plant and animal life, which is nowhere more manifest than in the alpine fell fields over Cottonwood Pass just west of Horseshoe Meadow, or around the subalpine meadows just south of Little Claire Lake over the crest from Mineral King. Here, in an incredibly brief 6-7 week span, some 40 varieties of hardy-yet-vulnerable grasses, sedges and flowering plants grow, bud, blossom, seed, and are harvested, running their appointed course under the daily threat of killing frost, and before the juggernaut deadline of the first winter snows. Caught in the complex "web of life," year-round resident animals like the cony, the marmot and the pocket gopher stake their very existence on the plants' explosively short summer tenure. Inexorably linked in the ecological chain, the migrating and hibernating carnivores, such as the coyote, mountain lion, black bear, red fox, marten, weasel and wolverine, would perish without their dependable rodent and squirrel food supply. So fragile and tenuous is this balance that the trampling by man and his live-stock of a high, grassy meadow—particularly during the early, wet days of spring—can have and has had catastrophic effects upon the food chain.

This is not to argue that man does not have a place in this setting. His trails, within strict practical and esthetic limitations, are as legitimate as those of the deer. He has the right to share the fish of the streams and the berries of the hillside with the bear. Like the marmot, he has his place in the sun—preferably a big flat rock where he too can laze away a warm afternoon. Man's propensity for mountaintops and places of quiet solitude is as valid as the bighorn sheep's. And, like the Hermit thrush at nesting time, or the Brewer blackbird at sundown, he has the right to sing of his exultation at being alive and here.

But, because he knows the devastation wrought by large, concentrated numbers of his species upon this country, he owes it to his co-habiters, and to himself, to expand rather than con-strict the size of primitive country, and to disperse his impact upon the country. Implicit within both of these obligations should be a profound respect for the ecological chain, of which man is a part, for this respect will give birth to a deeper knowl-edge and appreciation of the re-creating benefits of a region such as this. The authors hope that, beyond sharing their appre-ciation of and passion for this grand part of the Sierra, they might, with this modest guide, call the attention of the prospec-tive traveler to the less traveled byways and thereby contribute, in small measure, to the distribution of human impact. Because many of the routes described here are the lesser traveled, they are therefore sometimes faint, but that is as it should be. The passes are sometimes steeper than those used on the more traveled routes, but the rewards of scenery and solitude are commensurate.

As the quality of the wilderness experience is important, so is the quantity. For it is only through public support that requisite public legislation and administrative decisions will reflect man's desire and need for wild areas. The more people that are intro-duced to basic wilderness values, perhaps through guides like this, the greater will be the demand for more and better wilder-ness areas and national parks. If pieces of untrammeled country like that between the Kings-Kern Divide and the lower Kern River will remain bastions of peace and solitude, it will be not so much because government officials discourage and restrict wilderness travel as because more wilderness alternatives are created for people to use. The sooner people recognize this fact, the sooner the trend to wilderness attrition will be reversed.

There are seven trailheads cited in the text that give access to this region—three on the west side, and four on the east.

Lodgepole Campground (6800′). Go 50 miles east from Fresno on State Highway 180 to a junction with State Highway 198, then 26 miles southeast on 198 to a 0.6-mile spur road that leads east to a parking area. This spur road is 54 miles northeast from Visalia on Highway 198.

Crescent Meadow (6800′). Go about 2 miles south and east of Giant Forest Village on a road running past Moro Rock to the road's end.

Mineral King (7830′). Go 37 miles east from Visalia on State Highway 198, turn east, and go 23 miles on a mostly paved road. This narrow, winding 23 miles takes more than an hour to drive.

Symmes Creek Trailhead. Go 4½ miles west from Independence on the Onion Valley Road, turn left and go 1.3 miles to a fork, take the right-hand fork, and follow the *Shepherd Pass Trail* signs to the backpackers' trailhead (different from the horse-packers' trailhead).

Whitney Portal (8360′). Go 13 miles west from Lone Pine on the Whitney Portal road.

Cottonwood Creek Trailhead (9660′). From the center of Lone Pine on US 395 drive 3 miles west on the Whitney Portal Road, turn left, and go southward 20 miles to the Trailhead, beyond a pack station and a campground, and just before the road crosses Cottonwood Creek as the road swings south.

Horseshoe Meadow (9880′). Go 0.7 mile past the Cottonwood Creek Trailhead, to the end of the road.

South of Pinchot Pass on the John Muir Trail

Symmes Creek Trailhead to Wright Lakes   **68**

TRIP   From Symmes Creek Trailhead to Wright Lakes
via Anvil Camp and Shepherd Pass (round trip).
Topo map *Mt. Whitney*. Best mid or late season;
28 miles.

Grade	Trail/layover days	Total recommended days
Leisurely	....	....
Moderate	....	....
Strenuous	3/1	4

HILITES   This trip provides the great satisfacton of reaching
the high, remote backcountry via a tough climb up
the canyon of Shepherd Creek, one of the immense
gashes that typify the eastern Sierra escarpment.
The great elevation gain makes it a trip only for
those in excellent physical condition. Indeed, Shepherd Pass is *the* most difficult trail pass in the Sierra
Nevada.

DESCRIPTION (Strenuous trip)

1st Hiking Day (**Symmes Creek Trailhead** to **Anvil Camp**, 7½ miles):
The trail begins at the mouth of the Symmes Creek canyon and
gently ascends on the south side of the creek through piñon
pine, sagebrush and, at streamside, alders, willows and cottonwoods. The trail fords the creek four times (fill your water
bottle at the fourth), passing clumps of early and mid-season
columbine. From the fourth crossing the trail begins a long,
gruelling series of rocky switchbacks that climb a whopping

2300 feet to a saddle between Shepherd and Symmes creeks. Above 8000 feet red fir and then silver pine form a moderate forest cover, and the entire hot slope supports sagebrush, mountain mahogany and creamberry. From the saddle at the head of this slope, one may take a rest while inspecting the great peak to the south, Mt. Williamson, second highest in California— though, surprisingly, it is not on the Sierra crest. The deep, steep gash that contains Shepherd Creek falls away at one's feet, and it is an impressive introduction to the immense canyons of the eastern escarpment.

From the saddle, the sandy trail descends moderately over two small ridges high above Shepherd Creek before dropping 500 feet down to a dry creek bed. From here the trail rounds a ridge through a burned forest of piñon pines to arrive at the only year-round creek between Symmes Creek and Anvil Camp. Beyond this creek the trail switchbacks up to Mahogany Flat, where there is a poor campsite. At the upper end of this flat the trail begins a set of long brushy switchbacks to gain the elevation of the cascade visible to the southwest on Shepherd Creek. As the route crosses a large talus slope, the entire surroundings change dramatically within a few hundred feet. The trail has been largely on decomposed granite, and the vegetation generally sparse and desertlike. But as the trail reaches Anvil Camp (10,000') the experienced Sierra traveler suddenly recognizes that he is in the *High* Sierra: there is duff, a burbling stream, a campsite, willows, grass, and young lodgepole pines.

2nd Hiking Day (**Anvil Camp** to **Wright Lakes**, 6½ miles, part cross country): At Anvil Camp we ford Shepherd Creek and ascend moderately over rocky slopes on the south side of Shepherd Creek. After a mile the ill-defined trail to Junction Pass turns off to the right. (Until Forester Pass was opened in 1931 the John Muir Trail, in passing from the Kings River to the Kern River drainage, detoured to the east side of the Sierra crest over Junction Pass, descended to this trail junction, and recrossed westward over Shepherd Pass.) Our route crosses the area labeled "The Pothole" on the topo map, and ascends past great boulders to the giant declivity, below the pass, for which that label should have been reserved. Here is a gargantuan jumble of great jagged rocks that have been weathered out of the headwall of the cirque. The last 500 feet up to Shepherd Pass (12,050') are on a slope where the snow is thick in early season and may last all summer. Most of the trail here has been destroyed by erosion, and the snow may offer better footing than the scree.

At the pass, the route enters Sequoia National Park. Views of the Great Western Divide are excellent, and they get even better as the trail descends down a broad, boulder-strewn field to alpine meadows and stands of foxtail pine. Immediately to the south is the northern flank of Mt. Tyndall (14,018′), which the famous mountaineer Clarence King climbed in 1864 believing it to be the highest Sierra peak. He did not realize his error until he reached the summit.

At the 11,600-foot level the hiker should leave the trail and traverse southwest cross-country to the saddle between Peak 13540 and Peak 12345. The panoramic view from this saddle includes the noble series of summits of the Great Western Divide, Junction Peak, Mts. Keith, Brewer, Kaweah, Guyot and Young, and the top of Mt. Whitney, as well as the Kern River trench. Even in this high rocky saddle there are flowers, including prostrate purple-flowered pussypaws. Our route traverses down the east wall of the cirque that lies south of the saddle, to the fair campsites in a grove of foxtails where the outlet stream of Lake 11952 meets the other two draining the upper basin. Fishing is good for golden (to 8″).

3rd Hiking Day: Retrace your steps, 14 miles.

Rock glacier below Shepherd Pass

69 Symmes Creek Trailhead to Milestone Basin

TRIP   From Symmes Creek Trailhead to Milestone Basin via Anvil Camp and Shepherd Pass (round trip). Topo map *Mt. Whitney*. Best mid or late season; 38 miles.

Grade	Trail/layover days	Total recommended days
Leisurely	....	....
Moderate	....	....
Strenuous	4/1	5

HILITES   Milestone Basin is a fine choice for the lover of high country who wants to be alone. Many fish-filled lakes lie under the prepossessing heights of the Great Western Divide, where the delicate quality of the light and the air work their magic on all who come.

DESCRIPTION (Strenuous trip)

1st Hiking Day: Follow trip 68 to *Anvil Camp,* 7½ miles.

2nd Hiking Day (**Anvil Camp** to **Milestone Basin**, 11½ miles): Follow the 2nd hiking day, trip 68, from Anvil Camp to where that day's route leaves the Shepherd Pass Trail. Our route continues down the trail beside Tyndall Creek, through a huge, boulder-strewn, sloping meadow, with the 13,000-foot peaks of the Great Western Divide filling the western horizon. After fording Tyndall Creek, the trail diverges from the stream and enters a sparse cover of lodgepole and foxtail pine, meeting the stream again at the John Muir Trail. Our route turns right (north) onto the Muir Trail, fords Tyndall Creek (difficult in early season) and ascends a moderate slope to timberline. Three fourths of a mile from the last ford we turn left onto the Lake South America Trail. Then, a half mile farther on across alpine fell fields, we turn left again, onto the Milestone Basin Trail. Views in this upper Kern basin are at all times panoramic, and the traveler will mentally record pictures of the skyline he will not soon forget.

At the outlet stream of Lake 11440 the angler may wish to veer north and sample that lake's waters for the good fishing for golden (to 12″). The trail then skirts along the north side of a small lake, and makes a short, rocky climb to a ridge where the descent to the Kern River begins. From the ridge the traveler has closer views of Mt. Jordan, Thunder Mountain, Milestone Mountain, Midway Mountain—all on the Great Western Divide—and Kern Ridge and Red Spur in the south. Past this viewpoint the trail descends moderately through rocky and meadowy sections with a moderate cover of foxtail, lodgepole and some whitebark pine, and arrives at a picturebook lake that is fast (geologically speaking) turning to meadow. One may regret that all these high lakes are doomed, but one may enjoy the blend of meadows and lakes existing in the time to which he was born.

After climbing slightly, our route begins the last, steep descent to the Kern River, where it emerges at an unnamed lake at 10,650 feet elevation (good fishing for golden and rainbow-golden hybrids to 10″). Our route turns left at the east side of this lake and descends gently beside the infant Kern River for about 200 yards to the trail turning west to Milestone Basin. After fording the river, the trail contours to meet Milestone Creek and then veers west up a rocky slope away from the creek. After another ½ mile it rejoins the creek at a bench where, beside a waterfall, there is a good campsite (11,110′). Fishing in Milestone Creek is good for rainbow (to 10″). Those who wish to camp as high as possible may climb to the high lake (11,900′) just to the right of the words *Midway Mtn* on the topo map. The trail shown on the topo map beside Milestone Creek above the confluence of the north fork does not exist, and the hiker should follow the ducked route that turns right up the north fork, passes through a defile, skirts a small lake barren of fish, and traverses up to the high lake, where fishing is good for golden (to 12″). There are fair campsites below this lake on the outlet stream.

3rd and 4th Hiking Days: Retrace your steps, 19 miles.

70 Symmes Creek Trailhead to Mineral King

TRIP From Symmes Creek Trailhead to Mineral King via Anvil Camp, Shepherd Pass, Upper Kern River, Rattlesnake Creek and Franklin Pass (shuttle trip). Topo maps *Mt. Whitney, Kern Peak, Mineral King.* Best mid-to-late season; 53½ miles.

Grade	Trail/layover days	Total recommended days
Leisurely	....	....
Moderate	....	....
Strenuous	6/1	7

HILITES This long shuttle trip provides a grand sample of everything the High Sierra has to offer: sweeping vistas, intimate groves, barren granite, streamside meadows, rainbow, golden, brook and brown trout, pages of geological history, access to the highest Sierra peaks, the marks of great glaciers, thick pine forests, alpine fell fields—and that feeling of grandeur which calls the backpacker to the Sierra again and again.

DESCRIPTION (Strenuous trip)

1st Hiking Day: Follow trip 68 to **Anvil Camp,** 7½ miles.

2nd Hiking Day (**Anvil Camp** to **Lake on Upper Kern River,** 10 miles): Follow the 2nd hiking day, trip 69, to the lake on the Kern River at 10,650 feet elevation, where the Milestone Basin Trail meets the Kern River Trail. There are good campsites at the lake inlet, and fishing is good for golden and hybrids (to 10″).

3rd Hiking Day (**Lake on Upper Kern River** to **Junction Meadow**, 6 miles): Your trail proceeds south along the east shore of the lake, where red penstemon, or mountain pride, is especially abundant in the broken granite slopes. After 200 yards the Kern River Trail leaves the Milestone Basin Trail branching right, and soon begins the steep 600-foot descent of a granite-slabbed slope down which the young river cascades and falls. In the shade of lodgepole pines, one sees yarrow milfoil, paint-brush, penstemon, fleabane, and red mountain heather. Despite the topo map indication, the trail remains on the east side of the river. As the descent begins to level off, the trail passes through a bank of shield fern among which grows the delicate, white-headed Queen Anne's lace. At the foot of the descent our route enters a thick stand. Yellow groundsel flowers dominate the ground cover under these pines, complemented by the hues of orange tiger lily, purple swamp onion and red columbine.

After fording the outlet stream of Lake 11440, the trail begins a dusty section where the sagebrush is spottily shaded by a few lodgepole and foxtail pines. Shortly before the junction with the Tyndall Creek Trail there is a good packer campsite beside the river and here one begins to see red fir and aspen, indicating arrival in the Canadian life zone. The sandy, exposed trail continues its gentle descent to the Tyndall Creek ford (difficult in early season). Beyond this ford, the canyon becomes steeper, and the trail becomes more dufflike and tree-shaded. The first Jeffrey pines of this trip appear, along with a few mountain junipers. One-half mile beyond a roofless, decaying cabin our route meets the High Sierra Trail coming down from Wallace Creek, and from here down almost to Upper Funston Meadow the Kern River Trail and the High Sierra Trail are "superimposed."

From this junction it is a steep descent of 1 mile to Junction Meadow. Views on this descent are good down the Kern canyon, an immense U-trough which was given that shape by the main Kern glacier, which left the tributary valleys hanging. The forest cover on this descent is sparse lodgepole and Jeffrey, along with clumps of aspen, on a slope dominated by manzanita and currant. As the trail levels off, it enters a parklike grove of stalwart Jeffrey pines that provide a noble setting for the good campsites near the Kern River. Fishing is good for rainbow, golden and brook (to 10″).

4th Hiking Day (**Junction Meadow** to **Rattlesnake Creek/Kern River**, 11½ miles): This day's hike is entirely beside the young Kern River, but it is not lacking in contrasts and discoveries. After fording Wallace Creek (high water in early season) the trail descends gently down the U-trough of the Kern River. This trough is remarkably straight for about 25 miles, as it parallels the Kern Canyon fault. The fault, a zone of structural weakness in the Sierra batholith, is more susceptible to erosion than the surrounding rock. This deep canyon has been carved by both glacial and stream action: at least three times the glacier advanced down the canyon, shearing off spurs created by stream erosion and leaving some tributary valleys hanging above the main valley. The glacier also scooped and plucked at the granite bedrock, creating basins (like the lake at the start of the 3rd hiking day) which became lakes when the glacier melted and retreated. It is interesting to speculate that our trail probably passes over some of these ancient lake beds, now buried beneath river sediments.

The descending trail becomes a little steeper as it fords Whitney Creek, where a thirsty hiker can sample water that coursed down from the highest point in the contiguous United States. Tributaries cascading down the east face of Red Spur provide excellent views as the trail steepens again and fords the stream that drains Guyot Flat. Rounding the most salient part of Red Spur, the trail turns slightly west as it skirts the steep bluffs on the east canyon wall. The gravelly, flat canyon floor widens as the trail approaches the fords of the branchlets of Rock Creek. Just beyond the first of these is the delightful mountain spa of Kern Hot Spring—a treat for the tired, dusty hiker. To the traveler, the crude cement bathtub here becomes a regal, heated (115°) pool. Only a few feet away, the great Kern River rushes past, and its cold waters can be dipped into to cool the hot-spring water as desired. Beyond Kern Hot Spring the valley floor widens and the river bifurcates as it flows past Chagoopa Falls. Chagoopa Creek descends 1700 feet from its hanging valley on Chagoopa Plateau, but the actual waterfall drops only 150 feet.

A short distance to the south our route crosses a bridge to the west side of the Kern, and then continues its gentle descent past the Big Arroyo turnoff—thereby leaving the High Sierra Trail—to a ford of Funston Creek. Then, keeping away from the willow-infested banks of the Kern, the trail continues south past Upper Funston Meadow through a moderate-to-heavy forest cover of white fir, Jeffrey and sugar pine and some black oak, birch and aspen. Heavy patches of bracken fern inhibit the going in the wetter stretches, and the trail crosses through the site of an old burn before passing a drift fence and crossing the steel cantilever bridge spanning Big Arroyo Creek. From the bridge it is but a mile of level going to the good packer campsite at the confluence of Rattlesnake Creek and the Kern River. Fishing on the Kern is excellent for rainbow and brown (to 8″). Emergency services, should they be required, are usually available at the Kern Canyon Ranger Station 6 miles downcanyon. A cautionary note is warranted here: Rattlesnake Creek came by its name honestly, and one should exercise some care in hiking and climbing in the vicinity.

5th Hiking Day (**Rattlesnake Creek/Kern River** to **Upper Rattlesnake Creek**, 8 miles): Reverse the 2nd hiking day, trip 100.

6th Hiking Day (**Upper Rattlesnake Creek** to **Mineral King**, 10½ miles): Reverse the 1st hiking day, trip 96.

Kern Hot Spring   *J.C. Jenkins*

71   Symmes Creek Trailhead to Cedar Grove

TRIP

From Symmes Creek Trailhead to Cedar Grove Roadend via Shepherd Pass, Upper Kern River, Junction Meadow, Colby Pass, Scaffold Meadows and Avalanche Pass (shuttle trip). Topo maps *Mt. Whitney, Triple Divide Peak, Marion Peak.* Best mid-to-late season, 59½ miles.

Grade	Trail/layover days	Total recommended days
Leisurely	....	....
Moderate	....	....
Strenuous	8/1	9

HILITES

Staying entirely on trails sometimes limits one's experiences, but this route is diversified enough for any taste. Visiting four life zones, the trip offers a complete sampling of High Sierra ecosystems, and affords grand views of deep canyons and serrated skylines.

DESCRIPTION (Strenuous trip)

1st 3 Hiking Days: Follow trip 70 to **Junction Meadow**, 23½ miles.

4th Hiking Day (**Junction Meadow** to **Kern-Kaweah River**, 6 miles): Follow the 4th hiking day, trip 76.

5th Hiking Day (**Kern-Kaweah River** to **Big Wet Meadow**, 7 miles): Leaving the Kern-Kaweah drainage behind, the trail ascends steeply and quickly transcends the sparse cover of lodgepole pine. This steep climb offers magnificent views back into the headwaters of the Kern-Kaweah drainage and the backgrounding Kaweah Peaks Ridge. Just to the north of these distinctive summits rise the pyramidal heights of aptly named Triple Divide Peak—this landmark peak divides the drainages of the Kern, Kings and Kaweah rivers. The steep ascent levels briefly as it crosses the tributaries draining Milestone Bowl, and then, by a faint and unreliably ducked trail, resumes its steep, steady climb to Colby Pass (12,000'). Here one has grand views down Cloud Canyon, and of Glacier Ridge and the cockscomblike sentinels atop the Whaleback. This pass is often snow-covered until late in the season, but the route down to Cloud Canyon is easy to discern as it drops past occasional foxtail and white-bark trees and then around the northeast side of Colby Lake (campsites).

The poorly ducked trail follows the outlet stream from the wooded area at its source, zigging and zagging back and forth across the stream in the descent. Dwarfed and twisted white-bark pines dot the slopes on either side as the route dips steeply down over the unjointed granite shoulder of the Whaleback to the Cloud Canyon floor, where it soon fords to the west side of the infant Roaring River. Our trail turns right, and proceeds downstream through a lodgepole forest cover for about ⅔ mile to another ford, beyond which we reach the good campsites located just south of Big Wet Meadow (8700').

6th Hiking Day (**Big Wet Meadow** to **Scaffold Meadows**, 7 miles): North of Big Wet Meadow the moderate-to-heavy stands of lodgepole occasionally give away to clumps of aspen as the trail passes the "Big Wet Meadow Drift Fence" and a nearby packer campsite. The descent is moderate on a duff surface as it passes Cement Table Meadow and a nearby campsite. The gradual loss of altitude is reflected in the changing forest cover, which now shows red fir, juniper, and white fir mixed with the lodge-poles. Views of the glacially smoothed granite, particularly on the west wall of the canyon, continue as the duff-and-sand trail takes the traveler down past the beginning of the cross-country route to Brewer Lakes and Brewer Creek. After passing two more drift fences, our trail arrives at the campground at Scaffold Meadows (7400'). Fishing in Roaring River is fair for rainbow and some golden (to 10"), and a summer ranger is stationed here.

7th Hiking Day (**Scaffold Meadows** to **Campsites, Sphinx Creek Ford**, 9 miles): Crossing the bridge by the ranger station, our route takes the Avalanche Pass Trail northward on a steady ascent over a sandy trail, through a heavy forest cover of Jeffrey pine, red and white fir, and juniper. At the Scaffold Meadows drift fence the ascent becomes moderate to steep as the trail switchbacks up a lateral moraine whose morainal nature is identified by its rounded boulders and granite sand. From the crown of this moraine, views are good up Deadman Canyon to the head of the cirque near Elizabeth Pass. Here our route begins a short, steady descent to the easy ford of Moraine Creek. The moist sections near the creek support a variety of wildflowers, including shooting star, sneezeweed, cinquefoil, aster, groundsel and milfoil.

Beyond the ford, the duff-and-sand trail ascends steadily to moderately to the tributary that drains the Avalanche Pass area. The forest cover of lodgepole, red fir and a few junipers is moderate to heavy, and some aspen thrive along the creek. Our trail remains on the east side of the creek, and it has a number of switchbacks as it climbs from 8800 feet to 9200 feet. The trail becomes less steep, and finally level, as it nears Avalanche Pass (10,050′). Views from the pass are inhibited by the moderate-to-heavy forest cover. Along the moderate descent north of the pass, foxtail pines disappear and red fir and silver pine join the lodgepole to compose a heavy forest cover over the trail on granite sand. After fording the westernmost tributary of Sphinx Creek, our trail descends moderately to ford a second tributary, and then drops again on a moderate descent to Sphinx Creek and a packer campsite. An unmaintained, unmapped trail to the Sphinx Lakes leads south from here.

8th Hiking Day (**Sphinx Creek Ford** to **Cedar Grove Roadend**, 7 miles): Leaving Sphinx Creek via a short, steady descent, the trail makes a long, level traverse high above the creek on the east canyon wall. Part of the Sphinx Crest is visible to the south through the trees, and at the ford of a tributary stream one can pause to enjoy not only a drink but a mountain garden of wildflowers and ferns. The traverse ends as the trail begins a series of long, well-built switchbacks that descend to the banks of Sphinx Creek in its deep, **V**-shaped gorge. Both the creek and the trail follow along granite slabs for much of the way from the beginning of the switchbacks to the foot of the descent, and some of the trail has been blasted across these slabs. As the trail leads out onto the north side of a granite nose, there are very good views up the Bubbs Creek drainage, down the canyon to the flats around the roadend, and northwest to the peaks of the Monarch Divide, which separates the South and Middle Forks of the Kings River. The last part of the descent to Bubbs Creek is moderate, via many more switchbacks than are shown on the topo map. Then the forest cover thickens and our route meets the Bubbs Creek Trail, where it turns left to retrace part of the 1st hiking day, trip 57.

Whitney Portal to Outpost Camp

TRIP From Whitney Portal to Outpost Camp (round trip). Topo maps *Lone Pine, Mt. Whitney.* Best mid or late season; 7 miles.

Grade	Trail/layover days	Total recommended days
Leisurely	2/0	2
Moderate	....	....
Strenuous	day	....

HILITES This overnight trip offers an experience of the high country in the shadow of Mt. Whitney. Outpost Camp can be used as a base camp for climbing Mt. Whitney or for exploring the spectacular surrounding country.

DESCRIPTION (Leisurely trip)

1st Hiking Day (**Whitney Portal** to **Outpost Camp,** 3½ miles): From just east of the small store at road's end, our route follows the old stock trail from the defunct pack station as it steadily climbs through a moderate forest cover of Jeffrey pine and red fir. After ½ mile the trail crosses North Fork Lone Pine Creek and shortly enters the John Muir Wilderness. Soon the forest cover thins, and the slope is covered with a chaparral that includes mountain mahogany, Sierra chinquapin and sagebrush. This steep slope can get very hot in mid-morning, and the trip is best begun as early as possible. (Carry water.) Breather stops on this trail section provide a view down the canyon framing the Alabama Hills. Then the trail levels off somewhat through several willow-covered pockets having a moderate forest cover of lodgepole and foxtail pines, and passes fields of corn lilies, delphinium, tall lupine and swamp whiteheads as, in 1½ miles, it approaches the ford of Lone Pine Creek.

Beyond this log ford is a junction with a lateral that leads east to Lone Pine Lake, visible from the junction. The route leads up a barren, rocky wash, then switchbacks up another slope through a moderate lodgepole tree cover to Outpost Camp (10,365′—called "Bighorn Park" on the topo map), a willow-covered meadow that was once a lake. A very large abandoned stove near the upper end of this park is evidence of the days when a packer's wife ran a little camp here, renting tents and selling meals. The camp had to be removed when the area was made wilderness by Congress. There are many fair campsites here in Outpost Camp, but wood fires are forbidden, as they are on all of the Mt. Whitney Trail. Those bound for the summit of Whitney or for Crabtree Meadows and beyond may have enough steam left to climb on to Trail Camp, 3 miles ahead, the next legal camping place on the trail, which is above timberline.

2nd Hiking Day: Retrace your steps, 3½ miles.

Mt. Whitney over Long Pine

Whitney Portal to Crabtree Ranger Station **73**

TRIP
From Whitney Portal to Crabtree Ranger Station (round trip). Topo maps *Lone Pine, Mt. Whitney*. Best mid-to-late season; 30 miles.

Grade	Trail/layover days	Total recommended days
Leisurely	....	....
Moderately	5/1	6
Strenuous	4/0	4

HILITES
Despite the elevation at the pass where this route crosses the Sierra crest, it offers the fastest way into the high country of Sequoia National Park. Just beyond the pass is the lateral trail to the top of Mt. Whitney, an easy amble from there.

DESCRIPTION (Strenuous trip)

1st Hiking Day: Follow trip 72 to **Outpost Camp**, 3½ miles.

2nd Hiking Day: (**Outpost Camp** to **Crabtree Ranger Station**, 11½ miles): (This hiking day is a long one, owing to a lack of campsites short of Crabtree Ranger Station, and it involves an ascent of 3400 feet. The prudent hiker will start early.) Our trail veers away from the waterfall that tumbles down into Outpost Camp from the southwest, fords Lone Pine Creek and begins a short series of switchbacks beside the cascading creek past blossoming creambush, Indian paintbrush, Sierra chinquapin, mountain pride, currant, pennyroyal, fireweed and groundsel. Just after the trail crosses a footbridge it arrives at Mirror Lake (10,640′), cradled in its cirque beneath the south face of Thor Peak. This cold lake has fair fishing for rainbow and brook trout, but camping is no longer allowed here. The Forest Service closed the lake to camping in 1972 after severe overuse had created a montane slum. Since then, the lakeshore has begun to recover, and after a great many years it may look something like it did when first discovered.

Leaving Mirror Lake, the trail ascends the south wall of the cirque via switchbacks. Ascending steeply under the north flanks of Mt. Irvine, the rocky trail crosses the south fork of Middle Fork Lone Pine Creek and winds up past giant blocks and granite outcroppings. In the cracks in the boulders the hiker will find ivesia, cinquefoil, creambush, currant and much gooseberry, and looking across the canyon he will see the cascading outlet of Consultation Lake. Beside a rock bridge that crosses the stream are specimens of the moisture-loving shooting star. After ascending over some poured concrete steps—which unfortunately detract from the wilderness feel of this country—the trail arrives at the last campsites before the crest, Trail Camp (12,000'). Here beneath Wotan's Throne is also the last reliable water in late season. There are numerous level campsites.

As the trail begins the exactly 100 switchbacks to Trail Crest Pass, Mt. Whitney disappears behind its needles. The steep, rocky slope up to the crest is not entirely barren, for in season one may see a dozen species of flowering plants, climaxed by the multiflowered, blue "sky pilot." The building of this trail involved much blasting with dynamite, and the natural fracture planes of the granite are evident in the blasted slabs. Finally the 1800-foot ascent from Trail Camp ends at Trail Crest (13,780'), and the hiker suddenly has vistas of a great part of Sequoia National Park to the west, including the entire Great Western Divide. To the east, far below, are several small, unnamed lakes, lying close under the steep faces of Mts. Whitney and Muir. These lakes may be ice-covered well into summer.

From Trail Crest the route descends for a short 100 yards to a junction with the 2-mile lateral to Mt. Whitney (14,495'). The highest mountain in the United States until Alaska was admitted as a state, this peak was first climbed on August 18, 1873, by three fishermen, who made the ascent up the southwest slope. The present trail between this junction and the summit lies close to the crest on the west side of it, and is an easy hike if one doesn't try to fight bad weather and takes proper clothing.

As our switchbacking descent on the west side of the Sierra crest begins, one can make out the Hitchcock Lakes below in a cirque basin that has been changed but little since its glacier melted. The parallel avalanche chutes on the northeast wall of Mt. Hitchcock all terminate at the upper limit of glacial erosion.

Along the switchbacks, the most prominent flower is the yellow, daisylike hulsea, or alpine gold. After the long switchbacks end, the trail follows a moderate descent on a traverse of the "back" side of Mt. Whitney, leveling off at the first possible campsites, overlooking Guitar Lake (not named on the map). From these campsites our route crosses the outlet of Arctic Lake, descends on a moderately steep, rocky trail into a sparse cover of lodgepole, and arrives at Timberline Lake (no camping or grazing, but fair fishing for golden to 7"). After skirting the shore of this lake (viewpoints for focusing the camera on Mt. Whitney and its reflection), the trail fords Whitney Creek, passes a lovely meadow, and then descends the valley of Whitney Creek to the fair campsites near Crabtree Ranger Station, where emergency services are usually available. Fishing in Whitney Creek is fair for golden (to 7"). (During times of heavy trail traffic, the hiker who wants more solitude may choose to camp at Upper Crabtree Meadow, ½ mile southwest of the ranger station, or Lower Crabtree Meadow, 1 mile southwest. These sites are reached by taking the Rock Creek Trail at the junction west of the ranger station.)

3rd and 4th Hiking Days: Retrace your steps, 15 miles.

Mt. Whitney from Timberline Lake

74

Whitney Portal to Wallace Lake

From Whitney Portal to Wallace Lake via Trail
Crest, Crabtree Ranger Station and Wallace Creek
(round trip). Topo maps *Lone Pine, Mt. Whitney.*
Best late season; 47 miles.

Grade	Trail/layover days	Total recom-mended days
Leisurely	....	....
Moderate	8/1	9
Strenuous	6/0	7

HILITES Wallace Lake, lying in the heart of the Mt. Whitney region, is thought by many to be the finest
fishing lake in the region. Well off the "beaten
track" it is also a base from which to climb Mts.
Barnard and Russell.

DESCRIPTION (Strenuous trip)

1st and 2nd Hiking Days: Follow trip 73 to **Crabtree Ranger Station,**
15 miles.

3rd Hiking Day (**Crabtree Ranger Station** to **Wallace Lake,** 8½ miles):
From Crabtree Ranger Station our route branches right (north),
ford Whitney Creek and climbs the north slope of Whitney
Creek canyon into a foxtail-pine forest. On an overcast day, this
foxtail forest, with its dead snags, fallen trees, and lack of ground
cover, has an eerie, gloomy, otherworldly quality. The trail then
switchbacks up to a junction with the justly famous Pacific Crest
Trail. These switchbacks offer the hard-breathing hiker views
of Mts. Hitchcock, Pickering and Chamberlain, and the flanks
of Mt. Whitney, whose summit is over the horizon. From the
ridge, the route descends gently on a sandy trail through a mod-

erate cover of lodgepole and foxtail to a ford (10,636′) of an unnamed creek. Beginning here the trail skirts what is called "Sandy Meadow" on the topo map. Small meadowy sections of trail lie beside several little streams not shown on the topo map, and in season they are graced with the yellow blossoms of groundsel and monkey flower.

After these crossings the trail ascends a moderate slope with a lodgepole canopy and a heavy lupine ground cover to the saddle marked 10,964 on the topo map. From this saddle the route descends gently on a sandy trail around the west shoulder of Mt. Young. Leveling off, the trail winds among some massive boulders that make up a lateral moraine, and then leads down a rocky hillside from which the traveler has fine views of Mt. Ericsson, Tawny Point, Junction Peak, the flank of Mt. Tyndall, Mt. Chester Versteeg, Mt. Williamson, and, farthest right, Mt. Barnard. After the ford of a tributary of Wallace Creek the descent becomes gentle again, through a moderate cover of lodgepole, foxtail and whitebark pines. Beyond the next tributary ford the descent steepens, and the trail switchbacks ¼ mile down to Wallace Creek. Just past the ford (very difficult in early season) the High Sierra Trail and the John Muir Trail, which have been "superimposed" from the top of Mt. Whitney to here, diverge, the High Sierra Trail turning left (west) toward Giant Forest and the Muir Trail continuing north toward Yosemite.

Our route turns right (east) up Wallace Creek canyon. Under a forest cover of sparse-to-moderate lodgepole the trail ascends gently amid sprinklings of western wallflower, penstemon, groundsel, yarrow milfoil and Labrador tea. At the meadow where the outlet of Wales Lake joins Wallace Creek, the trail fords the creek and then fords the tributary, staying on the south side of Wallace Creek. Here the ascent becomes moderate for a short distance, and then reverts to a gentler grade. This route up Wallace Creek canyon is sometimes indistinct and sometimes confused by multiple trail sections and inadequate ducking. Careful negotiation of the indistinct sections will bring one to the fair campsites at timberline (11,400′) about ½ mile below Wallace Lake. Wallace Lake lies beneath the ridge that connects Mt. Barnard with Tunnebora Peak. Fishing in Wallace Lake is good for golden (to 14″), and the same is true of Wales Lake, reached by cross country southwest from the inlet of Wallace Lake.

4th, 5th and 6th Hiking Days: Retrace your steps, 23½ miles.

75 Whitney Portal to Milestone Basin

TRIP		From Whitney Portal to Milestone Basin via Trail Crest, Crabtree Ranger Station, Wallace Creek, Junction Meadow, Upper Kern River and Tyndall Creek (semiloop trip). Topo maps *Lone Pine, Mt. Whitney.* Best mid-to-late season; 59½ miles.

Grade	Trail/layover days	Total recommended days
Leisurely	....	....
Moderate	10/2	12
Strenuous	8/1	9

HILITES This trip samples both well-traveled trails and little-used trails, country above timberline and deep, dense forests. Milestone Basin, set under the giant finger of Milestone Mountain, is remote enough to suit the solitude-seeking hiker, and the lakes piscatorial enough to suit the most avid angler.

DESCRIPTION (Strenuous trip)

1st 2 Hiking Days: Follow trip 73 to **Crabtree Ranger Station**, 15 miles.

3rd Hiking Day (**Crabtree Ranger Station** to **Upper Kern River**, 8½ miles): Follow the 3rd hiking day, trip 74, to the junction of the John Muir Trail and the High Sierra Trail at Wallace Creek. Taking the High Sierra Trail from this junction, our route proceeds down Wallace Creek canyon on sandy underfooting, with views ahead of Mt. Kaweah and the Kaweah Peaks Ridge. The trail veers away from Wallace Creek and then meets it again after a short, moderate descent on an exposed slope. Our trail passes campsites lining both sides as it winds among sparse-to-moderate lodgepole and a great variety of wildflowers (in mid-summer), including fireweed, paintbrush, arnica, sulfur flower, wild buckwheat, pennyroyal, mountain pride and creamberry. After fording Wright Creek (difficult in early season), the trail descends more steeply through sparse lodgepole mixed with some foxtail pines.

As the canyon widens and the trail· veers more westward, the timber cover diminishes almost to nothing, and the slope (hot in afternoon) is covered with manzanita, creambush, holly-leaf redberry, mountain mahogany and Sierra chinquapin. The main splash of color in this chaparral is the red penstemon, or mountain pride. This exposed slope offers views down the great trough of the Kern River, south to Mt. Guyot and west to Kaweah Peaks Ridge. The descent now reaches the Canadian life zone as Jeffrey pines are seen, along with mountain juniper. Here our route turns northward and traverses down the Kern Canyon wall to meet the Kern River Trail, onto which it turns right (north), leaving the High Sierra Trail. One mile up the canyon our route passes a decaying roofless cabin. Beginning here there are several good campsites along the river, where fishing is good for rainbow (to 10″). These are the Kern River rainbow, *Salmo gairdneri gilberti,* found only in the upper Kern River.

4th Hiking Day (**Upper Kern River** to **Milestone Basin**, 6 miles): Once past the cabin, the trail ascends less steeply, and soon it reaches a ford of Tyndall Creek (difficult in early season). Beyond the ford, the trail becomes sandier and drier, and the red fir and aspen gradually disappear, leaving a forest cover of lodgepole and some foxtail that is sparse on the hillsides and moderate on the river terraces. There are numerous campsites along this stretch of trail, including a packer campsite ½ mile beyond the Tyndall Creek Trail. Beyond this trail, our route becomes more exposed, with considerable sagebrush. After the trail fords the outlet stream of Lake 11440, we soon come to a dell thick with lodgepole trunks. The excellent wildflower display in this large dell is dominated by groundsel, but also includes tiger lilies, swamp onions and red columbine. Then the trail ascends above the dell and passes through a bank of shield fern, Queen Anne's lace and bush chinquapin, staying on the east side of the river. Here our route ascends steeply through a sparse lodgepole cover on a rocky trail over granite slabs that rise 600 feet to the upper Kern plateau. After the trail levels off, it soon reaches a signed junction with the Milestone Basin Trail, where our route turns left (west). From this junction, continue as in the last part of the 2nd hiking day, trip 69.

5th Hiking Day (**Milestone Basin** to **Tyndall Creek Tributary**, 6 miles): Reverse the steps of the 2nd hiking day, trip 69, from Milestone Basin to the ford at the John Muir Trail/Shepherd Pass Trail junction, where our route turns right (south) on the John Muir Trail. The rocky trail ascends gently along the east flank of Tawny Point through a sparse-to-moderate cover of lodgepole and foxtail pines past many poor campsites, and then arrives at the good campsites on a tributary of Tyndall Creek (11,000'), near a small lake where swimming is good in late season.

6th Hiking Day (**Tyndall Creek Tributary** to **Crabtree Ranger Station**, 9 miles): Reverse the 3rd hiking day, trip 77.

7th and 8th Hiking Days: Retrace the 2nd and 1st hiking days, 15 miles.

Lakelet on Tyndall Creek tributary

Whitney Portal to Kern-Kaweah River   **76**

TRIP   From Whitney Portal to Kern-Kaweah River via
Trail Crest, Crabtree Meadow, Wallace Creek,
Junction Meadow (round trip). Topo maps *Lone
Pine, Mt. Whitney.* Best mid-to-late season; 61
miles.

Grade	Trail/layover days	Total recom- mended day
Leisurely	....	....
Moderate	10/2	12
Strenuous	8/1	9

HILITES   This route combines the high, rocky country along
the Whitney crest with the alluvial meadows on
the Kern River and the intimate camping in the
little-visited Kern-Kaweah River canyon.

DESCRIPTION (Strenuous trip)

1st and 2nd Hiking Days: Follow trip 73 to **Crabtree Ranger Station,**
15 miles.

3rd Hiking Day (**Crabtree Ranger Station** to **Junction Meadow,** 9½
miles): Follow the 3rd hiking day, trip 75, to the junction of the
High Sierra Trail and the Kern River Trail, and turn left (south).
From here the rocky trail descends steeply to Junction Meadow
through stands of aspen and past occasional Jeffrey and lodgepole pines, winding through a ground cover of manzanita and
currant. As the trail levels off, it enters a parklike grove of stalwart Jeffrey pines that provide the setting for the good campsites near the Kern River. Fishing is good for rainbow and some
brook trout (to 10").

4th Hiking Day (**Junction Meadow** to **Kern-Kaweah River**, 6 miles):
This day's route is unmaintained, but a backpacker with any
experience will have no trouble staying on the route. Soon after
the ford of the Kern River (very difficult in early season) the
trail begins the steep ascent up the Kern canyon wall to the
hanging valley above. Veering away from the Kern-Kaweah
River, it ascends to the north side of a granite knob, or spine,
and passes through what has been called "Kern-Kaweah Pass."
This difficult climb is repaid by the delightful valley above it,
one of the finest in the Sierra. From the "pass" the trail descends slightly to Rockslide Lake, with its crystal-clear, emerald-
green water. Just beyond the lake, the canyon widens into a
kind of granite amphitheater, where two tributary streams,
meeting, dash into the main canyon over a rocky ledge, to meet
the main river below the fall by which the river arrives at the
bowl. From here the ascent through a sparse-to-moderate lodgepole cover is moderate as the trail threads the deep canyon
lying between Kern Point and Picket Guard Peak. One more
steep ascent is required to reach the bowl that contains Gallats
Lake, a pond in a large, wet meadow (fishing is good for golden
to 8″). Fair campsites are here, but the traveler will prefer those
about 1 mile ahead where the trail turns away from the river
toward Colby Pass, where fishing is excellent for golden (to
7″). These campsites are a good explorer's base for excursions
into the lightly visited headwaters of the Kern-Kaweah River
and into Milestone Bowl.

5th, 6th, 7th and 8th Hiking Days: Retrace your steps, 30½
miles.

Mt. Whitney from the northwest   *Jim Barker*

Whitney Portal to Symmes Creek Trailhead   **77**

TRIP   From Whitney Portal to Symmes Creek Trailhead via Trail Crest, Crabtree Meadow, Tyndall Creek, Shepherd Pass (shuttle trip). Topo maps *Lone Pine, Mt. Whitney.* Best mid-to-late season; 39 miles.

Grade	Trail/layover days	Total recommended days
Leisurely	....	....
Moderate	6/2	8
Strenuous	5/0	5

HILITES   This high trip loops around "the Whitney group," the culmination of the Sierra spine, with five peaks standing over 14,000 feet. A spur trail will take the hiker to the highest point in the contiguous 48 states, 14,495 feet above sea level. The vast panoramas of the upper Kern basin along this route are unequalled in the Sierra.

DESCRIPTION (Strenuous trip)

1st and 2nd Hiking Days: Follow trip 73 to **Crabtree Ranger Station**, 15 miles.

3rd Hiking Day (**Crabtree Ranger Station** to **Tyndall Creek Tributary**, 9 miles): Follow the 3rd hiking day, trip 74, to the junction of the John Muir Trail and the High Sierra Trail. From Wallace Creek, this day's route continues north on the John Muir Trail.

The sandy and rocky trail ascends moderately through a sparse-to-moderate forest cover, to an overlook that photographers will want to utilize for photographs of the Great Western Divide. Here the trail becomes quite level as it crosses a sandy flat bearing a forest cover of lodgepole and foxtail pines. The trail crosses Wright Creek via a rocky ford (difficult in early season) and passes some campsites located east of the trail.

Several short but taxing ascents separated by level stretches bring the hiker out onto Bighorn Plateau, where the panoramic view begins with Red Spur in the southwest and sweeps north along the Great Western Divide and east along the Kings-Kern Divide to Junction Peak. In addition, one can see, to the southeast, Mts. Whitney, Young and Russell. A small lake west of the trail presents great photographic possibilities in the morning, and any time of day is good for photographing the lateral moraine of the Tyndall Creek glacier, which follows a contour along the west side of the plateau. Color is provided by a large field of lupine sweeping up the slope to the east. From here a gentle descent on a rocky trail through a sparse foxtail cover leads to the good campsites (11,100') where the trail crosses the outlet of a small lake (no fish) which offers good swimming in mid and late season.

4th Hiking Day **(Tyndall Creek Tributary** to **Anvil Camp**, 7½ miles): As this hiking day begins, the John Muir Trail descends gently on a rocky course through a forest cover of mixed lodgepole and foxtail pines to a junction with the Shepherd Pass Trail. Our route turns right (east) off the Muir Trail and begins a long, steady ascent up the meadowy, boulder-strewn upper basin of

The Great Western Divide from near Bighorn Plateau

Tyndall Creek. Views improve constantly as the traveler gains elevation, and the peaks of the Great Western Divide take on new aspects as they are seen from new angles. To the north, the southern escarpment of Diamond Mesa hides an upper surface that is one of the most level areas in this region. The traveler who has read the incredible first chapter of Clarence King's *Mountaineering in the Sierra Nevada* may speculate on where King and Richard Cotter crossed the Kings-Kern Divide and traversed this basin on their way to ascending Mt. Tyndall— which, in naming, they believed to be the highest Sierra peak until they were on top of it and saw other, higher ones nearby.

The appearance of Lake 12002 heralds the approach to Shepherd Pass (12,050'), which from this side of the crest is merely the end of a long, gentle ascent. The east side of the pass is a total contrast, with its steep scree and talus slopes which are often not passable to stock until August. From the pass, the trail switchbacks down a 500-foot scree slope into a gigantic, barren bowl scooped out by the plucking action of the Shepherd Creek glacier. After winding among boulders and topping a slight rise, the trail begins a moderate descent to timberline and a poor campsite near a junction with the Junction Pass Trail. Our rocky trail continues to descend moderately through a cover of sparse lodgepole to a ford of Shepherd Creek and the good campsites at Anvil Camp (10,000'), where fishing for rainbow (to 9") is fair.

5th Hiking Day (**Anvil Camp** to **Symmes Creek Trailhead**, 7½ miles): Reverse the 1st hiking day, trip 68.

78   Lodgepole Campground to Ranger Lakes

TRIP   From Lodgepole Campground to Ranger Lakes via Silliman Pass (round trip). Topo map *Triple Divide Peak.* Best mid-to-late season; 17 miles.

Grade	Trail/layover days	Total recom-mended days
Leisurely	....	....
Moderate	2/1	3
Strenuous	2/0	2

HILITES   Crossing the Silliman Crest on the boundary of Sequoia and Kings Canyon parks, this trip terminates at picturesque Ranger Lakes. En route, the trail passes through sedate fir forests, traces rambling brooks, and circles crystal-clear lakes.

DESCRIPTION (Moderate trip)

1st Hiking Day (**Lodgepole Campground** to **Ranger Lakes**, 8½ miles): The trail begins north of a bridge over the Marble Fork Kaweah River (6800′), and after a few yards of northward travel turns west on a moderate ascent through a dense forest cover of fir and cedar. This ascent, over alternating rocky and sandy stretches, then turns north and levels to a ford of Silliman Creek. These woods teem with wildlife, and the traveler is very apt to see a few mule deer, many squirrels, and a host of birds that will include Steller jay, pygmy nuthatch, Hammond flycatcher (until late summer), Williamson sapsucker, Brewer blackbird, fox sparrow and Lincoln sparrow. After two more fords of Silliman Creek, the trail continues the moderate ascent over duff and sand underfooting through patchy, dense stands of red and white fir and some meadow sections to Cahoon Gap. The trail then descends moderately to a ford of the unnamed tributary just south of East Fork Clover Creek. One fourth mile beyond this ford the trail veers east as the JO Pass Trail goes north, and then we ford East Fork Clover Creek.

The sometimes gentle, sometimes moderate ascent up East Fork Clover Creek witnesses the inclusion of lodgepole and silver pine in the forest cover, and as the trail approaches Twin Lakes, open stretches between the trees are a tide of colors. In season, one will find rank, knee-high corn lily, blue and white lupine, white mariposa lily, orange wallflower, purple larkspur, lavender shooting star, white cinquefoil, violet aster and golden groundsel. The last mile to the heavily timbered flats around Twin Lakes is a steep ascent, and the traveler may well contemplate a quick swim in the largest lake, whose shallow waters quickly warm to a midsummer's sun.

Continuing toward Silliman Pass, the view of the two large boulder stands of exfoliating granite (Twin Peaks) dominates the horizon during the steep progress to the pass' saddle. This ascent sees the end of the fir, and the almost exclusive domination of lodgepole pine. At the pass (10,165') one has a good view of flat-topped Mt. Silliman to the south, the heavily wooded Sugarloaf Creek drainage to the northeast, the Great Western Divide to the east, and the barren flats of the Tableland to the southeast. The descent from the pass drops steeply and then turns north to the nose of a granite ridge before switchbacking down. From the switchbacks one has fine views of Ball Dome, and of much of the Kings River watershed, including Monarch Divide. At the foot of the switchbacks a level duff trail leads off to the larger of the Ranger Lakes, and to the excellent campsites on the southwest side of the lake. Anglers working their way around the shallow lake plying their art on the fair-to-good fishing for rainbow trout (8–12″) will also enjoy the carpet of shooting stars and the rose-purple blossom of the heather. A layover day spent in this pleasant environment will allow the traveler to visit the nearby scenic settings of Beville (rainbow and brook), Lost (brook) and Seville (brook) lakes.

2nd Hiking Day: Retrace your steps, 8½ miles.

79 Lodgepole Campground to Scaffold Meadows

TRIP

From Lodgepole Campground to Scaffold Meadows via Silliman Pass, Ranger Lakes, Sugarloaf Valley (round trip). Topo map *Triple Divide Peak*. Best mid or late season; 43 miles.

Grade	Trail/layover days	Total recommended days
Leisurely	6/2	8
Moderate	5/2	7
Strenuous	4/2	6

HILITES

Scaffold Meadows, the terminus of this long trip, makes a superb location for a base camp. From here, one can explore the upper reaches of several remote drainages, and in the course of these explorations enjoy some of the finest fishing of the Roaring River country.

DISCRIPTION (Leisurely trip)

1st Hiking Day: Follow trip 78 to **Ranger Lakes**, 8½ miles.

2nd Hiking Day (**Ranger Lakes** to **Comanche Meadow**, 5½ miles): After rounding the east side of a rocky prominence on the east side of the larger Ranger Lake, the faintly ducked trail undulates northward, passes the turnoff to Lost Lake and circles Ball Dome. Passing through a moderate-to-heavy forest cover, the trail emerges at a meadowed crossing of the outlet stream from Seville Lake. Beyond this crossing, the junction of the Seville Lake/Marvin Pass Trail is poorly marked, but the trail is clear. Keeping right, on the northwest side of Sugarloaf Creek, our route descends sometimes steadily and sometimes moderately over duff-and-sand underfooting. This descent crosses an unnamed tributary, and a short distance beyond passes another trail to Marvin Pass. About 100 yards farther on, the trail passes the Kanawyer Gap Trail, which leads north and then west to Marvin Pass, and then fords the rocky creek emptying Comanche Meadow (7680′). Good campsites will be found on Sugarloaf Creek before and after this ford, and fishing for book trout (to 8′) is fair.

3rd Hiking Day (**Comanche Meadow** to **Scaffold Meadows**, 7½ miles): Beginning ¼ mile after the ford, the trail drops moderately on sandy underfooting over a heavily forested slope that shows the effects of a 1974 fire. Then, as the trail levels out on the floor of Sugarloaf Valley, the dome from which the name is derived can be seen through the trees. More resistant than the surrounding rock, this granite island withstood the onslaught of the ice, and today it stands as a round, smooth 1000-foot-high reminder of the ice river that carved the valley. Following the course of this old glacier through sporadic meadows, the trail parallels and then fords Sugarloaf Creek.

On the south side of this wide, shallow ford, the trail passes more campsites before crossing a series of sharp wrinkles in the terrain to reach Ferguson Creek and still more campsites. After fording this creek via logs or rocks, the trail rounds a long, dry, timbered ridge nose before dropping down a steady slope to the drift fence below Scaffold Meadows. Living up to its name, Roaring River can be heard a few yards to the left, and with this pleasant accompaniment the trail ascends the last, gentle mile to the good campsites (7360′), fording the Barton Peak stream on the way. Fishing for rainbow and some golden trout (to 10″) is fair to good. Emergency services are usually available from the resident summer ranger, whose cabin is nearby. These campsites make a fine base camp for further explorations of the surrounding headwaters of Deadman Canyon Creek, Roaring River and Brewer Creek.

4th 5th and 6th Hiking Days: Retrace your steps, 21½ miles.

Roaring River Ranger Station   *National Park Service*

80   Lodgepole Campground to Ranger Meadow

TRIP   From Lodgepole Campground to Ranger Meadow
via Silliman Pass, Ranger Lakes, Sugarloaf Valley,
Scaffold Meadows, Deadman Canyon, return via
Elizabeth Pass, High Sierra Trail, Panther Gap to
Crescent Meadow (shuttle trip). Topo map *Triple
Divide Peak.* Best late season; 50½ miles.

Grade	Trail/layover days	Total recommended days
Leisurely	....	....
Moderate	6/2	8
Strenuous	4/2	6

HILITES   The climax of this trip is the high, wildflower-filled
meadows at the head of Deadman Canyon. Seldom
visited because of its remoteness, this glaciated
canyon nestles against the craggy summits of Glacier Ridge in solitary splendor.

DESCRIPTION (Moderate trip)

1st 3 Hiking Days: Follow trip 79 to **Scaffold Meadows**, 21½ miles.

4th Hiking Day (**Scaffold Meadows** to **Upper Ranger Meadow**, 7
miles): Leaving Scaffold Meadows, our trail leads south while
veering away from the river on a gentle-to-moderate ascent past
well-charred Jeffrey pines. Views back over one's left shoulder
include a fine example of a lateral moraine in the form of Moraine
Ridge, the northeast wall of the canyon. About 1½ miles above
the Roaring River bridge, our route ascends past the upper drift
fence and several more campsites. At the right time of summer,
flowers seen during this short stretch include buckwheat, sagebrush, Indian paintbrush, white Mariposa, pennyroyal, penstemon and shooting star. Past the drift fence, the trail fords

Copper Creek, and in 1½ miles reaches a packer campsite and then a gravesite. Located at the north end of a large, wet meadow, about 50 yards southeast of the campsite, the grave marks the derivation of the name Deadman Canyon. The citation on the grave reads: "Here reposes Alfred Moniere, sheepherder, mountain man, 18–– to 1887."

From this grave our ascent continues, offering good views up the canyon of the spectacularly smoothed, unjointed, barren walls. Soon the trail refords the creek and then climbs alongside a dramatic, green-water, granite-slab chute. At the end of this ascent, the trail levels out as it passes through a dense stand of lodgepole and fir, and, passing a campsite, emerges at the north end of the open grasslands of Ranger Meadow. The precipitous canyon walls dominate the views from the meadow, and the cirque holding Big Bird Lake is clear on the west wall. By midsummer the meadow is a colorful carpet of wildflowers, including shooting star, penstemon and red heather.

From Ranger Meadow the trail resumes its steady ascent over duff and sand through stands of lodgepole and clumps of aspen. Just before the Upper Ranger Meadow flat, the route fords the creek to the east side. Here one has awesome glimpses of the headwall of the Deadman Canyon cirque, and this view continues to rule the skyline from the good campsites just beyond the drift fence at the north end of Upper Ranger Meadow. Fishing for rainbow, brook and hybrids is good (to 10").

5th Hiking Day (**Upper Ranger Meadow** to **Bearpaw Meadow**, 11 miles, part cross country): Just south of the campsites cited above, the trail passes a faint spur trail leading to scenic Big Bird Lake and ascends gently across grassy Upper Ranger Meadow. Low-lying willows line the stream, and clumps of wildflowers dot the green expanse. The ascent steepens to a moderate grade; then, as we begin the steep ascent of the headwall, we parallel a dramatic series of cascades and falls. Near the top of the falls, the trail fords the stream below a long, dashing granite chute, and then we climb steeply by a faint, infrequently ducked route up the southwest wall of the cirque. This barren, rocky climb over light-colored granite slabs contrasts with the darker metamorphic rocks (around an old copper-mine site) seen to the east, and this contrast is even more marked from the tiny saddle of Elizabeth Pass (11,380'). Views to the southwest from the pass include parts of the Middle Fork Kaweah River watershed, and the jumbled peaks of the southernmost prominences of the Tableland divide.

From the pass, the ducked trail descends steeply via a long, smooth granite trough to a ford of an unnamed tributary of Lone

Pine Creek. After a moderately descending traverse, the trail descends the steep northern wall of River Valley via a series of rocky switchbacks. At the foot of these zigzags, our route passes a spur trail to Tamarack Lake, and then, in ¼ mile, a trail that leads south to the High Sierra Trail. At the second junction our route swings southwest across the sparsely timbered nose of the ridge above Bearpaw Meadow. The descent from this ridge is steep, rocky and dry as it passes through stands of lodgepole and red fir and joins the High Sierra Trail 150 yards west of a ranger station. On this trail we go left a few yards and then turn right to reach a campground overlooking the Middle Fork Kaweah River canyon. Emergency services are usually available at the ranger station just east of where we left the High Sierra Trail.

7th Hiking Day (**Bearpaw Meadow** to **Crescent Meadow**, 11 miles): Reverse the 1st hiking day, trip 81.

Rae Lakes, Painted Lady   *Tom Ross*

Crescent Meadow to Whitney Portal

TRIP

From Crescent Meadow to Whitney Portal via Hamilton Lakes, Kaweah Gap, Junction Meadow, Wallace Creek, Crabtree Meadow and Trail Crest (shuttle trip). Topo maps *Triple Divide Peak, Kern Peak, Mt. Whitney, Lone Pine.* Best mid-to-late season; 68½ miles.

Grade	Trail/layover days	Total recom- mended days
Leisurely	....	....
Moderate	8/3	11
Strenuous	6/2	8

HILITES

Most of this dramatic trans-Sierra route follows the High Sierra Trail—a trail that is, in its early stages, literally carved out of the rock. After crossing the Great Western Divide, it descends to the Kern Trench, and later emerges on the east side at Whitney Portal. The scenic terrain it visits, and the fine trout waters it crosses or camps near, make it a justly famous and popular route.

DESCRIPTION (Moderate trip)

1st Hiking Day (**Crescent Meadow** to **Bearpaw Meadow,** 11 miles): From the parking loop, we circumvent the meadow on asphalt and begin climbing through a grove of giant sequoias. Soon after passing a trail leading to Giant Forest, we break out into the open above Middle Fork Kaweah River at Eagle View Overlook, and the view is indeed awesome. Moro Rock pokes up in the west, far below is the river, and to the east is the high country. Soon one is far enough from the road and its crowds to begin saying "hello" to people along the trail. One of the best things about wilderness is that many of the citified psychological barriers between a person and his fellows are fast discarded.

The trail erratically rises and falls as we move up-canyon in a forest of ponderosa and sugar pine, black oak, incense-cedar, bigleaf maple and even some bay trees, mixed with manzanita and whitethorn scrub. Across the canyon, those impressive sentinels of the valley, Castle Rocks, fall slowly behind as we march on. Soon we pass a cutoff to Wolverton Corral in the north. Innumerable spring-fed streams cross the trail here late into the season, and even a hot afternoon start on this hike is not too bad. Yellow-throated gilia and mustang clover are abundant along the trail until rather late in the year. Beyond Sevenmile Hill, a prominent ridge jutting out in the canyon below, we pass a junction with a trail that leads up to the Alta Trail 1300 feet above.

Our trail does not follow a "natural" route, but instead stays high on the north wall of the Middle Fork Kaweah River canyon. It is not a level traverse: frequently, the trail undulates over 400-foot rises, only to drop down into a secondary tributary canyon, and then emerge to climb again. From the Alta Trail junction, the trail descends to ford an unnamed tributary and then climb steeply. Views are all to the south and southeast, where the spectacular granite-dome formations of Sugarbowl Dome and Castle Rocks rise above the timbered valley floor. At each ford of the unnamed tributaries flowing from the slopes of Alta Peak, the trail passes precariously perched campsites, and then as it rounds a hot, dry, sparsely timbered slope to the Buck Creek bridge, it passes the faint, abandoned Moose Lake Trail. From here the route ascends through dense fir forest cover to the signed turnoff to a campground 200 yards south. Here, fair campsites (7700´) enjoy fine views of the canyon to the south and southwest. Emergency services are usually available from the ranger station just east of the campground turnoff.

2nd Hiking Day (**Bearpaw Meadow** to **Big Arroyo Trail Junction**, 11 miles): Returning to the High Sierra Trail, our route turns right (east), and soon passes expansive, green Bearpaw Meadow, said to have been named by early stockmen who found a bear's paw nailed to a tree. Today, most of the meadow is devoted to the outbuildings of Bearpaw Lodge (advance reservations for beds and board are advisable). Just across the trail from the lodge is the ranger's cabin. The magnificent views from the meadow and the subsequent trail include Mt. Stewart and Eagle Scout Peak on the Great Western Divide, Black Kaweah beyond, the Yosemite-like depths of Hamilton Creek and Middle Fork Kaweah River, and the Cliff Creek drainage below. Continuing past Bearpaw Ranger Station, the trail descends moderately through mixed, sparse forest stands. As the trail rounds the slope and descends toward River Valley, it traverses a section blasted from an immense, exfoliating granite slab. Educational views of clearcut avalanche chutes on the south wall of the canyon accompany the descent to the culvert fording wild, turbulent Lone Pine Creek. This stream cascades and plunges down a narrow granite chasm below the culvert, and the force of the torrent is clear evidence of the cutting power of the water. From the creek, the trail ascends an exposed slope, passing a side trail to Tamarack Lake and Elizabeth Pass (good campsites at this junction).

Continuing the steady ascent, the traveler is overwhelmed with the gigantic scale of the rock sculpting by ice, rock and snow to the east and southeast. The trail surface, while mostly rocky, passes occasional clumps of brightly colored wildflowers, including scarlet gilia, Douglas phlox, fleabane, Indian paintbrush, penstemon, mountain bluebell, red columbine and larkspur. Overshadowing the final climb to the ford of Hamilton Creek, the sheer granite wall to the north called Angel Wings, the sharply pointed granite sentinels atop the south wall, and the wall's avalanche-chuted sides are a constant source of wonderment and awe. Under these heights the trail climbs alongside the stream and then boulder-hops across it a few hundred yards below the lowest lake of the Hamilton Lakes chain. From this ford the trail climbs steeply over shattered rock to the good campsites at the northwest end of Lake 8235. Views from the campsites, including the silver waterfall ribbon at the east end, are superlative, and fishing for brook, rainbow and golden (to 10″) is fair to good, but the lake is highly overused, and we head for Kaweah Gap.

The steep climb to Kaweah Gap is an engineering marvel of trail construction, which has literally blasted the way along vertical cliff sections. Beginning at the northwest end of the lake, the trail ascends steadily up the juniper-and-red-fir-dotted slope with constant views of the lake and its dramatic walls. Despite the rocky terrain, many wildflowers line this ascent and among the manzanita and chinquapin one will find lush lupine, yellow columbine, penstemon, Indian paintbrush, white cinquefoil,

false Solomon's seal and Douglas phlox. After some doubling back, the trail turns south on a steep ascent to a point just above the north shore of Precipice Lake, at the foot of the near-vertical north face of Eagle Scout Peak. The jagged summits of the peaks of the Great Western Divide dominate the skyline to the east during the final, tarn-dotted ascent to U-shaped Kaweah Gap, but as one approaches the gap one can see the equally spectacular summits of the Kaweah Peaks Ridge beyond. This colorful ridge dominates the views from Kaweah Gap (10,700'), and one can see the Nine Lake Basin watershed to the north. Those with a bent for exploring barren high country, or interested in the good brook-trout fishing, may elect to detour across granite slab and ledge routes north to the Nine Lake Basin.

Our trail continues its steady-to-moderate southward descent along the west side of the headwaters of Big Arroyo Creek, fording over to the east side midway down. This descent crosses unjointed granite broken by substantial pockets of grass and numerous runoff streams even in late season, and the open stretches afford fine views of the U-shaped, glacially wrought Big Arroyo below, and the white, red and black rocks of Black Kaweah and Red Kaweah peaks to the east. The trail then reenters timber cover and arrives at some good campsites along the stream (9600'). These campsites and an abandoned trail-crew cabin are about ¼ mile above the Little Five Lakes/ Black Rock Pass Trail junction. Fishing for brook trout to 7" is fair to good. For those anglers with extra time, the 2-mile side trip to Little Five Lakes offers fine angling for golden trout.

3rd Hiking Day (**Big Arroyo Trail Junction** to **Moraine Lake**, 8 miles): Continuing past the Little Five Lakes Trail junction, the trail begins a long, steady traverse of the north side of Big Arroyo which culminates at the Chagoopa Plateau. This route parallels the course of a trunk glacier that once filled Big Arroyo, overflowed the benches on either side, and contributed to the main glacier of Kern Canyon. Our route climbs the wall of this trough, and the timber cover of this ascent is sparse, but there is no shortage of wildflowers tucked among the sage, manzanita and chinquapin. Most colorful are yellow columbine, Indian paintbrush and lupine. The sparse forest cover thickens near the Chagoopa Plateau, and one will find lodgepole and foxtail pines, and an occasional juniper.

The trail levels off near a small, mirror-faced tarn, and, swinging away north from the lip of Big Arroyo, it begins a gradual descent through alternating timber and meadow stretches. Tree-interrupted views of the jagged Great Western

Left: Moose Lake at lower left, Mt. Whitney tallest on skyline, Kaweah Gap near upper right

Divide skyline accompany the descent to a meadowed trail junction on the south side of a tributary of Chagoopa Creek. At this junction our route leaves the High Sierra Trail, and branches right (south) through meadowed clumps of shooting stars. This descent becomes steeper over coarse granite sand, through dense stands of lodgepole and foxtail pine. It is time well spent during this descent to step a hundred yards west of the trail for the superlative views down into Big Arroyo and across the Arroyo to the drainages of Soda and Lost Canyon creeks. This steadily down-winding trail brings one to the wooded shores of Moraine Lake. Good campsites on the south side of the lake (9290′) provide lake-fronted views back to the Kaweah Peaks, and gardens of wild azalea in season.

4th Hiking Day (**Moraine Lake** to **Kern Hot Spring**, 7 miles): After traversing a moraine just east of Moraine Lake, the trail descends moderately, then gently, passing an old stockman's cabin before reaching superb Sky Parlor Meadow. Views back across this flower-filled grassland to the Great Western Divide and the Kaweahs are excellent. A half mile beyond the ford of Funston Creek at the east end of the meadow, the route rejoins the High Sierra Trail and begins the moderate, then steep descent to the bottom of the Kern Trench. The initial descent sees the lodgepole being replaced by the lower-altitude white

Moraine Lake   *Ron Van Cleave*

fir and Jeffrey pine; and still lower down, the trail descends steeply through manzanita and snow bush that are overshadowed by an occasional juniper and oak. Views of the unmistakably U-shaped Kern Trench, typical of glacially carved valleys, are instructive—particularly to the south. The final climb down to the valley floor is accomplished via a series of steep, rocky switchbacks generally paralleling the plunging drop of Funston Creek. On the Kern Canyon floor our route turns north, upstream, on the Kern River Trail, drops into a marshy area, and then crosses the river on a wood bridge. Then the trail leads gently up through a forest of Jeffrey pine and incense-cedar. High on the western rim of the canyon one catches glimpses of Chagoopa Falls, a fury of plunging white water. Past a manzanita-carpeted open area the trail arrives at the southern fork of Rock Creek. Then, around a point, we arrive at the delightful mountain spa of Kern Hot Spring—a treat for the tired, dusty hiker. To the traveler, the crude, cemented bathtub here becomes a regal, heated (115°) pool. Only a few feet away, the great Kern River rushes past, and its cold waters can be dipped into to cool the hot-spring water as desired. In the river near the campsites, fishing is good for brown, rainbow and golden trout (to 10″).

5th Hiking Day (**Kern Hot Spring** to **Junction Meadow**, 8 miles): Continuing north, we ford the upper fork of Rock Creek and traverse the gravelly canyon floor below the immense granite cliffs of the canyon's east wall. Past the confluence of Red Spur Creek this route ascends gently, sometimes a bit stiffly, beside the Kern River, heading almost due north. The U-shaped trough of the Kern River, called the Kern Trench, is remarkably straight for about 25 miles as it traces the Kern Canyon fault. The fault, a zone of structural weakness in the Sierra batholith, is more susceptible to erosion than the surrounding rock, and this deep canyon has been carved by both glacial and stream action. Three times the glacier advanced down the canyon, shearing off spurs created by stream erosion and leaving some tributary valleys hanging above the main valley. The glacier also scooped and plucked at the bedrock, creating basins in the granite which became lakes when the glacier melted and retreated.

The walls of this deep canyon, from 2000 to 5000 feet high, are quite spectacular, and a number of streams cascade and fall down these walls. (The fords of the stream draining Guyot Flat, of Whitney Creek and of Wallace Creek can be difficult in early season.) Beyond the ford of Wallace Creek the trail enters a parklike grove of stalwart Jeffrey pines that provide a noble setting for the good campsites on the Kern River, where fishing is good for rainbow and some brook trout (to 10″).

6th Hiking Day (**Junction Meadow** to **Crabtree Ranger Station**, 8½ miles): Our trail leaves the parklike Jeffrey pines of Junction Meadow and ascends steeply on rocky underfooting over a slope covered by manzanita and currant. Views down the Kern Trench improve constantly, as the occasional Jeffrey, lodgepole and aspen offer frames for the photographer who would compose a "shot" of the great cleft. After one mile we arrive at the junction of the Kern River Trail and the High Sierra Trail, where our route turns right (southeast), back toward Wallace Creek canyon. From here, reverse most of the 3rd hiking day, trip. 75.

7th and 8th Hiking Days: Reverse the 2nd and 1st hiking days, trip 73, 15 miles.

Kaweah Peaks Ridge

Crescent Meadow to Mt. Whitney

	Trail/layover days	Total recommended days
Grade		
Leisurely	....	....
Moderate	13/3	16
Strenuous	10/1	11

TRIP   From Crescent Meadow to Mt. Whitney via Hamilton Lake, Kaweah Gap, Big Arroyo, Junction Meadow, Wallace Creek, Crabtree Ranger Station, return via Tyndall Creek, Upper Kern River to Junction Meadow (semiloop trip). Topo maps *Giant Forest, Triple Divide Peak, Kern Peak, Mt. Whitney*. Best mid to late season; 136 miles.

HILITES   Many people plan for years to climb Mt. Whitney
from Giant Forest, via the well-named High Sierra
Trail. This trip repays the planning, and adds the
dividend of getting off the main track during a
looping return from the great peak. A food cache at
Crabtree Ranger Station is almost a must.

DESCRIPTION (Moderate trip)

1st, 2nd, 3rd, 4th, 5th and 6th Hiking Days: Follow trip 81 to
Crabtree Ranger Station, 53½ miles.

Layover Day, 18 miles: This "layover" day is the most strenuous
of the trip. The hiker should begin as early as possible. He
might camp on the Mt. Whitney Trail ½ mile above Crabtree
Ranger Station in a small meadow on Whitney Creek, or hike
after dinner to Guitar Lake and sleep there. Those with stoves
can of course cook as high as they choose to.

From Crabtree Ranger Station our route ascends the narrow
canyon of Whitney Creek. Past a small meadow we arrive at
Timberline Lake (no camping, but fair fishing for golden trout).
Then the trail ascends somewhat steeply past the last pine trees,
crosses the outlet of Arctic Lake, and traverses above Guitar
Lake to a wet meadow where the "fun" begins. Switchback is
piled upon steep switchback until the panting hiker has to stop
for breath, only to confront another series of switchbacks. Little
windbreaks at the few flat places tell of westbound hikers who
were too tired to make it down to Crabtree Meadows. Finally,
after more than 1500 feet of climbing, we reach the side trail
that leads to the summit. If, while on top, you should wonder
how John Muir felt the first time he climbed Mt. Whitney, be it
noted that he later wrote, "I reached the summit needles about
11 o'clock that night and danced most of the time until morning,
as the night was bitterly cold and I was in my shirtsleeves."

7th Hiking Day (**Crabtree Ranger Station** to **Lake on Upper Kern
River,** 13½ miles): Follow the 3rd hiking day, trip 77 to the Tyndall Creek tributary. From this ford we descend gently on a
rocky trail through a forest cover of mixed lodgepole and foxtail pine to a junction with the Shepherd Pass Trail. From here,
our route northwest follows part of the 2nd hiking day, trip 69,
to the unnamed lake with elevation 10,650 feet. This natural
impoundment on the Kern River has good campsites and good
fishing for golden and rainbow-golden hybrids (to 10″).

8th Hiking Day (**Lake on Upper Kern River** to **Junction Meadow,**
6 miles): Follow the 3rd hiking day, trip 70.

9th–13th Hiking Days (**Junction Meadow** to **Crescent Meadow,** 45
miles): Retrace the steps of the first 5 hiking days.

Cottonwood Creek Trailhead to South Fork Lakes

TRIP
From Cottonwood Creek Trailhead to South Fork Lakes, return via cross country down South Fork Cottonwood Creek (loop trip). Topo map *Olancha*. Best mid or late season; 12½ miles.

Grade	Trail/layover days	Total recommended days
Leisurely	2/1	3
Moderate	....	....
Strenuous	day	....

HILITES
A fine weekend loop trip, this route affords grand scenery, and a good exposure to east-side ecology that will benefit both beginner and old hand.

DESCRIPTION (Leisurely trip)

1st Hiking Day (**Cottonwood Creek Trailhead** to **South Fork Lakes**, 6½ miles): From the trailhead (9660′) 0.4 mile west of the pack station, the trail leaves the road on a gentle ascent through a dense stand of lodgepole and foxtail pine, and soon enters Golden Trout Wilderness. Underfoot, the sand-and-duff trail of the forested trailhead area gives way to rock and sand as the trail climbs. Then, leveling out on the east fringes of open meadowland, the footing reverts to duff and sand. Cottonwood Creek, now close on the left, is frequently willow-choked, but the more open stretches reveal it to be a placid, clear-running stream—ideal for fly-rod action. Beaver reintroduced in this region in the 1940s have flooded many of these meadows with their penchant for damming running water. As a consequence, government officials of the Forest Service and the state Department of Fish and Games differ as to their continued value in this drainage. Rarely seen during daylight hours, these rodents still inhabit these waters, and a little scouting around should reveal some of the their latest handiwork.

In ½ mile the trail swings northward, skirts a meadow, and crosses Cottonwood Creek to pass the trail to Horseshoe Meadow on the left. This now steadily ascending route follows along the west side of Cottonwood Creek, passing Golden Trout Camp, a private resort. Near the camp we pass the Little Cottonwood Creek Trail, branching east, and then soon cross Cottonwood Creek. Beyond this crossing the trail swings west, passing through meadow clearings and moderate-to-dense stands of foxtail and lodgepole pines. The ascent levels during these meadowy stretches, and then the route comes to a trail junction, where we turn left and cross Cottonwood Creek again. Our route soon fords a fork of Cottonwood Creek not shown on the topo map and passes the South Fork Lakes Trail, branching left. Keeping to the right, we ascend a forested moraine via switchbacks to arrive at the meadowed east end of the lowest Cottonwood Lake, called Cottonwood Lake #1. Our trail skirts the south side of this lake, passing a trail leading to Old Army Pass. (Note: All the Cottonwood Lakes are closed to fishing.) These lakes were used at one time for research and breeding of golden trout.

Our route passes Cottonwood Lake #2 and then veers southwest through a jumbled area of near-white granite blocks. From the point where the trail turns west-northwest, a short spur trail descends a few yards to the good campsites at the west end of the westernmost South Fork Lake (11,000'). These campsites are located in a grove of sparse foxtail pines with fine views of Cirque Peak to the southwest. There are also nice campsites around the easternmost of the South Fork Lakes, reached via the lateral mentioned earlier. Anglers will fare better at this lake and at nearby Long Lake and Cirque Lake.

2nd Hiking Day (**South Fork Lakes** to **Cottonwood Creek Trailhead**, 6 miles, part cross-country): From the west side of the westernmost South Fork Lake, our route heads south and then east toward the easternmost lake, skirting the large talus area between the two lakes. We round the south side of the easternmost lake (golden to 7") and pick up a trail that leads downstream from its outlet. Keeping on the north and then the east side of the outlet stream, this route descends over heavily fractured granite past foxtail and lodgepole pines on a slope where the dashing stream cascades and falls from one rocky grotto to the next. Clumps of shooting star topped by showy yellow columbine and orange tiger lily line the stream.

The trail levels off in a meadow and then descends into a larger meadow, where the outlet of Cirque Lake joins South Fork Cottonwood Creek. Following the creek's course, we swing east and descend steeply in lodgepole forest to traverse another meadow. Beyond this meadow the trail drops steeply again, passing an old notched-log cabin where there are two cement fireplaces. The trail veers away from South Fork Cottonwood Creek and rounds the moraine between this fork and the main fork. Then our trail goes up the west side of the main fork for ⅓ mile to join the trail described in the 1st hiking day. Now our route fords Cottonwood Creek and turns south to retrace the steps of part of the 1st hiking day.

Foxtail pine

84

Cottonwood Creek Trailhead to Upper Rock Creek Lake

TRIP   From Cottonwood Creek Trailhead to Upper Rock Creek Lake via New Army Pass (round trip). Topo maps *Olancha, Kern Peak.* Best mid or late season; 26 miles.

Grade	Trail/layover days	Total recommended days
Leisurely	4/3	7
Moderate	3/2	5
Strenuous	2/1	3

HILITES   Beautiful Rock Creek and its spectacular headwaters are the goal of this high-country trip. The tiny, unnamed lake at the end of this trip makes a fine base camp for further exploration of Miter Basin and the Soldier Lakes.

DESCRIPTION (Leisurely trip)

1st Hiking Day: Follow trip 83 to **South Fork Lakes,** 6½ miles.

2nd Hiking Day: (**South Fork Lakes** to **Upper Rock Creek Lake,** 6½ miles): From the westernmost South Fork Lake, the trail ascends west through thinning timber to Long Lake. After skirting the south shore, our route begins a long, steadily rising traverse that takes the traveler above the campsites at the west end of the lake. Views of the lake from this traverse are favorites of photographers, but it is wise to save some film for the panoramic shots farther up. This traverse brings one above timberline as the trail skirts a wet area covered with grass, willows and wildflowers. The trail touches the south edge of High Lake, and a pause for a drink of the icy water at this lake's outlet will brace one for the upcoming rocky switchbacks.

The trail soon begins a series of long, gently graded zigzags which climb the cirque wall up to New Army Pass. The higher one climbs up this cirque wall, the better the views to the east of the lakes immediately below and of the Cottonwood Creek drainage.

Descending from New Army Pass into Sequoia National Park, the trail crosses a long, barren slope of coarse granite sand sprinkled with exfoliating granite boulders. A half mile north of the pass our route passes a trail that branches right to Old Army Pass. This pass, about ½ mile east, was the original pass constructed by an army troop stationed in Owens Valley in the 1890s. Beyond this junction the route swings west and descends steeply over rocky tread to level off on a more gentle descent in a barrne cirque. The trail crosses to the north side of the unnamed stream in the cirque and re-enters moderate forest cover. About 2 miles from New Army Pass the trail passes a trail to Siberian Pass, and there are good campsites on the south side of the stream just south of this junction.

Our route keeps to the right, continuing to descend through denser lodgepole pine, and when the forest gives way to the open spaces of a lovely meadow, our trail fords a little tributary of Rock Creek and turns left on the Rock Creek Trail. This trail descends steeply alongside a willow-infested tributary of Rock Creek until the rocky slope gives way to a meadow just above Upper Rock Creek Lake. (This name is not on the topo map but is generally used by hikers who frequent this country.) Around these meadows one may sight the relatively rare white-tailed jackrabbit. There are fair campsites at the head of this meadow, and others are located at the lake's outlet, but more primitive ones are to be found on the south side of the lake. The campsites at the outlet are reached by fording Rock Creek and rounding the north side of the lake. Fishing for golden (to 8″) in the lake and adjoining stream is good.

This marshy-meadowed lake makes a grand base camp for side trips to the rugged Miter Basin and adjoining "Soldier Lakes" (just south of the Major General, where there is good camping). Fishing for golden trout in most of the lakes below the Miter and The Major General is good. Other fine side trips include a looping cross-country exploration of the Boreal Plateau via Siberian Outpost, or the hardy and experienced backpacker with a yen for adventure may wish to take the Guyot Flat Trail to Crabtree Meadow and then take the scrambling cross-country route over Crabtree Pass, which rounds Mt. Chamberlin, Mt. Newcomb, Mt. Pickering and Joe Devel Peak and returns via Miter Basin.

3rd and 4th Hiking Days: Retrace your steps, 13 miles.

85 Cottonwood Creek Trailhead to Upper Rock Creek Lake

TRIP From Cottonwood Creek Trailhead to Upper Rock Creek Lake via New Army Pass, return via Cottonwood Pass (loop trip). Topo maps *Olancha, Kern Peak.* Best mid or late season; 24½ miles.

Grade	Trail/layover days	Total recommended days
Leisurely	4/3	7
Moderate	4/1	5
Strenuous	3/0	3

HILITES One of the finest circuits in the Sierra, this route tours peaks of spectacle and grandeur, visits unforgettable lakes, traces streams that plummet, seep and meander, and blends them all together with a carpet of green forest and open meadows that will give all who come a sense of accomplishment and peace.

DESCRIPTION (Leisurely trip)

1st and 2nd Hiking Days: Follow trip 84 to **Upper Rock Creek Lake,** 13 miles.

3rd Hiking Day (**Upper Rock Creek Lake** to **Chicken Spring Lake,** 6 miles): You begin this hiking day by retracing your steps for 1 mile to the meadowed Siberian Pass Trail junction passed during the 2nd hiking day. From the junction this trail ascends southward gently over a moderately-to-densely forested slope of foxtail and lodgepole pine. Our route crosses a barren area, climbs over an easy ridge and, ½ mile south of the junction with the New Army Pass Trail, turns left onto the Pacific Crest Trail. We now reverse the first part of the 2nd hiking day, trip 89, to Chicken Spring Lake.

4th Hiking Day (**Chicken Spring Lake** to **Horseshoe Meadow,** 5½ miles): Reverse the 1st hiking day, trip 89.

Cottonwood Creek Trailhead to Mineral King   **86**

TRIP   From Cottonwood Creek Trailhead to Mineral King via Army Pass, Rock Creek, Siberian Pass, Big Whitney Meadow, Golden Trout Creek, Kern River, Rattlesnake Creek, Franklin Pass (shuttle trip). Topo maps *Olancha, Kern Peak, Mineral King* (Wilderness Press version). Best mid or late season; 59½ miles.

Grade	Trail/layover days	Total recom- mended days
Leisurely	....	....
Moderate	7/4	11
Strenuous	6/3	9

HILITES   This excellent trans-Sierra route visits the finest fishing lakes and streams of the lower Kern River drainage. The severe altitude changes inherent in the route, however, recommend this trip for inter- mediate and experienced hikers only.

DESCRIPTION (Moderate trip)

1st and 2nd Hiking Days: Follow trip 84 to **Upper Rock Creek Lake**, 13 miles.

3rd Hiking Day (**Upper Rock Creek Lake** to **Big Whitney Meadow**, 7 miles): Follow the 3rd hiking day, trip 85, for the route to Siberian Outpost. From where the Pacific Crest Trail turns east, our route crosses the east end of Siberian Outpost and ascends gently past a snowmarker site to the easy rise called Siberian Pass (10,920′) where we leave Sequoia National Park and enter Golden Trout Wilderness.

Our trail crosses the headwaters of Golden Trout Creek midway down the descent from the pass, and then, climbing gently, crosses a ridge before descending a moderate slope to the west edge of Big Whitney Meadow. The underfooting of most of this descent has been dust and some rock, but as we near the meadow it is mostly sand. Mats of yellow monkey flower color the forest floor, and as the trail emerges in the opener sections, one finds lupine, penstemon, cinquefoil and sagebrush. Keeping to the forest fringes on the west side of the very large grassland, our trail passes the Cottonwood Pass Trail, and a few hundred yards beyond arrives at the fair campsites at the Rocky Basin Lakes Trail junction. These campsites are just north of the Big Whitney Tourist Pasture (fenced).

4th Hiking Day (**Big Whitney Meadow** to **Little Whitney Meadow**, 10 miles): Passing the fenced "Tourist Pasture," the winding meadow trail continues south over rolling terrain. Cattle-grazing permits are dispensed for this meadow and Little Whitney Meadow; hence the traveler may expect bovine company on these grassy sections. Many wildflowers line the route through the southern arm of the meadow and subsequent trail, including shooting star, monkey flower, lupine, wallflower, penstemon, mountain aster, cream cup, scarlet gilia, white cinquefoil, Bigelow sneezeweed and pussy paws. The sandy surface of the meadow trail continues into the moderate-to-dense forest cover of lodgepole and foxtail pine below. Shortly after re-entering forest cover, the trail fords Barigan Stringer and passes several nearby campsites. The polished granite canyon walls narrow, and the stream quickens for about ½ mile, and then as the canyon opens somewhat our trail passes the Barigan Stringer Trail (several campsites here). This creek was the original source for golden trout used in subsequent plantings throughout the higher lakes and streams of the Sierra.

Beyond the Barigan Stringer Trail junction our trail continues a moderate sandy descent past several more campsites to the ford of Golden Trout Creek. Mounting a sandy shelf above the creek, the trail descends gently past the Tunnel Air Camp Trail to the multibuilding complex of Tunnel Guard Station (emergency services available). The final descent to the guard station affords views of the open reaches of the valley, and of the red-topped volcanic hills to the southwest. Just beyond the Tunnel Guard Station our route passes the Ramshaw Meadows Trail branching east, and then turns west to ford Golden Trout Creek. Fishing on Golden Trout Creek below Tunnel Guard Station is restricted to artificial lures.

Across sandy, moderately forested, level terrain, the faint

trail, boggy and heavily trampled by cattle, stays well north of the creek, and passes an unmaintained trail to Groundhog Meadow. Rejoining the creek, the trail continues westward, winding along the northernmost edge of a large late Pleistocene volcanic flow (post-glacial) known as Malpais Lava. The largest single concentration of volcanic action in the upper reaches of the Kern, this basalt flow shows itself near the trail in brilliant displays of the colored rock. Predominant in the volcanic rock is a deep red, somtimes mixed with ochres and shades of tan. These colorful displays accompany the traveler all the way down this drainage, but the interested rockhound can see extensive fields of this rock by fording the creek and exploring the mile-wide strip of old lava flow to the south. Just east of Little Whitney Meadow, our trail drops steeply, and after passing the unmaintained trail to Salt Lick Meadow, fords Golden Trout Creek. On the west side of this meadowed ford are several good campsites (8420').

5th Hiking Day (**Little Whitney Meadow** to **Rattlesnake Creek/Kern River**, 11 miles): Our trail skirts the southern end of beautiful Little Whitney Meadow, and passes another "Tourist Pasture." Descending steadily over a dusty granite-sand surface, the trail then refords Golden Trout Creek. Then, as the route continues its steady descent, the trail surface becomes pumice, and the forest cover of lodgepole gives way to Jeffrey and juniper. Large concentrations of wildflowers daub the opener stretches with yellows (monkey flower), whites (white Mariposa), mixed blues and purples (larkspur and penstemon), and reds (red dogwood). Leveling out to a moderate descent, the trail then recrosses a tributary of Golden Trout Creek via a natural bridge of basalt. Easily eroded, this pink rock shows extensive water cutting and sculpting. After Natural Bridge, the grade of the trail steepens to a steady descent over pumice and sand through a forest cover of Jeffrey, white fir and some lodgepole. At the switchbacks dropping to the Kern Canyon floor, one can see the clearly delineated volcanic overlay with its subsurface of granite where the underlying rock has been laid bare by subsequent stream cutting that has knifed through the basalt layer and exposed a rainbow of blacks, reds, tans and whites. Some columnar basalt formations, usually associated with these lava flows, may also be seen to the north. Volcano Falls provides excellent views on the right as the trail twines steeply down over pumice and rock.

With the lower altitude come sugar pine and, on the canyon floor, quaking aspen, birch, black oak and incense-cedar. It is not until the canyon floor is reached that one has views of dome-like Tower Rock to the south. Through a sparse forest cover and clumps of sage, manzanita, willows and chinquapin, the trail veers south to cross the Kern River (footbridge), and then pass the Kern Canyon Ranger Station (emergency services usually available).

At the ranger station, our route meets and turns right onto the Kern Canyon Trail, and ascends the Kern Canyon by a series of moderate ups and downs. The forest cover is usually dense, with tiny wet sections that are made difficult of passage by dense concentrations of bracken fern. Their luxuriant growth is commonly associated with canyon bottoms, and they are frequently found in conjunction with riverside stands of alder, laurel, aspen and birch. The approach to Lower Funston Meadow is heralded by the lower drift fence, and then the trail begins a steady climb over the alluvial fan that results from Laurel Creek's contribution of silt and rock on the canyon floor. Fording Laurel Creek is accomplished via two crossings, each marked by a campsite; during high water, the second ford is sometimes hazardous.

Fishing in the Kern River, particularly near the confluences of the many tributary steams, is excellent. Angling is sometimes made difficult by the thickets of willows lining the river, but the rewards in rainbow trout (to 20″) more than make up for the casting problems. Fishermen, or those who simply enjoy the view from streamside, should keep a sharp eye out for beavers that work this section of the river. It is not surprising that one usually makes many wild animal sightings while traveling up this glacially carved trench. Animals, like men, are "channeled" down its steep-walled course, and within the canyon's relatively confined course, the hiker is apt to see bear, coyote, deer and the aforementioned beaver. From Laurel Creek the trail continues north through a moderate forest. Mostly duff, the trail surface makes pleasant walking, and the distance to the Rattlesnake Creek Trail junction is rapidly covered. At this junction, and just across the sometimes difficult ford of Rattlesnake Creek are excellent packer campsites (6600′). (Note: Yes, there are rattlesnakes in this area.)

6th Hiking Day (**Rattlesnake Creek/Kern River** to **Upper Rattlesnake Creek**, 8 miles): Reverse the 2nd hiking day, trip 100.

7th Hiking Day (**Upper Rattlesnake Creek** to **Mineral King**, 10½ miles): Reverse the 1st hiking day, trip 96.

Horseshoe Meadow to Rocky Basin Lakes **87**

TRIP From Horseshoe Meadow to Rocky Basin Lakes via Cottonwood Pass, Big Whitney Meadow (round trip). Topo maps *Olancha, Kern Peak.* Best mid season; 29 miles.

Grade	Trail/layover days	Total recommended days
Leisurely	....	....
Moderate	4/2	6
Strenuous	2/1	3

HILITES The fine angling enjoyed at the culmination of this trip should make it a good selection for the intermediate hiker who wants good recreation as well as a challenging route.

DESCRIPTION (Moderate trip)

1st Hiking Day (**Horseshoe Meadow** to **Stokes Stringer Campsites**, 5 miles): The trail leaves the end of the Horseshoe Meadow Road on an upgrade that quickly flattens out after forking right at a junction with the Tunnel Meadow Trail. After you enter Golden Trout Wilderness, breaks in the lodgepole and foxtail pine forest permit views of Mulkey Pass, Trail Pass, Trail Peak and Cottonwood Pass. The rerouted trail along the forest margin is giving the overrutted meadows a chance to recover something like their pre-man condition—although ecological changes never exactly reverse themselves. On the long, gradual ascent west up the meadow, hikers who get an early start are sure to come upon a few late-grazing deer, and along with many other birds they may well see a long-eared owl, a resident of these grasslands. Usually this predatory bird is seen while swooping down on its prey—meadow mice, deer mice and other rodents, but in very early season it is sometimes seen in family groups among the willows near the stream.

The meadowy path passes a lateral trail to Cottonwood Creek, and then boulder-hops an unnamed stream near a cabin with fair campsites nearby. Eighteen gentle switchbacks bring one to a meadow heavy with willows, paintbrush, columbine and penstemon. Then a replay of 13 more switchbacks suffices to mount a rocky saddle, Cottonwood Pass (11,200'). Views eastward include the Inyo and Panamint ranges, and to the west the more Sierralike Great Western Divide. A few feet west of the pass, the Pacific Crest Trail veers right toward Chicken Spring Lake, and from this junction our route descends sagebrush-covered slopes southwest for ½ mile to the several fair campsites on the right of the trail above Stokes Sringer.

2nd Hiking Day (**Stokes Stringer Campsites** to **Rocky Basin Lakes**, 9½ miles): Just 20 steep switchbacks are required to get down to a ford of Stokes Stringer before the trail zigzags down a more gentle slope to the eastern precincts of Big Whitney Meadow. Most of the tiny creeks meandering through this enormous graze-land are as unhealthy as they look, and need purifying tablets. After fording Stokes Stringer again, the trail crosses a forested ridge and descends past a snow-survey shelter about 25 yards to the right of the trail. We pass a sign indicating our arrival at Big Whitney Meadow proper before the trail makes a muddy ford of an unnamed creek. Then the trail tops another little rise before we arrive at a jump-across ford of upper Golden Trout Creek. The sandy path enters forest cover and passes the Siberian Pass Trail. Here we veer left and stroll 300 yards southwest to a junction from where the Rocky Basin Lakes Trail leads west.

Our westbound trail begins a moderate ascent through dense and sometimes moderate stands of pine trees. This ascent makes a long, dusty, southwestward traverse of the moraine just west of Big Whitney Meadow, then descends to a junction and turns right onto the Barigan Stringer Trail. The ascent beyond this junction is gentle, then moderate over increasingly rocky underfooting. The foxtail and lodgepole pine forest cover lining either side of this ravine ascent is a favorite habitat for a great variety of birdlife, including the long-eared owl, Steller jay, robin, chickadee, junco, calliope hummingbird, Clark nutcracker and rosy finch. The latter is often one's only contact with birdlife at the higher elevations, and is a frequently seen companion on exploratory trips around the rocky, barren expanses of Funston Lake, where fishing is good. Then the trail winds over a ridge and emerges at the east end of the westernmost Rocky Basin lake. The north and west walls of this cirque basin are heavily fractured granite, and are a haven for marmots. Our route rounds the north side of the middle lake and descends to the west side of the largest of the Rocky Basin Lakes, where fishing is good for rainbow (to 14"). Three more secluded campsites are on the northeast side of the lake.

3rd and 4th Hiking Days: Retrace your steps, 14½ miles.

Cottonwood Creek to Whitney Portal   **88**

TRIP From Cottonwood Creek Trailhead to Whitney Portal via New Army Pass, Rock Creek, Crabtree Meadow, John Muir Trail (shuttle trip). Topo maps *Olancha, Kern Peak, Mt. Whitney, Lone Pine.* Best mid or late season; 39 miles.

Grade	Trail/layover days	Total recom- mended days
Leisurely	....	....
Moderate	5/1	6
Strenuous	4/0	4

HILITES This fine shuttle trip surveys the Sierra crest from New Army Pass to Whitney Portal.

DESCRIPTION (Moderate trip)

1st Hiking Day: Follow trip 84 to **South Fork Lakes**, 6½ miles.

2nd Hiking Day (**South Fork Lakes** to **Lower Rock Creek Ford**, 10½ miles): Follow the 1st part of the 2nd hiking day, trip 84, to Upper Rock Creek Lake. The rest of this day is an easy 4-mile stroll down lovely Rock Creek canyon. This tumbling rill slows to a murmuring brook in the meadow flats, and its fresh-from-the-source waters are crystal clear and icy cold. The dense green canopy of lodgepoles overhead allows only clumps of shade-loving gooseberry to grow along the trail, but the virile willow maintains its verdant stream-bank growth, shade or sun. Willow growth is synonymous with birdlife, and Rock Creek has its share of robins, white-crowned sparrows, chickadees, juncos, woodpeckers and olive-sided flycatchers. It is often the *"oh-see view"* call of this flycatcher that reminds the passerby of the beauty of his surroundings—surroundings that, on this canyon descent, include a chain of lovely meadows. Unfortunately, this native tour guide leaves these environs in August, and the late-season traveler is left to rely on his own initiative.

Just before reaching a large meadow, the trail fords Rock Creek via logs (difficult in high water) and veers away from the stream. Interestingly enough, most anglers ignore the waters of this tiny creek and thereby miss some fine fishing for golden trout. The fish are not too large, but there are several in every hole. Past the west end of the large meadow, the trail descends to join the Pacific Crest Trail, and in 1 mile we reach the ford of lower Rock Creek (9500'), where fishing is good for golden (to 8").

3rd Hiking Day (**Lower Rock Creek Ford** to **Crabtree Ranger Station,** 7 miles): Beyond logs over the stream, the trail climbs steeply up the north wall of the canyon, then levels somewhat to the ford of Guyot Creek (last water for more than 4 miles). The jumbled, symmetrical crest of Mt. Guyot takes up the skyline to the west, and highly fractured Joe Devel Peak looms to the east as the trail begins another moderate ascent through a dense forest cover of lodgepole pine. This bouldery climb culminates at a saddle from which there are good views north across the Kern Canyon to the Kern-Kaweah drainage, Red Spur, Kern Ridge and the Great Western Divide. From the saddle, the trail descends moderately to the large, sandy basin of Guyot Flat. Like the Chagoopa Plateau across the canyon, this flat and the subsequent "shelf" traversed later in this hiking day were part of an immense valley floor in preglacial times. However, much of the granular sand deposits are a result of later weathering and erosion of the granite peaks to the east.

Beyond Guyot Flat the trail undulates through a moderate forest cover before dropping steeply into the Whitney Creek drainage. The descent into this drainage affords views eastward to Mt. Whitney—the long, flat-topped, avalanche-chuted mountain that towers over the nearer, granite-spired shoulder of Mt. Hitchcock. This descent concludes over a barren, rocky stretch to lower Crabtree Meadow, where, just beyond a good campsite, our route fords Whitney Creek and turns right (east) along its north bank. A half mile of gentle ascent ends at Upper Crabtree Meadow, where the route passes the Crabtree Lakes Trail. (This unmaintained trail leads to the good fishing on Crabtree Lakes for golden, to 14"). Continuing northeast beside Whitney Creek, the trail ascends gently to meet the John Muir Trail immediately east of a ford of Whitney Creek. Beyond this ford is the Crabtree Ranger Station (emergency services usually available) and fair campsites.

4th and 5th Hiking Days: Reverse the 2nd and 1st hiking days, trip 73, 15 miles.

Horseshoe Meadow to Whitney Portal   **89**

TRIP   From Horseshoe Meadow to Whitney Portal via Cottonwood Pass, Rock Creek, Crabtree Meadow, John Muir Trail (shuttle trip). Topo maps *Olancha, Kern Peak, Mt. Whitney, Lone Pine.* Best mid or late season; 38 miles.

Grade	Trail/layover days	Total recom- mended days
Leisurely	6/2	8
Moderate	5/1	6
Strenuous	4/0	4

HILITES   Crossing three passes, this route tarries in four drainages, offering a multitude of chances for angling that ranges from good to excellent. The scenery that graces most of this trail is exceeded nowhere in the Sierra, having an abundance of peaks exceeding 13,000 feet, and dozens of high, granitic cirque basins.

DESCRIPTION (Moderate trip)

1st Hiking Day (**Horseshoe Meadow** to **Chicken Spring Lake,** 5½ miles): Follow the 1st hiking day, trip 87 to Cottonwood Pass. At the pass we meet the Pacific Crest Trail and turn right onto it for 1 easy mile on level, dynamited footing to the good campsites east of the outlet of Chicken Spring Lake.

2nd Hiking Day (**Chicken Spring Lake** to **Lower Rock Creek Ford,** 9½ miles): There is no water until Rock Creek, so fill your canteen. The Pacific Crest Trail switchbacks westward up the wall of the Chicken Spring Lake cirque and then levels off over sandy slopes at the headwaters of Golden Trout Creek. After contouring above a meadow in another cirque, our route enters Sequoia National Park at an unnamed point (11,350′) on a ridge west of Cirque Peak. From here our route soon joins a new segment of the Pacific Crest Trail, which is rerouted to the north of Siberian Outpost. As the trail descends through the moderate -to-dense forest of lodgepole and foxtail pine, we get good views of Mt. Kaweah and the Great Western Divide, as well as large, bleak Siberian Outpost.

The trail descends steadily past a junction with the Siberian Pass Trail before the grade eases and our route begins a long, rolling descent along the forested ridge atop the south wall of Rock Creek canyon. Where the trail is close to the right side of the ridge, it is well worth stepping off to the right a few hundred feet to get the excellent views of the peaks surrounding Miter Basin. About 2½ miles from the junction our route makes a steep descent toward Siberian Pass Creek, but turns north before reaching it. Then it drops via rocky switchbacks through a dense forest down the north wall of Rock Creek Canyon. When the underfooting turns to duff, our route meets and turns left onto the Rock Creek Trail and descends one mile down the creek to the good campsites at the ford of lower Rock Creek (9500′), where fishing for golden trout (to 8″) is good.

3rd, 4th and 5th Hiking Days: Follow trip 88, the 4th through the 6th hiking days, 22 miles.

Siberian Outpost   *Kurt Rademacher*

Mineral King to Upper Cliff Creek

TRIP From Mineral King to Upper Cliff Creek (round trip). Topo map *Mineral King* (Wilderness Press version). Best midseason; 17 miles.

Grade	Trail/layover days	Total recom- mended days
Leisurely	....	....
Moderate	2/1	3
Strenuous	....	....

HILITES This is one of the easiest hikes into National Park wilderness in the western High Sierra, but still tough enough that the hiker will feel he has earned the privacy that awaits on the banks of Cliff Creek and at Pinto Lake.

DESCRIPTION (Moderate trip)

1st Hiking Day (**Mineral King** to **Upper Cliff Creek**, 8½ miles): From the Timber Gap/Sawtooth Pass trailhead one mile beyond the Ranger Station in Mineral King Valley, our route ascends the manzanita-and-sagebrush-flanked Sawtooth Pass Trail for ¼ mile, and then diverges left at a junction. Our fork climbs relentlessly up a southwest-facing slope that is warm indeed in midsummer, but blessed by some shade from juniper and red-fir trees. After a steep series of 10 swtichbacks, we traverse almost on the level across a treeless, flower-dotted hillside, and then enter a cool stand of red fir, which comes to include lodgepole and foxtail pine.

This ascent tops out at Timber Gap (9400´), where we begin to drop steeply in red-fir forest. During early summer in this forest, hikers may hear the thumping of blue grouse and the melodic flutings of hermit thrushes. As we descend above Timber Gap Creek, we find the rivulets on the slope sometimes disappearing into the loosely consolidated metamorphic rock. Soon we reach a mile-long flower garden, one of the largest and best in the whole Sierra. Although Timber Gap Creek is virtually inaccessible, there's plenty of drinking water in the rivulets that lace this high garden. Then the trail rounds the nose of the ridge on the east and switchbacks down to Cliff Creek through dense coniferous forest.

Beyond a ford of Cliff Creek (difficult in early season) are poor campsites and a junction with a trail to Redwood Meadow. Guard your food against bears at these campsites. After turning right, uphill through the campsites, our route climbs steadily through alternating brush and trees to reach a very verdant area watered in part by cold little streams that issue from the ground. In early summer the fine wildflower displays near the creek include Mariposa lily, rein orchid, wild strawberry, monkey flower, wallflower, corn lily, delphinium, yellow-throated gilia, yarrow and buckwheat. Beyond a grove of fir trees our route goes out onto what looks like an abandoned stream bed, and leads us right up to the base of the prominent falls of Cliff Creek. Here we finally veer away from the stream and climb the tough slope to the left through dense willow, sagebrush, whitethorn and bitter cherry. Then our trail crosses the outlet stream of Pinto Lake, tops a small rise in ½ mile, and arrives at a three-way junction. The left fork is the trail to Black Rock Pass, and the right fork is a short spur to good campsites near Cliff Creek. Just to the north, screened by willows, is little Pinto Lake, an excellent swimming pool much warmer than you'd expect.

2nd Hiking Day: Retrace your steps, 8½ miles.

Looking west from the Franklin Pass Trail

Mineral King to Little Five Lakes   **91**

TRIP
From Mineral King to Little Five Lakes via Cliff Creek, Black Rock Pass (round trip). Topo map *Mineral King* (Wilderness Press version). Best mid or late season; 31 miles.

Grade	Trail/layover days	Total recommended days
Leisurely	5/2	7
Moderate	4/1	5
Strenuous	....	....

HILITES
Next to the Sierra crest itself, the Great Western Divide is the most spectacular feature in Sequoia National Park. This trip crosses that sky-piercing divide at Black Rock Pass and leads to a large number of lakes to camp beside, all of them close under the colorful cliffs and peaks of the divide.

DESCRIPTION (Moderate trip)

1st Hiking Day (**Mineral King** to **Upper Cliff Creek,** 8½ miles): Follow the 1st hiking day, trip 90.

2nd Hiking Day (**Upper Cliff Creek** to **Little Five Lakes,** 7 miles): After crossing the meadows south of Pinto Lake, this day's route begins a gruelling 3000-foot ascent to Black Rock Pass. There's no decent campsite before Little Five Lakes, but given an early start, the hiker should be able to make it to the pass before the heat of the day reaches its maximum, and fortunately there is plenty of drinking water except in late season. Scattered foxtail pines dot the mostly open slopes, and in early summer wildflower gardens abound on the slopes above Cliff Creek, with their heather, yampa, larkspur, swamp whiteheads, Bigelow sneezeweed, paintbrush, phlox, wallflower, wild onion, groundsel and forget-me-nots. Soon Pinto Lake comes into view below, a very small pond at the base of a talus slope. Past a series of meadows the trail begins the switchbacking slog to the pass, and views of the upper basin of Cliff Creek include the cascades below Spring Lake, Spring Lake itself, Cyclamen Lake, and then Columbine Lake, icebound in early summer. The solitary traveler, moving quietly, will see numerous deer on these subalpine slopes. Finally the rocky path attains Black Rock Pass, and a good rest stop affords moments for viewing the vast scene ahead. The companion basins of Little Five Lakes and Big Five Lakes drop off into Big Arroyo, and beyond this chasm rise the multicolored, cliffbound Kaweah Peaks. In the east is the 14,000-foot Whitney Crest, backbone of the Sierra.

From the pass, the zigzagging downgrade trends southeast and then angles northeast to pass above the highest of the Little Five Lakes—actually over one dozen lakes. (When snow obscures the trail in early season, one should keep to the left so as not to get off-route too far to the right and come out onto some cliffs.) There are excellent campsites on the peninsula at the north end of the first lake whose shores the trail touches, and across the bay from these is a summer ranger who could provide emergency services. The grass, sedge and dwarf-bilberry ground cover around the peninsula-tip campsite is beautiful in the early-morning and late-evening light, and an evening meal here may be raised to four-star quality by the alpenglow on the Kaweah Peaks across Big Arroyo.

3rd and 4th Hiking Days: Retrace your steps, 15½ miles.

Mineral King to Nine Lake Basin

TRIP

From Mineral King to Nine Lake Basin via Timber Gap, Black Rock Pass and Big Arroyo (round trip). Topo maps *Mineral King* (Wilderness Press version), *Triple Divide Peak*. Best mid or late season; 42 miles.

Grade	Trail/layover days	Total recommended days
Leisurely	8/2	10
Moderate	6/2	8
Strenuous	4/1	5

HILITES

Nine Lake Basin offers the seclusion that places not reached by maintained trail always possess. Located in a south-facing amphitheater between the towering Great Western Divide and the blade-topped Kaweah Peaks Ridge, this lake basin is a perfect place to explore, fish, climb, photograph and recover your sense of marvel at nature's bounty.

DESCRIPTION (Moderate trip)

1st and 2nd Hiking Days: Follow trip 91 to **Little Five Lakes**, 15½ miles.

3rd Hiking Day (**Little Five Lakes** to **Nine Lake Basin**, 6½ miles): Just below the second of the Little Five Lakes, our trail fords the outlet and passes a trail to Big Five Lakes. We continue down beside the tumbling stream past the next lake in the chain, then ford the stream back to its north side. Soon the trail crosses the outlet of the northern cluster of Little Five Lakes, and the trout in this stream promise action to the angler who is willing to sweat his way up to the lakes above.

After an easy rise out of the basin, the trail begins to descend into Big Arroyo, a large right-bank tributary of the Kern River.

Diverging north of the topo-map trail, the actual trail reaches
Big Arroyo Creek about ½ mile upstream from the map ford.
Beyond the ford, an unsigned trail leads down Big Arroyo and
our trail in a few yards meets the High Sierra Trail near a
patrol cabin. (Numerous extra paths in this trail-nexus area
complicate the picture, and the hiker should take care that he
leaves the area on the trail he wants.) We turn left (northwest)
on this backcountry arterial and ascend gently up the broad
glacial valley past numerous possible campsites with great
views of granitic Lippincott Mountain and Eagle Scout Peak
towering in the west, and metamorphic Black Kaweah and Red
Kaweah piercing the eastern sky. The trail fords Big Arroyo
Creek again and then climbs over grassy pockets and granite
slabs toward Kaweah Gap, a distinctive low spot on the Great
Western Divide in the northwest. Where this trail swings west,
an unmapped trail takes off north into Nine Lake Basin, and it
soon arrives at the horseshoe-shaped first lake, with numerous
fair-to-good campsites and good fishing for brook trout. A base
camp here makes a springboard for excursions to the increasingly secluded and dramatic lakes north and east, and for climbing expeditions to the wealth of steep faces west and east of
this fine base camp.

4th, 5th and 6th Hiking Days: Retrace your steps, 21 miles.

Polemonium ("Sky Pilot")

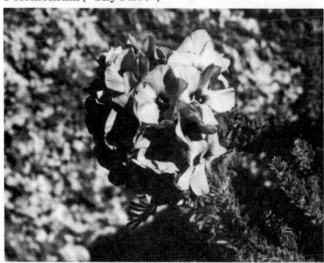

Mineral King to Hamilton Lakes

TRIP From Mineral King to Hamilton Lakes via Timber Gap, Black Rock Pass, Big Arroyo, Kaweah Gap; return via Bearpaw Meadow, Redwood Meadow, Timber Gap (semiloop trip). Topo maps *Mineral King* (Wilderness Press version), *Triple Divide Peak*. Best mid or late season; 44 miles.

Grade	Trail/layover days	Total recommended days
Leisurely	....	....
Moderate	6/3	9
Strenuous	4/2	6

HILITES Backpackers who want to sample the multifold attractions of Sequoia National Park will find in this one trip high passes and barren divides, sub-alpine stream valleys, inviting glacial lake basins, middle-altitude meadows, deep river canyons and giant sequoia groves.

DESCRIPTION (Moderate trip)

1st 2nd and 3rd Hiking Days: Follow trip 92 to **Nine Lake Basin**, 22 miles.

4th Hiking Day (**Nine Lake Basin** to **Little Bearpaw Meadow**, 9½ miles): After retracing the steps to the High Sierra Trail, this route turns right (west) and quickly climbs the few hundred feet to Kaweah Gap (10,640′). This pass on the Great Western Divide lies between the waters of the Kern River and the Kaweah River, and it affords views of many of the peaks whose snow-clad slopes give birth to these rivers. From the pass, our route drops moderately and then more steeply in granite sand. Early-season hikers are likely to see some gray-crowned rosy finches feeding on aphids and other insects that were blown onto the late-melting snow from lower elevations. The near-vertical faces of Mt. Stewart and Eagle Scout Peak "cradle" the trail as it passes aptly named Precipice Lake. Beyond the lake, the cirque widens and drops off. This stretch of trail is one of the most spectacular in the range: lush wildflowers and a multitude of cascades cover the valley wall and the hiker is awe-struck by the immensity of the colorful cliffs that rise from azure-blue Lower Hamilton Lake far below to the lofty crags above.

This vertical world will delight photographers, especially early in the day, and few of them will resist the spectacle of a channel for the trail that was blasted out of the canyon wall to create a "tunnel" open on one side—the cliff side. On these cliffs, white-throated swifts twinkle by, giving their mocking, laughlike cry as the trail drops and drops, 2000 feet in about 2 miles. A long switchback leg delivers the weary-kneed hiker to the west shore of Upper Hamilton Lake (8235'), where fishing is good for golden, rainbow and brook trout (to 16").

The trail crosses Hamilton Creek just below the lake and descends in or near the riparian vegetation along the stream. Below Lower Hamilton Lake the descending trail refords the creek and then contours along an increasingly steep rock face that gives a second and equally apt meaning to the name of this trail, the *High* Sierra Trail.

Now off the cliff face, our route climbs shortly as it swings north before descending to the cement bridge crossing of Lone Pine Creek. Below, in the gorge, the collapsed old bridge lies draped over a gigantic chockstone where the old trail crossed. From this creek to Bearpaw Meadow, the trail climbs more than it drops, as we traverse the steep walls high above River Valley. Views back toward the Great Western Divide and the glacier-carved canyons of Eagle Scout, Hamilton and Granite creeks emanating from it are awesome.

As we enter the Bearpaw Meadow area, the ranger station appears north of the trail, and south of it the tents of Bearpaw Meadow Camp, where meals, lodging (with reservations) and candy bars can be bought during the summer. We take the first trail to the left through the campground, toward Redwood Meadow. This campground gets heavy use, and it is dirty. More secluded campsites may be found at Little Bearpaw Meadow, about a mile south on a moderately-to-steeply descending trail that winds down under white fir, incense-cedar and sugar pine.

5th Hiking Day (**Little Bearpaw Meadow** to **Cliff Creek**, 6½ miles): Below Little Bearpaw Meadow we pass a marked trail on the right and continue our descent in mid-elevation mixed forest, with the spicy scent of mountain misery heavy in the air. At the bottom of this descent the trail passes a sign that points out the little used trail upstream and then fords the Middle Fork Kaweah River on logs and rocks (difficult in early season). Then our trail climbs the opposite bank and descends gently past a junction with a little-used trail down the Middle Fork, and we continue ahead, soon reaching cascading Eagle Scout Creek.

Rounding the next ridge, we come to Granite Creek, which is a roaring torrent in early season. An easy crossing by bridge and another short climb over a ridge in timber lead us to our last descent before Redwood Meadow. Even before we reach the meadow, we encounter red columnar giants standing tall among the lesser firs and pines in this forest. These are the giant sequoias, Sierra redwoods or big trees, earth's largest living things. However, as in most sequoia stands, there is not much reproduction of the giants here, because to reproduce they need disturbances like fires or landslides—ecological events which have not occurred here for some time—to clear the soil.

Our trail skirts the fenced meadow, where grazing is limited, and arrives at the Redwood Meadow Ranger Station. The building is an impressive two-story log house which is now used only by maintenance crews and park officials' guests. Camping is limited in this very peaceful place, as water is scarce. The trail climbs steadily, gradually leaving the big trees for mixed pine and fir, with patches of manzanita. Coralroot, a root parasite, grows here along the trail, commonly under firs and pines, where it feeds on living tree roots. Our route undulates through heavy forest for several miles, toward Cliff Creek and then away from it, and finally arrives at poor campsites near the junction by Cliff Creek. Guard your food against bears here.

6th Hiking Day (**Cliff Creek** to **Mineral King**, 6 miles): Retrace the steps of part of the 1st hiking day.

94

Mineral King to Spring Lake

TRIP   From Mineral King to Spring Lake via Glacier Pass (round trip). Topo map *Mineral King* (Wilderness Press version). Best mid-season; 10 miles.

Grade	Trail/layover days	Total recommended days
Leisurely	....	....
Moderate	....	....
Strenuous	2/0	2

HILITES   This "weekender" makes a fine exercise for the experienced backpacker in good condition. This route crosses the Empire Mountain ridge by a little-used pass to beautiful Spring Lake. Rugged peaks, mirror-like tarns, possibilities for exploring old "prospects" and cascading streams are the rewards for a difficult climb. This trip is recommended for the hardier breed of hiker with experience in the hazards of cross-country travel.

DESCRIPTION (Strenuous trip)

1st Hiking Day (**Mineral King** to **Spring Lake**, 5 miles, part cross country): Beginning from the dirt parking lot on the north side of the road, at the point where the road bends south '("Harry's Bend") our trail jogs north and then turns east on ascending switchbacks. This dusty, eroded trail winds up a dry, brushy slope, offering some views up the Mineral King valley to Farewell Gap. In ¼ mile, our trail passes the Timber Gap Trail branching north, and then continues east up the Monarch Creek drainage. Few trees screen this trail section from the sun, but the rank manzanita thickets along the trail are, as one oldtimer put it, "shoulder high to a growed elephant." Sometimes but not always visible from the trail, Monarch Creek splashes down to the valley in a series of granite-bottomed falls from the "false cirque" just above. This bowl does, at first glance, appear to be a true cirque—the womb of a glacial *mer de glace*—but as the traveler continues, he will see that it is merely where the river of ice midway down the slope discovered a schistic weakness in the underlying rock, and ground down on its heel, carving, scraping and sculpting the resulting amphitheater. Early local residents (the human sort) brought their eastern terminology to this country and, in honor of the many marmots that inhabit the rocky fringe of the grassy-bottomed bowl, named it Ground-hog Meadow.

At Groundhog Meadow we take the right trail fork across Monarch Creek. The left fork climbs directly up the canyon toward Sawtooth Pass and Glacier Pass. However, this trail is on unstable talus and it is no longer maintained.

We pass a fair campsite and begin several miles of long switchbacks which take us through open stands of red fir and silver pine with an understory of chinquapin, currant, goose-berry and lupine. Finally the trail crosses a ridge in timber that now includes some handsome foxtail pines, and just beyond the next hairpin bend is a nice lunch stop, where there are seats cut from logs, and where you can get drinking water by going 100 yards across the hillside. A short way up the trail from this lunch spot, a trail takes off to Crystal Lake.

Our trail, the new Monarch Lakes Trail, then rounds a shoulder, and now we can see the old trail across the canyon below, as well as Timber Gap, the Great Western Divide and Sawtooth Pass. We cross two forks of Monarch Creek and arrive at Lower Monarch Lake (10,380'), where camping is fair. A jumbled trail climbs around the north side of the lake through willows to upper Monarch Lake (10,640'), which is dammed and which lacks any decent campsites.

At the north end of Lower Monarch Lake we turn north and soon come to an unsigned trail junction going left. Keeping to the right, in ¼ mile we meet another unsigned junction, and take the right fork. (Many people coming down from Sawtooth Pass take the westbound fork here because it looks to be the more used trail. It connects with the old Sawtooth Pass Trail further down the canyon.) Soon the trail peters out and we follow ducks up a granite-slab-and-outcrop hillside. After nearly a mile of cross-country work, we arrive at a west-trending ridge lined with a few foxtail pines. From the top of this ridge we can see many sets of footprints leading north in the granite sand nearly horizontally over to the notch that is Glacier Pass.

Glacier Pass (11,000') is not named on the topo map, but is the next saddle west on the Sequoia National Park boundary. Views of the Cliff Creek drainage and barren Mt. Eisen are impressive, and they attend the hiker as he scrambles down the north side of the pass. Those with an exploratory bent may wish to detour across the barren granite slopes to the west, northeast of the summit of Empire Mountain, to the cairn-marked gold prospects and mines that dot the upper slopes.

This side of the pass is frequently covered with late-melting snow, and care should be taken to keep to the tundra-topped granite ledges east of and above the tarn beginning of the west tributary of Spring Lake. Here a faint trail (sometimes ducked, sometimes worn into the grass) descends steeply to ford the tributary just above its final plunge into Spring Lake. The trail then traverses the sparsely timbered west slope of the Spring Lake cirque to the good campsites (somewhat exposed) at the northwest end and at the outlet of the lake (10,050′). Fishing for brook (to 8″) is good. Views from the campsites of the sheer, smoothed granite headwall at the south end of the lake fill the viewer with a sense of awe and respect for the glacier's power.

2nd Hiking Day: Retrace your steps, 5 miles.

Mineral King Valley from the south   *Ron Felzer*

Mineral King to Lost Canyon

TRIP   From Mineral King to Lost Canyon via Sawtooth Pass, Columbine Lake (round trip). Topo map *Mineral King*. Best midseason; 15 miles.

Grade	Trail/layover days	Total recommended days
Leisurely	....	....
Moderate	....	....
Strenuous	2/1	3

HILITES   Strictly a knapsacker's route, this trail traces the Monarch Creek drainage to cross the Great Western Divide at Sawtooth Pass. High alpine scenery climaxed by the cold, often ice-filled waters of Columbine Lake make this a fine route for all who love the High Sierra. The excellent fishing in the upper Lost Canyon drainage will reward the angler who is willing to "walk for his supper."

DESCRIPTION (Strenuous trip)

1st Hiking Day (**Mineral King** to **Upper Lost Canyon,** 7½ miles): Follow the 1st hiking day, trip 94, to the ridge from where many tracks lead north toward Glacier Pass. From here we go north nearly to the notch, where we find many ducks doubling back southeast just below the ridgecrest. Stay high—all lower routes to Sawtooth Pass are difficult, especially with a full pack.

Sawtooth Pass is signed—and you may need the sign to tell you which notch is the pass, for it is not the low point on the ridge. From the summit of this high-ridged pass there are vistas of the surrounding country exceeded only by those from the tops of nearby Sawtooth Peak and Needham Mountain. One can see the length of the Monarch Creek drainage to the west, and on down into the wooded drainage of East Fork Kaweah River. Empire Mountain and the ridge to its southeast dominate the view to the north, Sawtooth Peak is on the skyline to the south, and to the east one looks across Columbine Lake, Lost Canyon and Big Arroyo to the timbered reaches of the Chagoopa Plateau. Far on the eastern horizon, one can see the Mt. Whitney complex of peaks, south as far as Mt. Langley and Cirque Peak.

The descent on the east side of Sawtooth Pass, like the western ascent, is a steep, sandy, zigzagging affair that will give the knapsacker little chance to look at the spectacular scenery. This route continues down, dropping steeply to the north side of Columbine Lake. Here glacially scoured granite slabs tilt into the lake's usually mirrorlike surface. The reflections of the nearby mineralized, rust-colored rocks blend with the chalkier whites of the lakeside granites to leave an indelible impression of mellowness in the passerby's mind—despite the basin's harsh, treeless condition.

After rounding the north side of the lake, our route drops steeply down to the head of Lost Canyon on a rocky surface that does not give way to grass and trees until one is almost due north of the westernmost spire of Needham Mountain. Here good campsites will be found in an open, grassy setting (10,200') amid a sparse forest cover of stunted lodgepole pines. Fishing for brook trout farther downstream is excellent.

2nd Hiking Day: Retrace your steps, 7½ miles.

Columbine Lake from Sawtooth Pass

Mineral King to Upper Rattlesnake Creek **96**

TRIP   From Mineral King to Campsites, Upper Rattle-snake Creek via Franklin Pass (round trip). Topo map *Mineral King* (Wilderness Press version). Best mid or late season; 19 miles.

Grade	Trail/layover days	Total recom-mended days
Leisurely	....	....
Moderate	....	....
Strenuous	2/1	3

HILITES   To call this trip a colorful one is an understatement. The peaks cupping the Franklin Lakes cirque are an artist's canvas of grays, shades of red, and various tones of green. Across Franklin Pass the fine fishing and beautifully intimate scenery of Rattle-snake Creek beckon to anglers and appreciative naturalists.

DESCRIPTION (Strenuous trip)

1st Hiking Day (**Mineral King** to **Upper Rattlesnake Creek,** 9½ miles): For this trip you may be able to park at the Sawtooth Pass/Timber Gap trailhead or you may have to park at the lot about halfway from the ranger station to that lot. You then walk up the road past the Mineral King Pack Station and go by a locked gate. A rough jeep road continues from this gate for about 1 mile, to an unimproved campground near the junction of Crystal Creek and East Fork Kaweah River. Looking up-canyon from this point, one can readily make out Farewell Gap at the top of V-shaped upper Farewell Canyon. Just west of the trail-road, the hurrying waters of the Kaweah River are hidden by a screen of willows, and the early-morning hiker is very apt to see a marmot surveying his territory. Scattered clumps of juniper and red fir contrast with the ghostly white

of cottonwood trunks just below the point where the route fords
Crystal Creek and, veering left where the road continues straight,
begins an unrelenting ascent of several miles. Along the shaley
trail, the savory odor of sagebrush assails the nostrils, and between the sagebrush and the gooseberry of these lower slopes,
spots of wildflower color are provided by purple Indian paintbrush, lavender fleabane, cream cow parsnip and red ipomopsis.
Soon the trail fords dashing Franklin Creek just below a lovely
fall (difficult in early season) and begins a steep, flowery, switchbacking ascent above a section of the Kaweah River that flows
through a deep, eroded gash.

About 1¼ miles north of Farewell Gap, our route doubles
back north, passes a junction with the trail to Farewell Gap,
and begins a long, stuttering traverse around the northwest
slopes of Tulare Peak. This traverse provides excellent views
back down the Kaweah River canyon to Mineral King and beyond to Timber Gap. The contrast between the green hillside
and the red of Vandever Mountain in the south is especially
pleasant in the morning light. Then your traverse enters a
sparse forest cover of mature foxtail pines and crosses red-hued
rocky slopes dotted with spring flowers and laced with little
snowmelt rills as you turn northeast into Franklin Creek's upper
canyon.

After descending briefly to ford the creek, the trail rises
steeply to the rock-and-concrete-dammed outlet of lower Franklin Lake. The colors in this dramatically walled cirque basin are
a bizarre conglomeration. To the northeast, the slopes of Rainbow Mountain are a study of gray-white marble whorls set in a
sea of pink, red and black metamorphic rocks. To the south,
the slate ridge joining Tulare Peak and Florence Peak is a hue
of chocolate red that sends color photographers scrambling
for viewpoints from which to foreground the contrasting blue
of lower Franklin Lake against this colorful headwall. Anglers
will find the fishing for brook trout (to 10″) good on the lower
lake, and better at the upper lake. There are a few poor, overused campsites along the northeast shore of Lower Franklin
Lake. Better ones, albeit treeless, are near the trail beside the
east inlet about 400 feet higher than the lake.

From this lake the trail rises steadily and then steeply on
switchbacks. Views of the Franklin Lakes cirque improve with
altitude, and it isn't long before both the upper and lower lakes
are in view. This ascent leaves the forest cover behind, as it
crosses and recrosses a field of coarse granite granules dotted
with bedrock outcropping. Despite the sievelike drainage of this
slope, flowers are frequently seen. High up on the slope two

adjacent year-round streamlets nourish gardens of yellow mimulus and lavender shooting stars. At windy Franklin Pass, views are panoramic. Landmarks to the northwest include Castle Rocks and Paradise Peak; to the east the immediate unglaciated plateau about the headwaters of Rattlesnake Creek, and Forester Lake (on the wooded bench just north of Rattlesnake Creek). East of the Kern Trench and plateaus, one can make out Mt. Whitney on the Sierra crest.

The initial descent from the pass, unlike the west-side ascent, is an ad-lib plunge down a slope mostly covered with a layer of disintegrated quartz sand and oddly dotted with small, wind-sculpted granite domes. After crossing this bench, the trail drops steeply down rocky, rough, blasted switchbacks that twine back and forth over some of the headwaters of Rattlesnake Creek. This steep descent levels out on the north side of the creek, and enters a friendly forest of young lodgepole pines broken by pleasant meadow patches. Several excellent campsites (10,300′) line the creek here. Fishing for brook trout (to 8″) is good to excellent, and the stream is ideal for fly fishermen. These streamside campsites are fine base camps for angling side trips to the several nearby lakes situated on the benches on each side of Rattlesnake Creek canyon.

2nd Hiking Day: Retrace your steps, 9½ miles.

Main Franklin Lake

Mineral King to Little Claire Lake

TRIP

From Mineral King to Little Claire Lake via Franklin Pass, Rattlesnake Creek, Forester Lake (round trip). Topo map *Mineral King.* Best mid-to-late season; 24 miles.

Grade	Trail/layover days	Total recommended days
Leisurely	....	....
Moderate	4/0	4
Strenuous	2/1	3

HILITES

For fine fishing, superlative scenery and a whole range of side-trip possibilities, this trip is hard to beat. As the opportunities for recreation are varied, so are the watersheds that this trip visits. After crossing Franklin Pass, this route hooks around to visit the alpine headwaters of two tributaries of the Kern River.

DESCRIPTION (Moderate trip)

1st Hiking Day (**Mineral King** to **Franklin Lakes,** 5½ miles): Follow the 1st hiking day, trip 96, as far as Franklin Lakes.

2nd Hiking Day (**Franklin Lakes** to **Little Claire Lake,** 6½ miles): Follow the 1st hiking day, trip 96, to the campsites on **Upper Rattlesnake Creek**. From the streamside campsites the trail descends moderately through an increasingly dense forest cover of lodgepole pine. In ¼ mile we pass the Shotgun Pass Trail, and in another 0.2 mile reach another junction. Leaving Rattlesnake Creek, we fork left here. A short distance beyond the junction, the trail fords a little stream and then ascends gently over a rocky slope. Soon the trail arrives at the charmingly meadowed west side of Forester Lake, where fine campsites look across the azure blue waters to a dense forest fringe, and an occasional dimpling on the surface indicates the presence of brook trout. Turning northwestward, the trail ascends through a moderate forest cover to a meadowed bench, and then makes another ascent to the sandy crown of the ridge dividing the Rattlesnake and Soda Creek drainages. From this rounded summit the crests of Sawtooth Peak and Needham Mountain are easily visible to the north, and they continue to be seen as the trail descends moderately to the south end of Little Claire Lake. The effervescent, burbling call of the Brewer blackbird and the raucous call of the Clark nutcrackers frequently are heard as the traveler skirts the east side of Little Claire Lake (10,450′) to the good campsites at the north end of the lake, around the outlet. Fishing for brook trout is excellent (to 11″).

3rd and 4th Hiking Days: Retrace your steps, 12 miles.

Mineral King road *Les Avery*

98

Mineral King to Little Five Lakes

TRIP   From Mineral King to Big Five Lakes via Franklin
             Pass, Rattlesnake Creek, Little Claire Lake, Soda
             Creek, Lost Canyon, return via Little Five Lakes,
             Black Rock Pass, Timber Gap (loop trip). Topo
             maps *Mineral King* (Wilderness Press version),
             Kern Peak. Best mid or late season, 39½ miles.

Grade	Trail/layover days	Total recom- mended days
Leisurely	....	....
Moderate	6/1	7
Strenuous	4/1	5

HILITES This is perhaps the best knapsacker's route for
             looping the fine fishing country east of Mineral
             King. Challenging passes and remote lakes are the
             attractions for the hiker. For the angler, the chance
             to wet a line in excellent golden-trout waters should
             be sufficient inducement.

DESCRIPTION (Moderate trip)

1st 2 Hiking Days: Follow trip 97 to **Little Claire Lake**, 12 miles.

3rd Hiking Day (**Little Claire Lake** to **Unnamed Lake at 10,000′**, 7
miles): The trail west of the outlet stream from Little Claire
Lake follows well-graded switchbacks down a steep, forested
slope for over a mile. At the foot of this precipitous duff-and-
rock slope, the route fords Soda Creek, descends gently over
duff and sand through a moderate forest cover, and then becomes steeper. Marmots on the rocky slopes south of the creek
whistle excitedly as unexpected visitors to their domain pass
by, but they do not usually stir from their watching posts
unless the traveler shows more than passing interest.

  During the next several miles of steady descent through
lodgepole forest, somewhat away from Soda Creek, we hop
across numerous refreshing tributaries and pass a half-dozen

campsites of uneven quality. Among the evergreens one finds an occasional silver pine, and then red fir appears. Clumps of sagebrush space the stands of timber, and nestled next to their aromatic branches are much Douglas phlox and Indian paintbrush. The appearance of Jeffrey pines heralds the approach of the junction where a trail down into Big Arroyo branches right and our route starts a steep, rocky, exposed ascent to the foot of Lost Canyon. Nearing the creek in this canyon, we double back to the northwest and suddenly leave the dry south slope for a cool, moist, verdant bower at a ford of Lost Canyon Creek (difficult in early season). Beyond the ford we veer away from the creek on a steady ascent up a duff-and-sand trail. More than a mile beyond the ford, just before a second ford of Lost Canyon Creek, the trail to Big Five Lakes branches right (north) and climbs the steep north wall.

This ascent makes a clear series of short, steep switchbacks which afford fine views west to the barren headwaters of Lost Canyon and the cirque holding Columbine Lake. Mostly lodgepole and foxtail pine, the timber cover thickens as the trail approaches a small, unnamed lake (due east of a granite spur, in the *Kern Peak* quadrangle). Fields of red heather highlight the luxuriant growth of the wildflowers around this lake's meadow fringes, and above the treetops in the north, the barren, massive, brown hulk of Mt. Kaweah rises just barely higher than the serrated Kaweah Peaks Ridge west of it. The excellent campsites at this little lake allow the dusty hiker to have a leisurely swim in water much warmer than can be found most places in the Sierra.

4th Hiking Day (**Unnamed Lake at 10,000'** to **Little Five Lakes**, 5 miles): From the north side of the little lake, our trail crosses a long ridge that is heavily overlaid with fallen snags. The ground trail is sometimes faint, but it is well-ducked. Above Big Five Lakes, the trail tops the ridge and we have views of Empire Mountain and Black Rock Pass to the west, and the lowest of the Big Five Lakes (9840') immediately below. The descent to the good campsites near the outlet and along the north side of this lake is a rocky, steep downgrade.

Beyond the log-jammed outlet of the lake, the trail leads west toward a reed-filled bay. At a junction we take the right fork and embark upon a steep, rocky, switchbacking climb of ½ mile. Just before the top of this climb, at a **T** junction where the left fork leads to another of the Big Five Lakes, our right fork is the Little Five Lakes Trail. Topping the ridge, we proceed to undulate for a dry mile, with periodic great views of Mt. Kaweah,

the Kaweah Peaks Ridge and, at the ridge's west end, Red
Kaweah and Black Kaweah. The Kaweahs are prime climbing
territory, and most serious mountaineers sooner or later sur-
mount them all.

The dry stretch ends when the trail dips into a small, intimate
valley where a stream flows at least until late summer. From
this brook we ascend for several hundred vertical feet in a
moderate lodgepole forest, level off, and then gain sight of the
main Little Five Lake and its large bordering meadow. In a few
minutes our trail reaches the base of the lake's north-end peninsula, which contains many good-to-excellent campsites. The one
nearest the peninsula's tip is surrounded by a wonderful carpet
of grass, sedge and dwarf bilberry which shimmers in the delicate light of late afternoon, and an evening meal here may be
raised to four-star quality by the alpenglow on the Kaweah
Peaks across Big Arroyo. Across the bay is a summer ranger
station where emergency services are usually available.

5th and 6th Hiking Days: Reverse the 2nd and 1st hiking days
of Trip 91, 15½ miles.

Glacial erratic

Mineral King to Big Five Lakes

TRIP
From Mineral King to Big Five Lakes via Sawtooth Pass, Columbine Lake, Lost Canyon, return via Little Five Lakes, Black Rock Pass, Spring Lake, Glacier Pass (semiloop trip). Topo maps *Mineral King, Kern Peak*. Best mid or late season, 21½ miles.

Grade	Trail/layover days	Total recommended days
Leisurely	....	....
Moderate	4/2	6
Strenuous	....	....

HILITES
This fine, short, looping trip is an angler's delight. In this route's short mileage 5 creeks and 15 lakes are touched, providing a variety of fishing water—and trout—that the fisherman will certainly want to try.

DESCRIPTION (Moderate trip)

1st Hiking Day: Follow trip 95 to **Upper Lost Canyon**, 6½ miles.

2nd Hiking Day (**Upper Lost Canyon** to **Lower Big Five Lake**, 4½ miles): From the alpine-meadowed bench below Columbine Lake, the trail enters forest cover (sparse lodgepole and foxtail), and then drops steeply over broken granite and meadowy sections. This stepladdering descent keeps to the north side of Lost Canyon Creek for about 1 mile, and then fords the creek twice in the space of the next mile. The second ford returns to the north side of the creek, where our route branches north, away from Lost Canyon, on the poorly signed Big Five Lakes Trail. From this junction, proceed as described in the second half of the 3rd hiking day and the first half of the 4th hiking day, trip 98.

4th Hiking Day (**Lower Big Five Lake** to **Spring Lake**, 5½ miles, part cross country): From the junction near the reed-filled bay on the north side of the lowest Big Five Lake, our trail goes west around the lake's north side and then ascends along the north side of the inlet through rank growths of ferns amid moderate stands of foxtail pine. This moderately ascending trail fords the stream ¼ mile below the outlet of the largest lake in the Big Five chain, and climbs over glacially smoothed granite to that lake's east shore. Our route fords the outlet and passes a packer campsite and several primitive campsites before crossing the swampy area around the north inlet of the lake. Just west of this inlet, our trail passes a trail to Little Five Lakes (or back to the lowest lake in the chain) branching right and continues west up the Big Five Lakes basin. Fishermen will find the angling for golden trout good to excellent in all the lakes of the upper basin except the highest.

The ascent to the third lake we pass is gentle over grass and swampy areas, and, near the outlet of this lake, the trail passes two primitive, exposed campsites. The grassy trail continues around the lake, but our cross-country route turns right (north-west) and ascends the steep granite ridge separating the Big Five Lakes and Little Five Lakes drainages. This ascent climbs by grass-topped ledges to the cairned saddle just south of the uppermost lake of the Little Five Lakes chain.

From this ridge one can see across Big Arroyo to the Kaweah Peaks and Red Spur. To the west, aptly named Black Rock Pass stands out in startling relief from the surrounding white granite. The steep, difficult, rocky descent on the north side of the ridge is clearly ducked, but some scrambling is required to bring one to the edge of the uppermost lake. (Fishing for golden in the two lower lakes of this chain is good.) Crossing the outlet stream from this lake, our ducked route meets and turns left onto the Black Rock Pass Trail. First ascending across alpine meadows, the trail veers north and then climbs a steep, very rocky series of switchbacks to the summit of Black Rock Pass (11,630'). This pass provides one of the finer viewpoints on this trip. Looking east one can see the Kaweah Peaks Ridge, the wooded flats of Chagoopa Plateau, a considerable length of Big Arroyo, and both the Little and the Big Five Lakes basins. On the south side of the pass, there are heart-stopping panoramas of the deep Cliff Creek drainage and towering Empire Mountain, seeming to be almost at fingertip distance.

Descending on the west side of the pass, the rocky trail makes one long traverse and then drops by steady and steep zigzags toward the grass-bottomed basin just north of Spring Lake. Where we almost touch a year-round stream, at a hairpin bend in the trail, a trail of use takes off for Spring Lake, visible in the distance. This route contours around the head of this basin.

After fording the tributary stream northeast of Spring Lake, our route ascends the waterfall outlet of Spring Lake itself, and arrives at the good campsites (somewhat exposed) on the east side of the outlet and in the sparse timber cover of the northwest shore (10,050′). Views from these campsites of the massive cirque headwall and the ribboned waterfall inlets are satisfying, and fishing for brook trout (to 8″) is good. (Less experienced backpackers should not go via Spring Lake but should stay on the trail from Black Rock Pass down Cliff Creek to the Timber Gap Trail and return via it; 1st hiking day, trip 90.)

5th Hiking Day (**Spring Lake** to **Mineral King**, 5 miles, part cross country): Reverse the 1st hiking day, trip 94. Note that Glacier Pass is the third saddle to the left of Empire Mountain.

Northeast from Black Rock Pass　　　　　*Ron Felzer*

100   **Mineral King to Crescent Meadow**

TRIP   From Mineral King to Crescent Meadow via Franklin Pass, Rattlesnake Creek, Kern River, Hamilton Lakes (shuttle trip). Topo maps *Mineral King* (Wilderness Press version), *Kern Peak, Mt. Whitney, Triple Divide Peak.* Best mid or late season; 56 miles.

Grade	Trail/layover days	Total recom- mended days
Leisurely	....	....
Moderate	8/2	10
Strenuous	6/1	7

HILITES   This loop trip is one that should be taken by all who would say, "I know the Great Western Divide country" or "I know the Kern Trench and its wooded plateaus." This route surveys a 5000-foot range of Sierran biota, and the scope of the glaciated terrain one travels over reads like the synopsis of a geology textbook.

DESCRIPTION (Strenuous trip)

1st Hiking Day: Follow trip 96 to the campsites on **Upper Rattlesnake Creek**, 10½ miles.

2nd Hiking Day (**Upper Rattlesnake Creek** to **Rattlesnake Creek/Kern River**, 8 miles): Traveling down through the upper reaches of Rattlesnake Creek is a delightful study in intimate meadows, dense stands of lodgepole pine and a classic, murmuring mountain creek. About ¼ mile from the timberline campsites, our trail passes the Shotgun Pass Trail leading south across the creek, and in another 0.2 mile passes the turnoff to Forester and

Little Claire lakes. Then it fords the winding meadow stream, only to return to the north side a few hundreds yards downstream. Soon we pass the Upper Rattlesnake Creek drift fence, the first of four seasonal stock fences in the canyon. As we descend, the creek picks up speed as its meandering course is constricted by narrowing canyon walls, and the trail climbs briefly on the north wall. In the narrow canyon the trail stays fairly close to the swiftly tumbling creek waters as it descends on a long, steady, rocky traverse of the canyon wall. After rounding the fractured granite nose of a ridge, the trail descends steeply to ford an unnamed tributary cascading down from the north wall, and then rejoins Rattlesnake Creek in the level stretches at Cow Camp Meadows.

This green grassland is frequented by the many mule deer in the vicinity and an occasional bear. Reflecting the lower altitude, the meadow's fringes show a forest cover of lodgepole, fir and some juniper, and as the trail continues to descend steadily, Jeffrey pine, aspen and birch begin to make their predictable appearance.

Just above the final steep descent into the Kern Trench, our trail passes a trail to Big Arroyo, branching north, and then it switchbacks down abruptly to the good packer campsites just south of the junction with the Kern River Trail. (Those wishing to take in the geologically instructive views from Rattlesnake Point should follow the fire trail leaving the Rattlesnake Creek Trail at the Big Arroyo Trail junction. From this point, one has unobstructed views of the canyon's distinctive, glacially formed **U** shape, and the wooded plateaus that were part of a pre-uplift valley floor.) Fishing for rainbow in the Kern is excellent (to 20″).

3rd Hiking Day (**Rattlesnake Creek/Kern River** to **Moraine Lake**, 7½ miles): Reverse the last part of the 4th hiking day, trip 70 to the junction of the Kern River Trail and the High Sierra Trail. Then proceed west on the High Sierra Trail, reversing the steps of the first part of the 5th hiking day, trip 81.

4th, 5th and 6th Hiking Days: Reverse the first 3 hiking days, trip 81, 30 miles.

Trip Cross-reference Table

Trip No.	No. Hiking Days	Season			Pace			Trip Type			
		Early	Mid	Late	Leis.	Mod.	Stren.	Round	Shuttle	Loop	Semiloop
1	2	x		x	x			x			
2	4		x	x	x			x			
3	3	x		x		x				x	
4	6		x	x	x			x			
5	7		x	x	x						x
6	4		x	x		x		x			
7	6		x	x		x					x
8	4		x	x		x			x		
9	7		x	x		x					x
10	7			x		x					x
11	6		x	x	x			x			
12	2		x			x		x			
13	4		x		x			x			
14	5		x	x		x				x	
15	7		x	x		x				x	
16	2		x	x	x			x			
17	3		x	x		x		x			
18	4		x	x	x				x		
19	2		x	x	x			x			
20	2		x	x	x			x			
21	2		x	x	x			x			
22	2		x	x	x			x			
23	2	x	x		x			x			
24	2	x	x			x			x		
25	2	x	x		x			x			
26	4	x	x		x			x			
27	4		x	x	x			x			
28	6		x	x	x						x
29	6		x	x	x			x			
30	7		x	x	x						x
31	6		x	x	x			x			
32	5		x	x		x				x	

Trip No.	No. Hiking Days	Season			Pace			Trip Type			
		Early	Mid	Late	Leis.	Mod.	Stren.	Round	Shuttle	Loop	Semiloop
33	6		x	x			x		x		
34	4	x	x		x			x			
35	6		x		x			x			
36	4	x	x		x						x
37	2	x			x			x			
38	4	x	x		x			x			
39	7		x	x	x			x			
40	2		x	x	x			x			
41	2		x	x	x						x
42	2		x	x		x		x			
43	2		x		x			x			
44	6		x	x		x					x
45	8		x	x		x			x		
46	8		x	x		x			x		
47	4		x	x			x	x			
48	5		x	x			x	x			
49	2	x					x	x			
50	4		x	x			x	x			
51	4		x				x		x		
52	3		x	x			x	x			
53	4		x	x			x		x		
54	2	x		x			x	x			
55	4	x		x			x	x			
56	6		x	x			x		x		
57	3	x	x			x		x			
58	5		x	x	x			x			
59	7		x	x	x			x			
60	5			x		x		x			
61	6			x		x				x	
62	5			x		x			x		
63	4		x	x		x		x			
64	6			x			x				x
65	9		x	x		x					x
66	2	x	x		x			x			

Trip No.	No. Hiking Days	Season			Pace			Trip Type			
		Early	Mid	Late	Leis.	Mod.	Stren.	Round	Shuttle	Loop	Semiloop
67	6		x	x	x				x		
68	3		x	x			x	x			
69	4		x	x			x	x			
70	6		x	x			x		x		
71	8		x	x			x		x		
72	2		x	x	x			x			
73	4		x	x			x	x			
74	6			x			x	x			
75	8		x	x			x				x
76	8		x	x			x	x			
77	5		x	x			x		x		
78	2		x	x		x		x			
79	6		x	x	x			x			
80	6			x		x			x		
81	8		x	x		x			x		
82	13		x	x		x					x
83	2		x	x	x					x	
84	4		x	x	x			x			
85	4		x	x	x					x	
86	7		x	x		x			x		
87	4		x			x		x			
88	5		x	x		x			x		
89	5		x	x		x			x		
90	2		x			x		x			
91	4		x	x		x		x			
92	6		x	x		x		x			
93	6		x	x		x					x
94	2		x				x	x			
95	2		x				x	x			
96	2		x	x			x	x			
97	4		x	x		x		x			
98	4		x	x			x			x	
99	4		x	x		x					x
100	6		x	x			x		x		

Index